Conrad C. Reining
Oxford, 1951

THE SANUSI
OF CYRENAICA

BY

E. E. EVANS-PRITCHARD

PROFESSOR OF SOCIAL ANTHROPOLOGY
AND FELLOW OF ALL SOULS COLLEGE
IN THE UNIVERSITY OF OXFORD

OXFORD
AT THE CLARENDON PRESS
1949

Oxford University Press, Amen House, London E.C.4

GLASGOW NEW YORK TORONTO MELBOURNE WELLINGTON
BOMBAY CALCUTTA MADRAS CAPE TOWN

Geoffrey Cumberlege, Publisher to the University

PRINTED IN GREAT BRITAIN

PREFACE

THIS account of the Sanusi of Cyrenaica would not have been written if a number of accidents had not led me to their country during the late war, but the seed of it was planted long before the war. I had acquired during three years' residence in Egypt and through travels in other Arab lands some knowledge of Arab history and culture, a little experience of Bedouin, and proficiency in spoken Arabic. During the war a year spent as Political Officer in the Alawite Territory of Syria added to both knowledge and enthusiasm. I had been acquainted with some of the Sanusi exiles in Egypt as far back as 1932 and had visited Darna and Banghazi by sea; and it had long been my hope that I might some day, when the Italians had ceased to rule the country, have a chance to visit the interior. This wish came true when in November 1942 I was posted as Political Officer to the (third) British Military Administration of Cyrenaica. I spent over two years in the country, the greater part of them among the Bedouin, particularly the more nomadic sections. Inhabited Cyrenaica is a small country and as in the course of my wanderings, mostly in its southern steppes and the desert beyond them, I covered more than two thousand miles by horse and camel I came to know something of its Bedouin tribes. My duties, it is true, prevented me from carrying out any systematic inquiries of a sociological kind, but the contact with the Bedouin they entailed enabled me to read the literature which forms the basis of this study in the light of my own experience. My labours have been but a small return for the hospitality of the tents and the many kindnesses of my Bedouin hosts.

I have not attempted to write a history of Cyrenaica, but only of the development of the Sanusiya Order among the Bedouin tribes of the country. I have, therefore, said nothing of the centuries of Greek colonization and Roman and Byzantine rule, nor of the little known centuries of Arab and Turkish rule until 1843, when the Grand Sanusi founded his first zawiya, or religious lodge, on the Cyrenaican plateau. Also, I have not aimed at giving a comprehensive account either of the Sanusiya Order or of the Bedouin tribes, but I have described both only in so far as seemed necessary to an understanding of the political development of the Order which sprang from their association. The Sanusi of Cyrenaica, and elsewhere, are so called because they adhere to the Islamic Order of the Sanusiya which takes its name from its founder al-Sayyid Muhammad bin 'Ali al-Sanusi and has been directed by his descendants. I have, therefore, described briefly the nature of an Islamic Order and how this particular Order became established and spread. The Sanusiya differs from most other Orders not so much in its teachings and rites as in its political and economic organization, a development arising from its absorption into the Bedouin tribal structure, but owing much also to opposition from the outside, particularly to the Italo-Sanusi wars. For this reason I have described in the latter part of the book Italo-Sanusi relations at some length. If in doing so I have sometimes expressed indignation, I do not wish it to be thought that I have any but friendly feelings for Italy and her people, or that I believe the Italian colonial record to be very different from the records of other Colonial Powers.

I have transliterated Arabic words in the simplest way. The Arabist will know, or can easily discover, how they are written in Arabic, and those who do not know the language would be little the wiser had I transliterated them differently. For the uninitiated it need only be said that the letter 'q', which stands for the Arabic letter *qaf*, has in Cyrenaica the value of a hard 'g' as in the English word 'goat', that 'gh', which stands for the Arabic letter *ghain*, has the value the Parisian gives to the 'r' in 'Paris', and that ', which stands for the Arabic letter *'ain*, is a guttural sound peculiar to Arabic. I have not been entirely consistent in the spelling of Arabic words in that I have retained the usual English spelling of such words as Cairo, Mecca, Kufra, Caramanli, and Koran, and that I have treated some Arabic words as though they were English words and have, therefore, not italicized them and have given them the common English plural form, e.g. Shaikhs, qadis, Sharifs, mudirs, and zawiyas. I have used the Arabic names of places instead of classical or Italian names: Shahhat, Marsa Susa, and al-Marj instead of Cirene, Apollonia, and Barce. If I need to excuse myself for this on the grounds that Cyrenaica is to-day an Arab country, no apology is needed for using the Arab names for the sites of recently built Italian colonial settlements, in naming which the Italians commemorated persons who for the most part might well be forgotten. To aid the reader I have listed at the end of the book the chief place-names mentioned in the text with their Italian equivalents. It will be observed that the Italian way of writing Arabic words is different from our way: where we write Suluq, Tubruq, Banghazi, and Jaghbub, they write Soluch, Tobruch, Bengasi, and Giarabub.

I have cut the book to half its original size and have consequently been compelled to omit a mass of detail. I have also restricted references to quotations and to statements which seem particularly to require the citation of an authority. Much of the omitted detail and many of the deleted references will be found in various articles and papers I have published on the Sanusi elsewhere. In a few instances I have not been able to check references because the books cited are unobtainable in England.

I acknowledge the generous help of many British and Arab friends, especially of Major-General D. C. Cumming, Muhammad Shafiq Effendi Hamza, and the warm-hearted companion of my travels Salih bu 'Abd al-Salam.

I thank Mr. E. L. Peters and Miss Sonya Gregory for help in preparation of the maps.

E. E. E.-P.

OXFORD
April 1948

CONTENTS

LIST OF PLATES

MAPS

CHAPTER I

ORIGIN AND EXPANSION OF THE SANUSIYA (1837–1902)

I

THE Sanusiya is an Order of Sufis or, as they are sometimes called, Darwishes. They are Sunni or orthodox Muslims. This means that in faith and morals they accept the teachings of the Koran and the *Sunna*, a collection of traditions about the life and habits of the Prophet, whose example in all matters should be followed by believers. Most orthodox Muslims recognize two further doctrinal sources, *ijma'*, general agreement among those of the faithful capable of holding an opinion on such matters, and *qiyas*, determination of what should be believed or done by analogy with the teachings and life of the Prophet. The founder of the Sanusiya Order, like other teachers of some of the more rigidly orthodox groups, such as the Wahhabi, rejected both, though, in practice, he made use of what amounts to analogy. Of the four canonical rites of orthodox Islam the Sanusi of Cyrenaica, like the founder of their Order, follow the Maliki, the rite dominant throughout North Africa.

The Sanusiya is, therefore, a highly orthodox Order. It is not a sect, but a fraternity. The enemies of its founder were never able to convince any disinterested person that he was guilty of heresy, though they attempted to do so; and it was only in very small matters that they were able to accuse him of departing from the Maliki rite. Even its Sufism is conventional and austere. The Wahhabi, those stern and ruthless critics of the sects and Orders of Islam, found in it no *bid'a*, innovation, which in the eyes of these fanatics amounts to heresy, and, alone among the Sufi Orders, they have tolerated its presence in the Hijaz.

Sufism is Islamic mysticism. Orthodox Islam tends to be a cold and formalistic religion. The gulf between God and man, spanned by the bridge of the Imams among the Shi'ites, is too wide for simple people, and its rules and regulations deprive it of warmth and colour. The need for personal contact and tenderness finds expression in the cult of saints, in Sufi

B

mysticism, and in the ritual of the Darwish Orders, all of which tend to be frowned on by the puritans and Pharisees of Islam and sometimes by its secular rulers.

In every religion there will be found people who, like the Sufis, feel that while formal acceptance of the tenets of the faith and conscientious performance of its duties are sufficient for righteousness and salvation, they do not satisfy the deeper longings of the soul which seeks always by entire love of God a perfect communion with Him. Human souls are rays of the divine sun imprisoned in the material world of the senses. The aim of Sufism has been to transcend the senses and to attain through love identification with God so complete that there is no longer a duality of 'God' and 'I', but there is only 'God'. This is brought about by asceticism, living apart from the world, contemplation, charity, and the performance of super-numerary religious exercises producing a state of ecstasy in which the soul, no longer conscious of its individuality, of its bodily prison, or of the external world, is for a while united to God.

In the first centuries of Islam the Sufis were quietists, individuals, often with a speculative bent, pursuing their lonely quest of God, and tending to become hermits. In the twelfth century Darwish Orders impregnated with Sufi ideas and ideals began to come into prominence and in course of time they became widespread and immensely popular with the common people, the poor, the humble, and the unlettered, especially in the towns. Indeed, there is a good deal of truth in Père Lammens's claim that the Darwish Orders 'have really flourished only among the intellectually backward . . . . and in regions where anarchy reigns'.[1] The popularity of these Orders, which have many social functions, is doubtless to some extent to be accounted for by the almost complete absence of corporate life in Islam. In becoming social institutions, and sometimes political movements, in the Arab lands they have shed most of their original content of mysticism.

The very wide following which these Orders attracted and the great influence thereby gained by their leaders excited the suspicion, and often the open hostility, of the official exponents of Islamic doctrines and traditions, the 'Ulama, or clergy, who

[1] Le R. P. H. Lammens, *L'Islam*, 2nd ed., 1941, p. 181.

furthermore scented heresy in them. To protect himself against accusations of doctrinal irregularities, it was customary for the founder of a new Order or sub-Order to demonstrate in his initial treatise, as the Grand Sanusi did, his orthodoxy by showing how his teachings followed those of some famous theologian whose orthodoxy was acknowledged by all. The Orders also aroused the enmity of the religious aristocracy of the Sharifs, descendants, or supposed descendants, of the Prophet Muhammad, who saw the common people looking to the Shaikhs and Brothers of the Orders for the blessing they had considered their exclusive privilege; and of the secular rulers, often themselves Sharifs, whose duty it was to support the clergy in the preservation of orthodoxy and who, on their own account, mistrusted popular movements of any kind, especially when, as was often the case with the Darwish Orders, they were associated with particularist aspirations. Opposition from these sources has not lessened—it has probably increased—the popularity of the Orders among the masses, who, rather dumbly but quite rightly, are irritated by governments and meddlers of all kinds. The humble have always sympathized with the Orders and have supported them as they support all those who, standing on common ground, can yet point the way to Heaven, and a brighter way than that offered by the cold learning of the official clergy.

For an Islamic Order is a way of life, and so it is called in Arabic a *tariqa*, a road, a path, a way. The various Orders counsel their followers to take different paths, stressing the role of reason or intuition, and differing from one another in the means they advocate of reaching the goal, but the paths lead to the same end, the identification of the soul with God by the elimination of all worldly desires and distractions.

The followers of an Order are aided to reach the desired state in which the body sheds its corporeal garment of the senses by the recitation of a *dhikr*, a religious formula, often accompanied, but not among the Sanusi, by violent rhythmic jerkings of the body and, in certain of the Orders, by music. According to Sufi teachings it should be repeated until even the words no longer make any impression on the senses and nothing but the form of the Divine Name is left. There results a completely passive, or empty, state, known to mystics of all religions, in which the soul experiences God. It is suffused with knowledge: not with *'ilm*, intellectual and traditional knowledge, but with *ma'rifa*, gnosis, wisdom. The Grand Sanusi and his successors very strongly disapproved of external aids to this end, such as processions, music, movements of the body inducing convulsions, piercing the flesh with sharp implements, and such other means as are used by some Orders, and steered a middle course between the illuminative, or intuitive, school of Sufi writers and the rational, or intellectual, school. Thus Sayyid Ahmad al-Sharif, his grandson, has in his writings, as Moreno points out,[1] exhorted followers of the Order not to depart from the rational, the chief aim of the Sanusiya being to make a man a good Muslim rather than a good mystic. Mysticism is something added to orthodox faith and morals, not a substitute for them.

It is for this reason that, as Sayyid Ahmad insists, perfection is to be sought through spiritual identification with the Prophet Muhammad rather than with God, at any rate for ordinary people. This is to be attained by contemplation of the essence of the Prophet and by an inner knowledge of him through constant imitation of his actions, attention to his words, and blessing him. The contemplation should be so intense that veneration of the Prophet pervades the adept till at last he hears only his name and has only his form before the eyes of the intellect. Then the Prophet becomes his sole guide and counsellor.

As this is not a treatise on Sufism there is no need to give further details about the mystical content of the Sanusiya. It should, however, be stressed that the rigorous orthodoxy of the Order, and especially its insistence on conformity to the original teachings of the Prophet, meant that the faith and morals which the Prophet preached to the Bedouin of his day, and which they accepted, were equally suited to the Bedouin of Cyrenaica, who in all essentials were leading, and still lead, a life like to that of the Bedouin in Arabia in the seventh century. In particular, the refusal of the Grand Sanusi to allow the more demonstrative forms of ecstasy, which, together with lack of organization and direction, characterize so many of the Sufi Orders of North Africa, enabled the Bedouin to adopt his teachings and ritual, for Bedouin are an undemonstrative people and it is difficult to imagine them piercing their cheeks with skewers, eating glass,

[1] M. M. Moreno, *Brevi Nozioni d'Islam*, 1927, p. 58.

or swaying into convulsions. Indeed, it is noticeable that the Orders which permit such practices, notably the 'Arusiya, 'Isawiya, Rifa'iya, and Sa'adiya, so popular in the towns of Libya, have made no converts among the true Bedouin.

It is unnecessary to discuss further the mystical side to the Sanusiya for another reason. The Bedouin of Cyrenaica with whom this book is concerned have only the slightest knowledge of either the religious teachings or the ritual of the Order, and are interested in neither. They belong to the illiterate class of the *Muntasabin*, the simple adherents of the Order who follow its Shaikh personally and politically. It is very seldom, if ever, that the Bedouin know the special prayers and litanies of the Order, and their use of them, if any, is restricted to getting a scribe to write them on paper so that they can sew them up in leather and tie them to their bodies. It is only a tiny educated minority who regularly recite the prayer formulas and litanies. These are the *Ikhwan*, the Brothers of the Order. They live in the lodges of the Order and hold prayer-meetings there. Among the Brothers are some who have been raised to the position of Shaikhs of lodges, generally, in past times, after special training at the University of the Order at Jaghbub oasis, where they have received a diploma from the Head of the Order or from one of his family or inner circle. This inner circle, the *Khawass*, consists vaguely to-day of a few senior members of the Sanusi family and two or three learned Brothers and does not function as a Body, but in the past it was, according to Sayyid Muhammad Idris, an official Council controlling the affairs of the Order and was composed of four Shaikhs of the Order, who were not of the Sanusi family, under the presidency of the Head of the Order, who had to be a member of the founder's family. As Dr. Adams points out,[1] the fact that this inner circle is no longer a determinate Body indicates a change in the character of the Order, a development of its political, to the detriment of its religious, functions. This development has favoured the interests of the Sanusi family to the disadvantage of the Order as a whole.

The *Shaikh al-Tariqa*, Head of the Order, advised in past times by his Council, appoints the Shaikhs of the lodges and these Shaikhs can ordain Brothers and the Brothers can receive

[1] C. C. Adams, 'The Sanusiya Order', *Handbook on Cyrenaica*, 1944, p. 31.

into the Order ordinary members. This is done simply by the two persons concerned shaking hands and reciting the *fatiha*, the opening verse of the Koran, together. These categories can hardly be regarded as grades and I can cite the authority of Sayyid Muhammad Idris to support the opinion that they have never meant more than that some persons were recognized as more learned than others and therefore better qualified to recite the longer and more advanced religious exercises.

II

The Grand Sanusi's desire to create around him a society living the life of primitive Islam and his missionary zeal gave an impression, enhanced by the austerity of his Bedouin followers and the remoteness of the Sahara, of excessive puritanism and fanaticism; and some writers have compared the Sanusi movement to the Wahhabi movement on account of these supposed traits. Duveyrier's account,[1] used very uncritically by other writers, is largely to be blamed for the exaggerated stories of the secrecy, puritanism, fanaticism, power, and numbers of the Order that were current at the end of the last century and in the first decade of the present century and which much prejudiced it in the eyes of European Powers with interests in North Africa. With Duveyrier it was an axiom that any foolhardy European who got himself killed in North and Central Africa had been assassinated by Sanusi agents and that any setback to French interests was due to their propaganda.

It is true that the Grand Sanusi, like the founder of the Wahhabi movement, aimed at restoring what he conceived to be the original society of the Prophet. Neither was peculiar in doing so, for every Muslim preacher must have the same aim. The Grand Sanusi forbad the drinking of alcohol and the taking of snuff and at first, though not absolutely, smoking. But all Muslims are forbidden alcohol and many who are neither Sanusi nor Wahhabi think that smoking is best avoided. It is untrue, as has been asserted, that the Sanusi are forbidden coffee. The Bedouin of Libya do not drink coffee, only tea, in

[1] H. Duveyrier, *La Confrérie Musulmane de Sidi Mohammed ben 'Alî es Senoûsî et son Domaine géographique en l'Année 1300 de l'Hégire = 1883 de notre ère*, 1884.

praise of which many poems have been written by Brothers of the Order. The Grand Sanusi forbad music, dancing, and singing in the recitations of the Order, but in this he was at one with all the official spokesmen of Islam. Most reformist movements in Islam tend towards asceticism.

Far from being extreme ascetics, however, the Sanusi Brothers eat and dress well, even using scent, and are amiable and merry companions. The Tunisian scholar and traveller Muhammad 'Uthman al-Hashaishi, who travelled in 1896 via Malta, Tripoli, and Banghazi to Kufra to visit al-Sayyid al-Mahdi and met the leading Brothers of the time, remarks that 'they are fond of diversions, honest jesting. I have visited many of their zawiyas and I have made the acquaintance of many of their notables: I have seen only cheerful and smiling faces, welcoming me with benevolence and kindness. May God reward them!'[1]

The Grand Sanusi discouraged the trappings of poverty by his example, his exhortations, and his insistence on the Brothers being self-supporting. Although the Heads of the Sanusiya Order, like the Wahhabi leaders, encouraged settlement on the land, they can hardly have hoped to have greatly influenced the Bedouin to this end; but they insisted on the lodges of the Order supporting themselves by agriculture supplemented by stock-raising, and thereby took a stand against *ittikal*, the dependence for livelihood on alms and not on labour which some mendicant Orders have advocated.

The Order has always been, in fact, conventional as well as orthodox. In its early period it was essentially a missionary Order with the limited aim of bringing by peaceful persuasion the Bedouin Arabs and the peoples of the Sahara and the Sudan to a fuller understanding of the beliefs and morals of Islam, while giving them at the same time the blessings of civilization: justice, peace, trade, and education. Its principles were, as Shaikh Muhammad 'Uthman says, simply 'to do good and avoid evil'.[2]

The accusation of fanaticism is not borne out by either the character of the Bedouin adherents of the Order or by its actions.

---

[1] Mohammed ben Otsmane el-Hachaichi, *Voyage au Pays des Senoussia à travers La Tripolitaine et les Pays Touareg,* 1912, p. 128 (1st ed., 1903).

[2] Ibid., p. 86.

The desire to establish in North Africa conditions in which Muslims might live by their own laws and under their own government, as they did in Arabia under the first four Caliphs, led the Grand Sanusi and his successors to oppose the Turkish way of life and the influences and innovations of Western Christendom, but their intransigence in these matters did not imply intolerance, far less aggressiveness. Though some writers have made assertions to the contrary, the Sanusi have never shown themselves more hostile than other Muslims to Christians and Jews, and the Grand Sanusi and Sayyid al-Mahdi scrupulously avoided all political entanglements which might bring them into unfriendly relations with neighbouring States and the European Powers. The Brothers of the Order were discouraged from discussing political questions. Nor were the Sanusi intolerant towards fellow Muslims who differed from them. Shaikh Muhammed 'Uthman records of Sayyid al-Mahdi that 'the persons he dislikes the most are those who speak ill of Muslims'.[1] The leaders of the Sanusiya have always tolerated other and rival Orders, even when they have disapproved of their rites. The Grand Sanusi had himself been a member of a succession of Orders before he started his own and he allowed, as his successors have done, members of other Orders to belong to the Sanusiya at the same time.

The leaders of the Order have also been tolerant towards the cult of saints, unlike the iconoclastic Wahhabi, who have destroyed even the tombs of those nearest to the Prophet himself. The view held by the doctors of orthodox Islam is that, though intercession through a saint is unlawful and the only mention of him during prayers at his tomb should be to ask the mercy of God on his soul, it is permissible to show respect to his tomb and his memory. The heads of the Sanusiya have, however, always tolerated among their Bedouin followers a regard for holy men and their tombs which goes beyond mere respect. It is unlikely that they felt any repugnance to the cult, because they counted among their forbears several saints and were themselves brought up in North Africa where the cult of saints is widespread and very near to the hearts of the common people; and they could not have remonstrated with the Bedouin for believing that holy men and their tombs are sources of *baraka*,

[1] Op. cit., p. 121.

divine blessing, since it was because the Bedouin believed the Sanusi family had the same virtue that they accepted their leadership.

The resemblance often alleged between the Sanusi and the Wahhabi movements, on the grounds of like puritanism, literalism, and fanaticism, cannot be substantiated. It is obvious that there must be resemblances between new religious movements: they usually claim to be a return to primitive faith and morals and they are generally missionary and enthusiastic. There is no great significance in such common characteristics of the two movements. Nor is there any reason to suppose that the Grand Sanusi was directly influenced by Wahhabi propaganda. A more significant comparison between the two might be made by tracing their developments from religious into political movements. Both started as religious revivals among backward peoples, chiefly Bedouin, the Wahhabi movement in the Nadj in the eighteenth century and the Sanusi movement first in the Hijaz and then in Cyrenaica in the middle of the nineteenth century; the *Ikhwan* organizations of the two movements have much in common; and both ended in the formation of Amirates, or small Islamic States.

Both movements have created States, the Wahhabi in Arabia and the Sanusi in Cyrenaica, based explicitly on religious particularism. In doing so they have only done what any movement of the kind is bound to do in a barbarous country if it is to continue to exist, namely, to create an administrative system which would ensure a measure of peace, security, justice, and economic stability. A religious organization cannot exist apart from a polity of a wider kind. But they did not create the sentiment of community which made the growth of governmental functions and the emergence of a State possible.

Religious divisions in Islam have commonly been the expression of a sense of social and cultural exclusiveness. The support given to the 'Alids in Persia and Arabia, to the Umayyads in Africa and Spain, to the Fatimids in Egypt, to the Kharijites by the Berbers in North Africa, and the adoption of extreme Shi'ite doctrines by the mountaineers of Syria and by the Kurds, and of Isma'ili teachings in parts of India, were all reactions against foreign domination as much as revolts against orthodoxy. The religious deviation was the expression of the intense desire

of a people to live according to their own traditions and institutions. To-day this desire is expressed in the political language
of nationalism. In the past it was expressed in religious movements. Arab nationalism is not a new phenomenon. Only its
dress is new.

As will be seen in the chapters which follow, conditions in
Cyrenaica were particularly favourable to the growth of a
politico-religious movement such as the Sanusiya became. It
was cut off by deserts from neighbouring countries, it had a
homogeneous population, it had a tribal system which embraced common traditions and a strong feeling of community
of blood, the country was not dominated by the towns, and the
Turkish administration exercised very little control over the
interior. It was, as will be seen, the tribal system of the Bedouin
which furnished the Order with its political foundations just as
it was the tribesmen of the country whose hardiness and courage
enabled it to stand up to the succession of defeats it had to
endure.

The reasons for the political success of the Sanusiya Order in
Cyrenaica will appear in the course of this account, and here I
wish to draw attention to one of them only. It has been said
that its rites and teachings were, like the Bedouin character,
austere without being fanatical, and that it tolerated the cult
of saints to which the Bedouin were accustomed, the Grand
Sanusi becoming, in fact, a kind of national saint; but it must
be added that the acceptability of its teachings and the fact
that the Grand Sanusi could at once be placed by the Bedouin
in the familiar category of *Marabtin*, holy men coming to
preach and settle in Cyrenaica from the west, cannot alone
account for the remarkable success of the Sanusiya movement.
The Bedouin of Cyrenaica had heard similar teachings before
from similar teachers and had paid them the same degree
of attention as they paid to the Grand Sanusi, but these
earlier missionaries won only a personal and local following for
themselves and their descendants, whereas the Grand Sanusi
established himself and his family as leaders of a national
movement, a position they have now held for three generations.
Leaving aside the remarkable personality of the Grand Sanusi
and without here discussing whether the time at which he
taught was particularly favourable to the growth of the move-

ment to which his teachings led, it may be said that the great difference between the Grand Sanusi and the earlier holy men whose tombs are homely landmarks all over Cyrenaica was that, while they were, all of them, in the eyes of the Bedouin, Marabouts, the Grand Sanusi was also the head of an Order which gave to him and his successors an organization. Moreover, unlike the Heads of most Islamic Orders, which have rapidly disintegrated into autonomous segments without contact and common direction, they have been able to maintain this organization intact and keep control of it. This they were able to do by co-ordinating the lodges of the Order to the tribal structure.

III

The more recent Islamic Orders are to be found principally in North and West Africa. The Sanusiya is one of the most recent of them. Its founder was an Algerian scholar, al-Sayyid Muhammad bin 'Ali al-Sanusi al-Khattabi al-Idrisi al-Hasani, a very remarkable man, mystic, missionary, and Marabout. The Sayyid Muhammad bin 'Ali al-Sanusi is usually spoken of in Cyrenaica as *al-Sanusi al-Kabir*, the Grand Sanusi, and I generally refer to him thus in this book.

The Grand Sanusi was born of a distinguished family of Sharifs at a village near Mustaghanim in Algeria about 1787. Early in life he became noted for his intelligence, piety, and profound learning, considered fitting ornaments to his noble birth. He studied first at Mustaghanim, then at Mazun, and later at the famous mosque school at Fez in Morocco, where he learnt theology, jurisprudence, exegesis of the Koran, and the other usual subjects of a Muslim student of the time. There he seems to have developed an interest in mysticism, having come under the influence of the Moroccan Order of the Tijaniya Darwishes. He left Fez when in the early thirties in order to make the pilgrimage to Mecca, though a Turkish biographer says that one of his reasons for leaving Morocco was to avoid possible unpleasantness with the authorities, who were alarmed lest his propaganda for the greater unity of Islam, his life's aim, might have political consequences.[1] They had small cause for alarm as his efforts seem to have made little impression on the

[1] Salim bin 'Amir, *Majallat 'Umar al-Mukhtar*, No. II, 1943-4, p. 2.

people of Fez, but, if the story is true, the suspicion of those in authority would have been his first experience of the kind of opposition he was later to encounter in Cairo and Mecca.

He went from Fez to southern Algeria and thence to Qabis, Tripoli, Misurata, and Banghazi, preaching everywhere on his way. He had already gathered around him his first disciples (*Ikhwan*), mostly Algerians, and in their company he made his way to Egypt by the coastal route from Banghazi and stayed there a few weeks. He had intended to study at al-Azhar, but he seems to have aroused the jealousy of the Shaikhs of the University and to have irritated them by his reforming zeal and his speculations, and so departed for Mecca. Short though his stay in Cairo had been it is probable that the independence of the Khedive Muhammad 'Ali and the cultural and intellectual revival going on there left their mark on his mind.[1]

He remained in the Hijaz for about six years, studying under a number of Shaikhs at Mecca and al-Madina. He is said to have returned to Mustaghanim in about 1829 and not to have visited the Hijaz again till 1833. On this second visit, which lasted for eight years, he was accompanied by a considerable number of disciples from the west. He continued his reformist agitation and his studies under learned Shaikhs at Mecca. The man who influenced him most, and whose favourite pupil he became, was Sayyid Ahmad bin Idris al-Fasi, the fourth Head of the Moroccan Order of the Khadiriya or Khidriya Darwishes, a branch of the Shadhiliya Order, and later the founder of a new sub-Order of his own, the Idrisiya or Khadiriya-Idrisiya. Sayyid Ahmad Idris had aroused the hostility of the doctors of the Maliki rite at Mecca, by whom he was regarded as un-orthodox, and went into exile into the Yaman, where he was accompanied for two years by the Grand Sanusi. On Sayyid Ahmad Idris's death in the Yaman, his two chief disciples organized his followers into two new sub-Orders, the Mirghaniya and the Sanusiya, the latter being organized and led by the Grand Sanusi, who established its headquarters at Mt. Abu Qubais, near Mecca, in 1837. This year is regarded as the official date of the foundation of the Order.

It will have been noted that the Grand Sanusi was influenced by a wide range of Sufi tradition and had affiliated himself to a

[1] Salim bin 'Amir, *Majallat 'Umar al-Mukhtar*, No. I, p. 12.

number of Orders before he founded his own. It has been recorded that he was influenced by the Moroccan Tijaniya Order and that at Mecca he became the favourite pupil of the founder of the Idrisiya Order, which derived its tenets from the basic Shadhiliya Order. In his student days he became a member of other Orders: Shadhiliya, Nasiriya, Qadariya, and perhaps others.[1] His catholicism was not peculiar among the Sufis, and in his case he seems to have joined a large variety of Orders with the deliberate intention of learning their rites and doctrines at first hand so that he could combine all that was best in each of them in a new Order which would be the crown of Sufi thought and practice. It must not be supposed that on this account his teaching was a mere amalgam of the tenets of earlier Orders. Original it was not, but it was a consistent and carefully thought out way of life.[2]

The new Sanusiya Order made such rapid progress, especially among the Bedouin of the Hijaz,[3] that it excited the jealousy and fear of the various authorities in Mecca, the 'Ulama, the Sharifs, and the Turkish Administration. There can be little doubt that the real objections to the Order were that it threatened the prestige and privileges of these authorities, but they were framed in less revealing language. It seems to have been held against the Order that it lowered Sufi standards to accommodate itself to Bedouin laxity in religious matters, and that it verged on heresy.

Faced with serious opposition the Grand Sanusi did what his teacher Sayyid Ahmad Idris had done in similar circumstances: he left the Hijaz, in about 1841, accompanied by many of his disciples, to return to his native land. After spending some months in Cairo, he continued his journey westwards to Siwa oasis, where he was taken sick and spent several weeks recuperating and instructing the people of the oasis in the faith. In the following year he reached Tripoli by the desert route. On his way to Qabis from that town he heard of the new French advances in his homeland and decided in view of them to return to Tripoli and thence to Banghazi. It would appear therefore

---

[1] Ibid., p. 6; Adams, op. cit., p. 22.
[2] Carlo Giglio, *La Confraternità Senussita dalle sue Origini ad Oggi*, 1932, p. 17.
[3] A. Le Chatelier, *Les Confréries Musulmanes du Hedjaz*, 1887, *passim*.

that he did not choose Cyrenaica as his field of labour but was compelled to settle in Libya for a time because the road to the west was closed by the French and the road to the east by the authorities in Cairo and Mecca. The Grand Sanusi was a cosmopolitan, a townsman, and more at home in the schools and libraries of Fez, Cairo, and Mecca than amid the lentisk and juniper of the Cyrenaican plateau or the thyme and wormwood of its rolling plains. Even after founding in 1843 what has become the Mother Lodge of the Order, al-Zawiya al-Baida, on the central Cyrenaican plateau, not far from the ancient city of Cyrene, and while the Sanusi movement was still young in the country, he returned in 1846 to Mecca and stayed there till 1853. Altogether he spent only about ten years of his teaching life in Cyrenaica, whereas he spent some twenty years in the Hijaz.

On his return to Cyrenaica he seems to have felt the need for greater solitude. He was then nearing seventy years of age and doubtless felt that what was left to him of life should be given to contemplation, prayer, and study. It may be true also, as is commonly stated in books written by Europeans, that he desired to place a wide stretch of desert between himself and the Turkish authorities who, as the Sanusiya movement grew, began to take greater interest in it. He therefore first went to live for a short while at al-'Azziyyat on the southern edge of the plateau, where he built a zawiya, and afterwards at Jaghbub, about 160 km. from the sea.

Jaghbub, now to become the centre of the Order and the seat of an Islamic University second only in Africa to al-Azhar, was till 1856, when the Grand Sanusi made it his seat, an un-inhabited oasis, in which the water was brackish, highly sulphurous, and insufficient to irrigate more than a small area of gardens. It was not a place for luxurious living, though it seems to have been healthy and, unlike Siwa, free from malaria; but it had certain political advantages. It was out of reach of the Turkish, French, or Egyptian governments, it was on the main pilgrimage route from North-west Africa through Egypt to Mecca, and this pilgrimage route bisected at the oasis one of the trade routes from the coast to the Sahara and the Sudan. Moreover, since Cyrenaica is a peninsula, it was the most central point he could have chosen at that time to be in equal touch with the lodges of his Order in Cyrenaica, Tripolitania, the Western Desert of Egypt, and the Sudan.

In moving the seat of his Order to Jaghbub, the Grand Sanusi was probably most influenced by his decision to direct his missionary propaganda southwards. It is understandable that he should have made this decision. His was a missionary

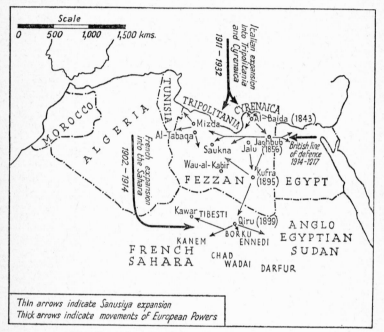

The Spread of the Sanusiya in North Africa.

mind and the Order he had founded a missionary Order, and the pagan and semi-pagan countries of the Sahara and the Sudan, and of Equatorial Africa beyond them, offered endless scope for conversion to the faith. Moreover, his Order was already reaching the limits of its expansion in North Africa. It had won over the nomad and semi-nomad Bedouin tribes of Cyrenaica, Tripolitania, and Egypt, and the oases folk under their influence, but was not making, and was not even in its heyday to make, much impression on the peasants and townsmen up against whom it now found itself in Northern Tripolitania and the Nile Valley. Dammed to west and east the Order poured its vitality southwards along the trade routes to the interior of Africa, into Fazzan and the various regions that are to-day called the French Sahara and French Equatorial Africa. Until France opened up the Atlantic seaboard, much of the Central African trade found its way along the oases-routes to the ports of Cyrenaica and Tripolitania and there were, there-fore, well-established social connexions running from the Bedouin tribes of Cyrenaica and southern Tripolitania through the oases-dwellers to the tribes of the interior, for the nomads of Libya controlled the routes and to a large extent supplied the transport for the caravans. These connexions allowed an easy ingress to the Sanusiya. The two Cyrenaican tribes who chiefly traded with the Sahara, the Majabra and the Zuwaya of the oases of Jalu and al-Jikharra, had already been won over to the Order. The Zuwaya, who had date groves in the distant oasis archipelago of Kufra, over 700 km. to the south of Jaghbub, had already promised the Grand Sanusi a liberal donation of palms and water if he would build a zawiya there, and he had sent one of his followers to supervise the erection at al-Jauf of a lodge which became known as Zawiyat al-Ustad. Also, the Order had gained a foothold in the Wadai. While still a student at Mecca the Grand Sanusi had made friends with Muhammad Sharif, a prince of the Wadai, who in 1838 became Sultan of that country and furthered the interests of the Order there. It is said also that the Grand Sanusi bought a caravan of slaves on its way from the Wadai through Jaghbub to the coast and, having freed and educated them, sent them back to the Wadai as his missionaries.[1] The Order was also infiltrating from Mizda in southern Tripolitania, where a lodge was founded in 1845, and from the lodges in the oases of the Sirtican hinterland into Fazzan.

In Jaghbub oasis the Grand Sanusi set about the construc-tion of his headquarters, a large mass of stone buildings, some of them two-storied, enclosing a mosque and school which were, for Cyrenaica, on an imposing scale. Around these central buildings and courts were the houses of the *Ikhwan*, many of them teachers in the school, of the students, of whom Shaikh Muhammad 'Uthman says that there were over 300,[2] and of the Sayyid's family. There were also guest-rooms, quarters for the

[1] Duveyrier, op. cit., pp. 18–19.   [2] Op. cit., p. 88.

THE TOMB OF THE GRAND SANUSI (HASANAIN PASHA)

slaves, kitchens, and wells. The oasis depression was studded with date palms and just outside the main entrance to the village were small irrigated gardens and wind-mills. The people had to use the brackish water for ordinary purposes, but sufficient fresh water for tea was obtained from infrequent showers by hollowing out cisterns in the rocks at the top of the western escarpment of the oasis.

The Grand Sanusi was not only a very learned man and a writer of distinction but also a bibliophile with a fine library of some 8,000 volumes,[1] mostly works on Islamic law and juris-prudence, mysticism, philosophy, history, koranic exegesis, poetry, and astronomy and astrology. Round him were many men capable of making good use of this substantial library. Indeed, it would have been difficult to have found anywhere in the Islamic world at that time, outside Cairo, a circle of better scholars. Poetry was one of the arts most cultivated at the oasis and I have been told by Arabs that it reached a high level of excellence. Shaikh Muhammad 'Uthman, himself a poet, wrote that at Jaghbub one meets 'literary men of distinction, whose writings eclipse those of the poets of Iraq and of Andalousia'.[2]

The whole community at Jaghbub may have numbered round about 1,000, but it is not possible to make more than a guess at the figure. As the oasis produces little except dates, the supply problem must have been considerable, and we know that the Grand Sanusi kept herds of camels to the west of the oasis, where there is scrub grazing, and at al-'Azziyyat, to transport supplies from the coast. The community lived very largely on the surplus revenues, mostly goods in kind, sent annually by all the zawiyas of Cyrenaica.

The community was centred round the University. It was, in fact, almost purely a University society, and its importance as such in the history of the Sanusiya Order is very considerable. Here, under his personal supervision and the supervision of his disciples, far from worldly distractions, the Grand Sanusi was able to train the future leaders of the Order. The Shaikhs of the lodges of the Order were appointed by him from among his intimate circle of disciples, many of whom had followed him

---

[1] Duveyrier, op. cit., p. 24; Muhammad bin 'Uthman, op. cit., p. 88; Sir Richard Burton, *Personal Narrative of a Pilgrimage to al-Madinah and Meccah* (Memorial Edition), 1893, vol. ii, pp. 24–5.   [2] Op. cit., p. 88.

from Algeria and the other countries of the Maghrib on his travels backwards and forwards to Arabia. He found in Cyrenaica a tribal structure of a simple kind on which it was possible to build a missionary organization, but not out of which it could be built. He brought this organization with him to Cyrenaica, a band of devoted followers whose allegiance had been tried by many vicissitudes. It must be remembered also that these intimates of the Grand Sanusi were foreigners to the Bedouin of Cyrenaica, with whom they had no ties of kinship, so that they stood always outside the tribal system and were not involved in the ancient loyalties and feuds inherent in Bedouin society. The missionary organization, the Sanusiya Order, was separate from the tribal system, and by centring it in the distant oasis of Jaghbub the Grand Sanusi prevented it from becoming identified with any one tribe or section of the country, as it might have become had it been centred in Cyrenaica proper. As we will see, it was the local attachment of the tribes to the zawiyas in their territories, and the attachment of the Shaikhs of these zawiyas to the Head of the Order, which made the Order so effective a missionary Body, and eventually enabled it to become a political force.

The Grand Sanusi died at Jaghbub on 7 September 1859 and was buried there. Later a magnificent shrine, furnished with ornate trappings, was erected over his bones and was surmounted with a white cupola, which gleams several miles away as one approaches the oasis. The shrine is of Egyptian craftmanship and seems incongruous in its desert surroundings and unfamiliar among a simple people.

There can be no gainsaying that al-Sayyid Muhammad bin ʻAli al-Sanusi was a great man and his life's work a great achievement. He is said to have been tall and of a distinguished appearance, an eloquent speaker, and a wise teacher.[1] His religious personality may be estimated by the fact that many Algerians, Tunisians, and Moroccans were so inspired by his teaching and example that they left their homes and followed him on his travels and at his orders went as missionaries into new lands, and by the fact that the Bedouin of Arabia and Libya, who are a reserved and unheeding people, accepted him as their guide in things both spiritual and temporal.

[1] Adams, op. cit., p. 10.

The mere physical achievement of the man was remarkable. He had studied assiduously since he was a small boy in the Koranic school of his home and in other schools of North Africa and Arabia, and was still acquiring and sifting knowledge in his library at Jaghbub up to his death. He had taught in the schools in Morocco, Algeria, Tunisia, Tripolitania, Cyrenaica, Egypt, the Hijaz, and the Yaman. Months of his life had been spent in travelling by the slow camel caravans of those days. He had thrice made the pilgrimage to Mecca. In spite of these activities he had found time to write a number of treatises. He had started his career as the head of a new missionary Order late in life—he was about 50 years of age when he founded his first zawiya in Arabia, and in the next twenty years he had made the Sanusiya the dominant Order in western Arabia and in North Africa from the Nile Valley to the borders of Tunisia and from the Mediterranean to the Sahara. When he died it was still intensifying its activities in the areas where it was already dominant, building everywhere new lodges, and was still expanding, mainly into the Sahara and the Sudan.

IV

When the Grand Sanusi died his two surviving sons, al-Sayyid Muhammad al-Mahdi and al-Sayyid Muhammad al-Sharif, were minors, so a regency of ten Shaikhs was appointed to control the affairs of the Order till the elder, Muhammad al-Mahdi, was old enough to take over their direction. When he did so he dealt primarily with the general affairs of the Order, leaving religious instruction in the hands of his brother.

The Grand Sanusi had been typical of the great itinerant teachers of his day: international in outlook and intent on the pursuit of holiness and learning rather than guided by secular distractions and ambitions. Mecca was the centre of his world and to it he tended always to gravitate. The Sayyid al-Mahdi was more definitely a Cyrenaican. Born in 1844 in a cave at Massa, near the Cyrenaican Mother Lodge of al-Baida, he was brought up among the religious families of the country and among the Bedouin. He studied under his father, the erudite Moroccan Sidi Ahmad al-Rifi, Sidi 'Ali bin 'abd al-Maula, Sidi 'Umran bin Baraka, and others of his father's circle of pupil-

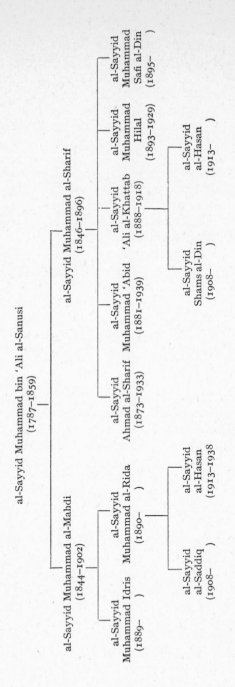

al-Sayyid Muhammad bin 'Ali al-Sanusi
(1787–1859)

al-Sayyid Muhammad al-Mahdi
(1844–1902)

al-Sayyid Muhammad al-Sharif
(1846–1896)

al-Sayyid
Muhammad Idris
(1889–   )

al-Sayyid
Muhammad al-Rida
(1890–   )

al-Sayyid
Ahmad al-Sharif
(1873–1933)

al-Sayyid
Muhammad 'Abid
(1881–1939)

al-Sayyid
'Ali al-Khattab
(1888–1918)

al-Sayyid
Muhammad
Hilal
(1893–1929)

al-Sayyid
Muhammad
Safi al-Din
(1895–   )

al-Sayyid
al-Saddiq
(1908–   )

al-Sayyid
al-Hasan
(1913–1938)

al-Sayyid
Shams al-Din
(1908–   )

al-Sayyid
al-Hasan
(1913–   )

savants, and later at Mecca. He is said to have been an eloquent
and inspiring leader and he was evidently an able organizer.
Unlike his father the Grand Sanusi and his nephew Sayyid
Ahmad al-Sharif he has left no writings behind and he seems
to have had less interest than they in literature and speculation.
He lived an austere life and was considered by his followers to
have been a saint and worker of miracles as great, or greater,
than his father.

The Order expanded considerably under Sayyid al-Mahdi's
leadership, particularly into the Sahara and the Sudan, and its
greatly extended missionary enterprises demanded his personal
attention. The conversion of the heathen and semi-heathen
tribes of these regions created political problems and the trading
activities of the Order required organization. The trade routes
through the Libyan oases to the coast had increased in importance since the rise of the Sudanese Mahdi in 1881 had closed
the Nile route. Personal direction was difficult from Jaghbub,
so in 1895 Sayyid al-Mahdi moved the seat of the Order to
Kufra, a more central position than Jaghbub in the theocratic
empire being slowly built up. He first went to live at the
zawiya of al-Ustad but shortly afterwards built a new zawiya,
in which he resided, on a site which became known as al-Taj.
He departed from Jaghbub amid the lamentations of his
followers, only some of whom he was able to take with him to
Kufra, leaving the rest behind at Jaghbub, with his nephew al-
Sayyid Muhammad 'Abid as his titular representative there.

There are few places in the world so remote as Kufra oasis,
but it was at the centre of the Sanusi empire and the meeting-
place of a number of important desert routes. Before Sayyid
al-Mahdi made it the seat of his Order, Kufra had been little
more than a watering place for caravans and the centre for the
wandering Tibbu tribes of the region, though the Zuwaya of
al-Jikharra went there each year to collect dates. It now became
an emporium through which caravans were constantly passing
and exchange was carried on. The Sanusiya profited both
by directly engaging in trade and transport and through
customs dues.

The little village of mud and palmwood houses at al-Taj also
became a centre of religious life and propaganda. The missionary efforts of the Order intensified all over Fazzan and into

the territories of Kawar, Tibesti, Borku, Ennedi, Darfur, Wadai, Kanem, Chad, the Azger, the Air, and Baghirmi. Its teachings were spread as far as Senegal. The work of organizing this propaganda fell largely to Sayyid al-Mahdi's two principal lieutenants. Sidi Muhammad al-Barrani operated in Kanem, where he founded a lodge at Bir Alali on the route to Chad and organized bands among the Aulad Suliman, Zuwaya, Majabra, Tibbu, and especially the Tuwariq, to oppose the advance of the French into Central Africa; and afterwards in the Borku. Muhammad al-Sunni, and his son al-Mahdi, operated in Bornu and Baghirmi, where he entered into relations, politically un-fruitful, with the Sultans of those countries, and in the Wadai, where he strengthened the good relations existing between the Sultan of that country and Sayyid al-Mahdi. In 1899 Sayyid al-Mahdi transferred the seat of his Order to Qiru (or Quru) oasis, between Borku and Tibesti, to direct better its propaganda, to administer the extensive regions won to it, and to organize resistance to the French.

It is sometimes said in European books that one reason why Sayyid al-Mahdi went from Jaghbub to Kufra was his desire to increase the distance between himself and the Turkish Administration of Cyrenaica, but I have not found any evidence to support this view. On the other hand there can be no doubt that he was alarmed by the military and political activities of the French, about which he seems to have been well informed. The French were hastening to reach the limits of the sphere allotted to them by the agreements with England of 1898 and 1899 about the partition of Central Africa. In January 1902 they seized Bir Alali (Kanem) and destroyed the Sanusiya zawiya there. At the end of May, or at the beginning of June, in the same year Sayyid al-Mahdi died. His brother, Sayyid Muhammad al-Sharif, had predeceased him at Jaghbub in 1896.

In general the energies of the Sayyid al-Mahdi had been directed to the Sahara and the Sudan and the main events during his headship of the Order took place off the Cyrenaican stage. I have not thought it necessary, therefore, to give more than a brief summary of his career and of the political history of the Order in Central Africa. He saw the Order his father had founded rise under his direction to the height of its expansion and political importance. Except for two or three lodges founded after his death the distribution of the lodges shown on the map—two in Algeria, and some elsewhere which were not completed, are not marked—is that of 1902. All the Bedouin of Cyrenaica and of the Sirtica, and most of those in the Western Desert of Egypt, followed the Order and there was no part of these regions which had not established in it a Sanusiya lodge; and even in the towns of Cyrenaica it had an influential following in the more cultured administrative and commercial circles. In southern Tripolitania the Order had slowly increased its authority and advanced it to the west, while it was the dominant power in Fazzan and in the central Sahara. It had retained a powerful following among the Bedouin of the Hijaz.

After Sayyid al-Mahdi's death the fortunes of the Order declined. This was chiefly due to the attack on it by the powers of Europe whose greed for possessions in Africa and Asia was bringing them rapidly to disaster. For his part Sayyid al-Mahdi showed himself anxious to avoid any action which might enable these powers to accuse him of political designs. He wished only to be left alone to worship God according to the teachings of his Prophet, and when in the end he fought the French it was in defence of the religious life as he understood it. In its remarkable diffusion in North and Central Africa the Order never once resorted to force to back its missionary labours. Shaikh Muhammad 'Uthman says of Sayyid al-Mahdi that the only orders he gave his followers were to pray and to obey God and His Prophet, that he avoided making any show of his power, considerable though it was, and that he held himself apart from political questions, fleeing from all considerations of that kind.[1] The Sanusiya Order co-operated with the Turks in the administration of Cyrenaica, although the Sanusi family and the Brothers of the Order disapproved of their way of life, but it resisted Turkish demands for assistance in their war of 1876–8 against the Russians. It refused the aid asked for by 'Arabi Pasha in Egypt in 1882, and by the Sudanese Mahdi in 1883, against the British. Sayyid al-Mahdi likewise rejected diplomatic overtures by the Italians and Germans. But when the French invaded its Saharan territories and destroyed its religious houses, and when later the Italians, also without

---

[1] Op. cit., pp. 118–19.

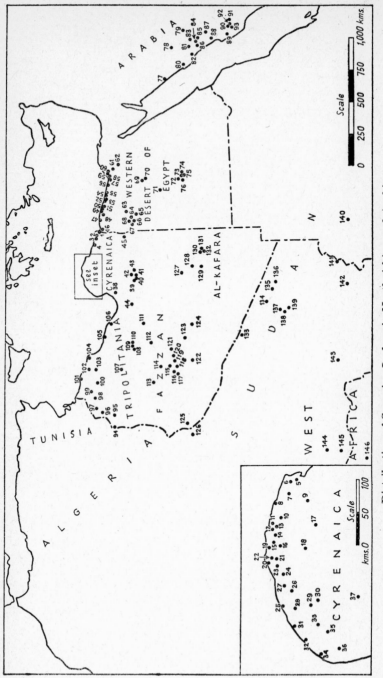

Distribution of Sanusiya Lodges in North Africa and Arabia.

CYRENAICA

1 al-Jarfan
2 Umm Rukba
3 Janzur
4 al-Marassas
5 Umm al-Razam
6 Umm Hafain
7 Martuba
8 Darna
9 al-'Azziyyat
10 Mara
11 Khashm Rzaiq
12 Maraziq
13 Bishara
14 Tart
15 Shahhat
16 al-Fayidiya
17 al-Makhili
18 al-Nayyan
19 al-Hamama
20 al-Haniya
21 al-Zawiya al-Baida
22 Qafanta
23 al-'Arqub
24 al-Qasrain
25 Talmaitha
26 Anbalu al-Huwaiz
27 Mirad Mas'ud
28 Qarabarbi
29 al-Marj
30 al-Qasur
31 Taukra

32 Dariyana
33 Asqafa
34 Banghazi
35 Umm al-Shakhanab
36 al-Tailimun
37 Msus
38 al-Qatafiya
39 Aujila
40 al-'Arq
41 al-Libba
42 al-Jikharra
43 al-Khatt
44 Marada
45 Jaghbub

EGYPT

46 al-Akhsab
47 al-Shih (Barrani)
48 al-Mithnan
49 Shammas
50 Najaila
51 Umm al-Rakham
52 Baqush (Sidi Harun)
53 'Ailat Bin Musa
54 Fuka
55 al-'Awama
56 al-Jamaima (al-Dhaba)
57 Abu-Shinaina
58 al-Hammam
59 Sidi Musa
60 Yadim al-Abairish
61 al-Ghait

62 Haush 'Isa
63 al-Qara
64 Gharmi
65 al-Zaitun
66 al-Sabukha
67 al-Gharbiya
68 Taba'
69 al-Bawiti
70 Mandisha
71 Farafra
72 al-Qasr
73 al-Rashda
74 Balat
75 Ismant
76 al-Qalamun

ARABIA

77 al-Wajh
78 al-Ais
79 al-Madina
80 al-Haura
81 Yanbu' al-Nakhl
82 Yanbu' al-Bahr
83 al-Khaif
84 al-Safra
85 Subh
86 Badr
87 Ziba
88 Rabigh
89 Jidda
90 Abu Qubais (Makka)
91 al-Tayif

92 Muna
93 al-Husainiya

TRIPOLITANIA

94 Ghadamis
95 Darj
96 Sinawin
97 al-Haraba
98 al-Rujban
99 al-Qal'a
100 Mizda
101 Tarabulis
102 Masallata
103 Bani Walid
104 Misurata (2)
105 Sirt
106 al-Naufiliya
107 al-Tabaqa
108 Hun
109 Saukna
110 Waddan
111 Zalla

FAZZAN

112 al-Fuqha
113 Birqin
114 Sabha
115 Ghudwa
116 Dlaim
117 Murzuq
118 Taghaghan
119 Umm al-Aranab

120 Zuwila
121 Tamassa
122 al-Qatrun
123 Wau al-Kabir
124 Wau al-Namus
125 Ghath
126 Qanit

AL KAFARA

127 Tazirabu
128 Bazima
129 Ribiyana
130 al-Hawari
131 al-Taj
132 al-Jauf

SUDAN

133 Bardai
134 Quru
135 Wajanqa al-Kabira
136 Wajanqa al-Saghaira
137 Yarda
138 'Ain Kalak
139 Faya
140 al-Fashir
141 Jabal Murrah
142 Abaish
143 Bir Alali
144 Jajiduna
145 Zinder
146 Kano

provocation, did the same in Cyrenaica, the Order had no choice but to resist.

But though it was attacks from the outside which destroyed the theocratic empire of the Sanusiya, it may be considered doubtful whether in any case such extensive territories could have been maintained under single direction. The economic and political organization of the Order was crude, even when elaborated in the days of Sayyid al-Mahdi in response to increased trading activities and to the need of maintaining peace in the petty and barbarous states that had come under its influence. Its administrative machinery was at no time adequate for effective control over such wide domains, with their poor communications and their manifold tribal, racial, and cultural divergencies. To these weaknesses must be added, after Sayyid al-Mahdi's death, personal rivalries within the Sanusi family on the lines of which cracks began to appear in the loose empire, and it is probable that even if it had not been attacked by the Powers of Europe it would have broken up into a number of principalities, or spheres of religious influence, ruled by various members of the family. It might indeed be possible to sustain the thesis that it was the Italian occupation of Libya which prevented the complete break-up of the Order by rallying the outraged sentiment of the Bedouin to its side as the symbol of their common resistance to conquest and alien rule.

The administrative organization of the Order in the time of Sayyid al-Mahdi was simple indeed. Each lodge of the Order lived on its own revenues, derived from endowments, tithes, contributions of money, goods, transport, and labour, and sent its surplus to Jaghbub and Kufra for the maintenance of the University and of the Sanusi family and for the general purposes of the Order. The Shaikh of each lodge arbitrated in disputes in the district in which it was situated and could generally wield spiritual sanctions sufficiently weighty to compel acceptance of his awards. The Shaikh of a lodge was appointed by the head of the Order and was responsible to him. There was, however, so little centralized planning that new lodges seem occasionally to have been founded by the initiative of influential families without the head of the Order hearing of the new foundation till its completion. In the more distant parts the lodges were largely autonomous, or came under the control of a local Mother Lodge, such as Mizda in Tripolitania and Abu Qubais in Arabia. After the death of Sayyid al-Mahdi, a member of the Sanusi family sometimes installed himself as local director of the affairs of the Order, as Sayyid Muhammad 'Abid did in Fazzan. Without going into further detail it may be said that though central control existed it was cumbersome and that though there was an organization it was inadequate to deal with situations such as that which faced the Order on the death of Sayyid al-Mahdi, which demanded a rapid marshalling of its dispersed resources.

V

The dynastic situation which had formed after the death of the Grand Sanusi formed again after the death of Sayyid al-Mahdi: his surviving sons, Sayyid Muhammad Idris and Sayyid Muhammad al-Rida, were minors. The leadership of the Order therefore passed to Sayyid Ahmad al-Sharif, son of Sayyid Muhammad al-Sharif, Sayyid al-Mahdi's younger brother; though for the first few years its political direction seems to have been largely in the hands of the experienced old Shaikh Ahmad al-Rifi, the last of the intimates of the Grand Sanusi and the principal adviser of Sayyid al-Mahdi.

Sayyid Ahmad al-Sharif's leadership of the Order falls into three periods, from 1902 to 1912 when he was resisting the French in the Sahara, from 1912 to 1918 when he was in Cyrenaica directing the Bedouin against the Italians and the British, and from 1918, when he went into exile, to 1933, the year of his death at al-Madina in Arabia. It is only the second period with which this book is directly concerned and I will therefore summarize very briefly the events in the Sahara, leaving to a future chapter a more detailed account of the events in Libya which led to the Sayyid's appearance in Cyrenaica at the head of the Sanusiya Militant.

The French advance continued. After the loss of Bir Alali in 1902 Sayyid Ahmad moved his headquarters from Qiru back to Kufra, where he was protected by an immense desert and diplomatic immunity, since the British took the view that the oasis belonged to Turkey. In 1906 the French took Kawar and

Bilma and in the following year occupied 'Ain Kalak, killing Sidi Muhammad al-Barrani, the Shaikh of the Sanusiya lodge there and the foremost of al-Sayyid al-Mahdi's missionaries in the Sahara. In 1909 they occupied Abaish in Wadai and sent an expedition against Masalit. As they advanced they everywhere destroyed or suppressed the lodges of the Order. In 1913 and 1914 they occupied Tibesti, Borku, Wajanqa, and Ennedi, at the same time as the Italians occupied Fazzan from Tripolitania. Though the Sanusiya had minor military successes and temporarily regained some of its territory, it had lost all political control in what is now known as the French Sudan. While the Franco-Sanusi war was in progress in the Sudan Italy, in 1911, declared war on Turkey and landed troops at various points on the Libyan coast, the conquest of Tripolitania being the primary objective. From the first the Sanusiya entered the fray and when Turkey abandoned the contest in 1912 the Order continued the struggle in its own name.

At this point I must break off my account of the history of the Order to show how it achieved its paramountcy in Cyrenaica, because the development of the Order is tied up with a certain set of social relations in Cyrenaica and has been circumscribed by them. Only in Cyrenaica did the Sanusiya in the end establish itself firmly because only there existed conditions which permitted its taking root strongly.

CHAPTER II

THE BEDOUIN OF CYRENAICA

I

In the last chapter I recorded the development of the Sanusiya. In this chapter I give a brief description of Cyrenaica and of the way of life of the Bedouin who live there and an equally brief account of the history of these Bedouin and of their tribal system.

The geographical isolation of Cyrenaica proper, the large peninsula which juts into the Mediterranean from the Bay of al-Sallum to the eastern Sirtica, has greatly affected its history. It is cut off from the Nile Delta by 700 km. of semi-desert and from Tripolitania by 650 km. of the Sahara round the shores of the Sirtica, while to the south of it stretch endless desert wastes, for Cyrenaica proper is only just over 200,000 sq. km. with a Saharan hinterland of over 500,000 sq. km. On the other hand the coast of Cyrenaica lies only 300 km. from Crete and 400 km. from the Greek mainland, and it belongs by climate and vegetation to Europe.

The physiographic features of the country which influence to any extent the life of its people can rapidly be summarized. Northern Cyrenaica is a calcareous mountain rising to a table-land, *al-Jabal al-Akhdar*, the Green Mountain, so called from its evergreen forests. To the north its slopes rise steeply from the sea or its littoral, while to the south it billows gently towards the great Saharan desert. The two major divisions of the country are known as *al-jabal*, the mountain—or *al-ghaba*, the forest, since its northern part is covered with bush—and *al-barr*, the steppe. The mountain and the steppe alike fall into a number of zones, the principal of which are shown in the accompanying sketch-map. There is a narrow strip of coastal plain which broadens towards Banghazi and then spreads south-westwards into the great *barqa* plain. Animal transport can only mount the plateau from the coast by steep and infrequent paths which lead up deep ravines to the first terrace, the so-called *arqub* country, a succession of thickly wooded ridges broken into myriad bosses and cut deep by many wide wadis,

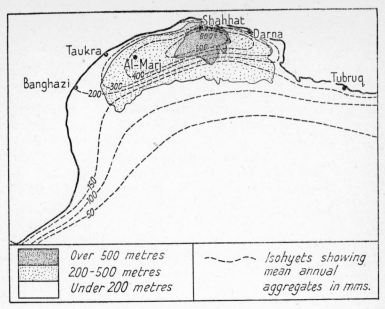

Rainfall and the Plateau Area.

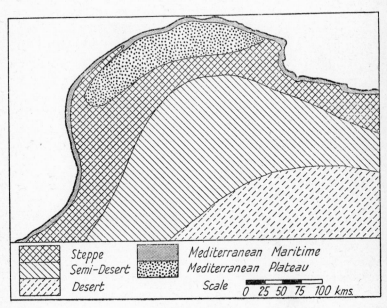

Climatic Zones.

the steep sides of which make east–west journeys slow and arduous. To the west this broken country levels down, and in a bay in the hills lies the extensive treeless, but very fertile, basin of al-Marj, known to Europeans as the Barce Plain. It was colonized in classical times and again recently by the Italians. The Arabs call this first terrace *lusaita* (*al-wasaita*), the middle part, because it lies between the coastal plain and the plateau tableland formed by *al-zahir*, the second terrace. This table-land is famous for its Graeco-Roman ruins and is dotted also with the deserted farms of Italian colonists. It mounts to a narrow third terrace, at about 875 metres above sea level, from the top of which one can look down on these settlements.

The plateau slopes southwards through a juniper belt. There forest ends and it continues to roll to the southern steppe in stony undulations dissected by many wadis. In the plain at its foot there is plenty of grass and low scrub, and vegetation is thick in depressions, but the country becomes increasingly desolate the farther to the south one journeys towards the life-less wastes of the Sahara. The eastern part of Cyrenaica is more arid than the west or centre. The Marmarica, the *batnan* of the Arabs, is characterized by low hills rising from the coastal belt and prolonged towards the south to create a succession of crests of several kilometres in depth. The mean annual rainfall is low and wells are restricted to the coastal belt. However, there is, probably in most years, a certain amount of grazing to some fifty miles from the coast during the rains. The Sirtica, the extension of Cyrenaica to the west, is a vast rolling treeless plain traversed by a series of wadis running north–south which in their spread provide most of the summer grazing. Wells are found only near the coast but pasturage is plentiful till the Wadi al-Farigh is reached.

The rainfall very exactly determines the vegetation belts and thereby limits human distribution and imposes a certain way of life. The amount of precipitation depends on a number of circumstances. Mean annual rainfall decreases from west to east. Altitude also affects it. More significant, however, are the variation with latitude, the seasonal rhythm, and annual irregularities. The accompanying map shows how rainfall decreases rapidly from the coast, how only the very limited plateau area is subject to heavy precipitations (400–550 mms.),

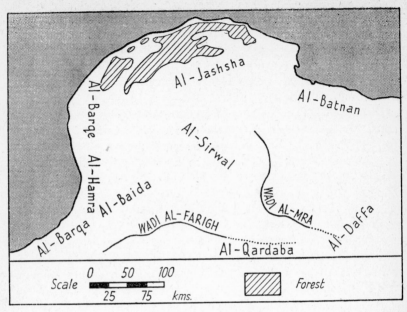

Distribution of Forest.

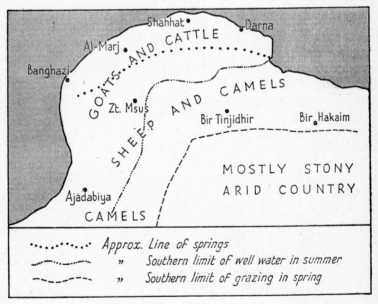

Pastoral Zones.

and the insufficiency of the fall elsewhere. It follows that only on the plateau can there be forest, and only there is a settled and purely agricultural way of life possible; and it was there and on the coastal fringe that in ancient and modern times European colonists settled.

The rains in Cyrenaica fall only in winter, from October to April. In the absence of irrigation the planting season is thus clearly delimited. So is the grazing season to the south of the plateau, for in summer the grasses wither and the wells dry up, compelling shepherds to drive their flocks northwards to the plateau, thus producing the kind of seasonal nomadism known as transhumance. The variation in total rainfall from year to year and the distribution of its fall over the winter months are of the utmost importance for agriculturalists in Cyrenaica. There is still some obscurity, but it is an observed fact that every few years in Cyrenaica there is a year in which the fall of rain is insufficient, or too badly distributed, to raise an adequate crop. In a mixed economy this fact must have given an overwhelming bias towards pastoralism.

The water supplies of the plateau, which depend entirely on rainfall, are sufficient for the needs of the Bedouin and their flocks. The clayey soils are, however, very exacting and running spring water is rare, being for the most part restricted to the triangle Darna–Slanta–al-Haniya. On the western part of the plateau water is conserved in cisterns and wells and on the maritime and *barqa* plains, in the Sirtica and Marmarica, and generally to the south of the plateau, in wells.

The distribution of vegetation in Cyrenaica follows variation in degree of precipitation. Where there is much rain there is forest. Where there is little rain there is steppe. Where there is no rain there is desert. The forest is thick but mainly squat and of very limited extension. An Italian estimate[1] of its distribution is shown on the accompanying map. It is predominantly Mediterranean in type, the juniper and the lentisk being the two commonest trees of the country. Forest ceases a few miles to the south of the high watershed of the plateau and gives way to steppe. The well-known route Tariq 'Aziza is generally regarded as the dividing line between the two kinds

---

[1] Dott. Giovanni Manzoni, 'Memorie sui boschi della Cirenaica', *Notiziario Economico della Cirenaica*, 1929.

of country. The whitish soils of the steppe support worts and other scrub bushes and some drought-resisting trees in the beds of wadis and they are well covered with annual and perennial grasses and other plants which yield excellent pasturage in the springtime. However, except in the Wadi al-Mra, where camels can be kept the year round, there is little grazing beyond the line Msus–Bir Tinjidhir–Bir Hakaim.

The Bedouin of the forest area are essentially a goat people, though they also keep many sheep and cattle, and it is mostly through the medium of the goat that the vast natural wealth of the forests of Cyrenaica is transformed into human wealth. The animal is hardy and frugal, and has the great merit of preferring tree and shrub to grass and of being a catholic feeder. Just as the forest would be useless to the Bedouin without the goat so the much vaster stretches of steppe would be useless to them without the sheep and camel which turn its grasses and scrub into food. Thus Cyrenaica is fundamentally a pastoral country, primarily a country of sheep farming, and its people, as they say themselves, have the hearts of shepherds and not of peasants. While agriculture and pastoralism are both practised, the bias of nature and tradition is towards animal husbandry, by which the rich vegetation of the country is turned into milk, butter, meat, wool, hides, and draught and transport.

II

In Cyrenaica stand always contrasted the mountain and the plain, the forest and the steppe, the red soils and the white, the region of goats and cows and the region of sheep and camels, settled life and nomadism.

True nomadism is very rare. A few Fawakhir, Minifa, Huta, and other tribal fragments herd only camels, or if they possess other animals keep them with kinsmen near the plateau, and can therefore wander pretty well where they please. They may be found anywhere between the Nile, Fazzan, and the Sudan. Their spirit is that of an Aulad 'Ali tribesman who said to me: 'We call no place our home. It is wherever there is grass and water.' Semi-nomads are numerous. Those with land on the plateau cultivate there, then graze southwards, and return again to the plateau in the dry season to water their flocks.

Those of the *barqa* plain may never camp on the plateau but they move freely between grazing grounds, permanent water supplies, and ploughland.

Of the plateau tribes, the Darsa, the 'Arafa, most of the Hasa, and a number of 'Abaidat and 'Awaqir sections remain there throughout the year. The Bedouin met with wandering about in the southern grazing grounds after the rains are the 'Abaidat Ghaith, 'Awakla, and Shahin, some of the Hasa Shabarqa and Bakhayit, the whole of the small *'Ailat* Fayid tribe, large numbers of Bara'asa Husain, Tamiya, and Masa'id, 'Abid Mansur and Jabar, 'Awaqir Sdaidi and Brahim, and numerous small client groups more or less affiliated to these tribal sections. The nomadic sections are generally richer than the others in sheep and camels, and are also more vigorous, independent, and warlike. Politically, they are the leading sections of the tribes to which they belong. The foremost Shaikhs of the 'Abaidat, Hasa, Bara'asa, 'Abid, 'Awaqir, and Magharba are all to be found during the rains farther away in the steppe than most of their fellow-tribesmen.

The move southwards starts in December after the barley has been sown, or part of a group may take the animals south while the rest finish the ploughing. Most of these semi-nomads return to the plateau in May, when water becomes scarce, but some, including some of the most powerful elements, remain to the south of it permanently. There are many advantages in this annual move to the south. Rain falls and the grasses spring up in advance of the plateau, and grazing is more abundant and of a better quality. On the other hand, the grasses of the plateau and its southern slopes are still green when the desert grasses, except in specially favoured depressions, are withered. By their annual oscillation the Bedouin thus give their animals the best grazing at all seasons of the year. Sheep mostly lamb round about November, which is the month in which new grasses spring up in the *barr*, so that the move southwards gives the sheep the richest grazing at a time when they need it most; and the warmer conditions prevailing in the south suit the lambs. At the same time, the Bedouin in southern grazing grounds are compelled to live very largely on milk food, and the combination of rich pastures with the dropping of their young by sheep, goats, and camels, enables them to live on the country to a great extent. In normal times the Bedouin drive their animals on the hoof to Egyptian markets, slowly, along this rich southern pasture belt, grazing as they go, so that they arrive in good condition. Finally, there can be no doubt about the correctness of the Arab claim that a few weeks residence in the open steppe is a tonic for man and beast.

It must be remembered that there are no water problems at this time of year. Sheep, goats, and camels do not have to be watered from the time the first rains make grass till the end of April or early in May: even horses do not drink until well into April. This fact is important, because it means that the prolific pastures can be grazed by all without dispute, since the wells, which belong to tribal sections or families, are not drawn on. While rain is still falling regularly human re-quirements are met from pools. To the south of the Tariq 'Aziza, generally speaking, there is no ownership in land—there are no *hudud*, boundaries, as the Arabs say—and anyone may cultivate or graze where he pleases, but there is strict ownership in wells; whereas to the north of the Tariq 'Aziza there is less narrowly restricted ownership in water, which is here spring water in abundance, but there are well-defined rights in arable.[1] The water of the southern wells is essential for the Bedouin who own the country and who live in it all the year round, and their rights are respected by those who graze there. Sheep and goats need only drink every second or third day, even in the hottest weather, so that in the period of meagre pasturage they have a wide range of grazing from the wells, and the dry grasses, supplemented by evergreen shrubs of the goosefoot family, are sufficient nourishment for them. Wells are numerous in the steppe but few of them last out the summer.

The animals grazed in the southern steppe are mostly sheep and camels. The Bedouin say 'Cattle and goats do not migrate; camels and sheep do'. Camels are essential to nomadic life as it is impossible to move camp without them, and the richer Bedouin are in camels the more frequently they move, seeking richer pastures. Cyrenaican dromedaries are heavy beasts,

[1] Enzo Savarese, *Le Terre della Cirenaica*, Pt. II, 1928, Chap. VII; Massimo Colucci, *Il Regime della Proprietà Fondiaria nell' Africa Italiana*, vol. i, 1942, pp. 210 seq. and 220 seq.

useful mostly for transport and ploughing, though they give a good milk yield and a fair harvest of wool. There are horses, of Berber rather than of Arab type, in every big camp. They are kept for the saddle alone, being much used in old days for hawking, and are a sign of wealth and social position.

The census figures for domesticated animals are probably highly inaccurate. The flocks and herds were certainly much greater, especially for camels and horses, before the Italians ravaged the country. The Turkish figures for 1910 were 713,000 sheep, 546,300 goats, 83,300 camels, 23,600 cattle, and 27,000 horses, and it has been reckoned that by 1933 these had been reduced to 98,000 sheep, 25,000 goats, 2,600 camels, 8,700 cattle, and 1,000 horses.[1] Before the outbreak of the second Italo-Sanusi war in 1923 the normal export to the markets of Egypt was 80,000 sheep and goats a year, and it was reckoned that a settled Cyrenaica could produce annually for export at least 100,000 to 150,000 sheep and goats and 6,000 camels. The country used to satisfy a considerable portion of Egypt's meat requirements. It also exported clarified butter in big quantities, 91,835 kilograms being the figure for 1922 and 75,462 the figure for 1923.[2]

Although the Bedouin are by practice and inclination shepherds first and cultivators afterwards, all plough. Barley and some wheat are a staple food. Indeed, in most years they cultivate a surplus of barley which they trade, and it may be said that for the most part they are self-supporting as far as their flour requirements go. On the southern slopes of the plateau and in the *barqa* plain ploughing begins from the middle of October to the middle of November, according to the rains. The coastal belt is sown a little later and the plateau in December and January when the grasses begin to sprout. By mid-April the first harvest, that of the *barqa* and the southern slopes of the plateau, is being reaped, and on the plateau reaping goes on from May to the end of August. Everywhere barley is sown greatly in excess of wheat, for wheaten bread is not considered a necessity and barley is required for horses as well as for men.

[1] Jean Despois, *La Colonisation Italienne en Libya: Problèmes et Méthodes*, 1935, p. 44; Hans w: son Ahlmann, *La Libia Settentrionale*, 1930, p. 78. (First published in 1928.)

[2] *L'Oltremare*, Mar. 1930; *Rivista delle Colonie Italiane*, 1934, p. 885; Francesco Coro, *Settantasei Anni di Dominazione Turca in Libia*, 1937, p. 82.

They could not sow a better crop. There are wild varieties of barley in Cyrenaica and the country is in every way suited to its culture. It is very hardy, stands up to drought, and easily holds its own against the grasses, which are ploughed in with the seed on the plateau. When the barley and wheat have been reaped, the grain is stored in *kuf*. On the plateau these are ancient tomb-caves; elsewhere they are holes dug in the ground.

In a bad year, and even more in a succession of bad years, the Bedouin have experienced famine, but in most years the barley, and to a lesser extent the wheat, give an abundant yield. Bedouin have told me that they expect from sowing in the beds of wadis up to a hundredfold of barley and in the *barqa* up to fiftyfold. On the plateau the yield is smaller and in the Marmarica and Sirtica much smaller. In Turkish times there was a large export of grain from Cyrenaica. Mondaini says that it was to the mean annual value of 40,000 Lire Sterling for the years 1885 to 1900.[1] Much of this surplus was bought by English brewers.

The Bedouin way of life is well adapted to their environment. Given the inconstancy of the rainfall and the distribution of water supplies they would be foolish indeed were they not, at any rate in part, shepherds. They are not, of course, in all respects self-supporting. They make their winter tents and a good part of their equipment, carpets, sacks, and so forth, from the wool of their beasts, but some things the Bedouin regard as necessities have to be imported, notably tea, sugar, some rice, and cloth, especially the *jird*, the woollen cloak of the country. They trade these with surplus stock on the hoof, skins, wool, clarified butter, surplus barley, and honey and wax, so that they are in an economic sense self-supporting.

Cyrenaica is a rich country for Bedouin, a poor country for Europeans. Bedouin generally have no overhead expenses in production. I say generally, because rich men sometimes employ shepherds, though this is usually the practice of urban merchants engaged in the sheep trade. Bedouin use their own labour and that of their families and animals. What is perhaps more important is that they are prepared to live on what

[1] G. Mondaini, *Manuale di Storia e Legislazione Coloniale del Regno d'Italia*. 1927, p. 308.

Europeans consider to be a low level of civilization. They do not feel the need for expensive roads and ports, electric light, wireless sets, telephones, schools, churches, newspapers, and so forth; and clearly their economy could not support them. Time and again colonists, tempted from their homes by the short sea routes and the wooded plateau, have settled in the country and dispossessed the Bedouin, but in the end it is the Bedouin, and not the colonists, who have survived. When one looks at the massive Phoenician, Greek, Egyptian, and Roman ruins and the already half-ruined Italian towns, villages, and farms, and then on the flimsy tents of the Arabs, one cannot but reflect that the race is not always to the swift nor the battle to the strong.

III

Even in the steppe country it is difficult to find a Bedouin *naja'*, camp, for the camps are pitched in hollows and on the slopes of wadis and their feeders for shelter from rain and wind and too many visitors. On the plateau they are hidden in the forest. One cannot, therefore, make more than a very approximate estimate of the population of any part of the country, or of its distribution, by bare observation. It can, however, be said that at present the country is underpopulated and that the population is badly distributed between town and country, the urban part of it, which is almost entirely unproductive, being too large in relation to the whole.

There have been a number of estimates of the population by early travellers who visited the country in Turkish times. They had to make a guess at the population figure, aided by Turkish censuses. It has been suggested on the basis of their reports that the country then supported round about 250,000 souls.[1] The Turkish census of 1911 gave the population as 198,345, excluding Kufra.[2] Taking into account the various estimates which were made during the Italo-Sanusi wars, in the interval between them, and since, it may be said that to-day the total population of Cyrenaica is probably round about 200,000, of whom about a quarter live in the towns, the remainder being tented Bedouin and a few thousand oasis dwellers.

[1] Dr. Gotthold Hildebrandt, *Cyrenaïka als Gebiet künftiger Besiedelung*, 1904, p. 317. [2] Coro, op. cit., p. 20.

If the Bedouin of the country number no more than 150,000 it is evident that density of population outside the towns must be very low indeed. Ricci's map, based on Col. De Agostini's census, shows a density of 0 to 5 per sq. km. for all the tribes of Cyrenaica except the 'Arafa, the Darsa, and the Hasa, all plateau tribes, for which he gives a density of 5 to 10.[1] Col. De Agostini, in his exhaustive monograph,[2] written before the worst Italian excesses, reckoned the native population of Cyrenaica at 185,400, of whom 181,750 were Arabs and 3,650 Jews. Of the Arabs about 25,000—I give round figures—were living in urban centres, about 7,000 in the oases, and about 150,000 were tented Bedouin. Of the Bedouin he classed only 16,000 as nomads, 35,000 as semi-nomads, and 99,000 as stable. His classification into nomads, semi-nomads, and stable was, as he recognized, arbitrary, since there is no reliable criterion of stability among a tented people, but it gives a useful indication of relative mobility. By 'stable' Col. De Agostini meant normal residence in a determined area within which the tents are pitched here and there for watering or other reasons and with periodic movements for sowing and pasturing, even though some days away from their usual seat, as we find among the 'Arafa tribe and a considerable part of the Hasa, the Darsa, and the 'Abaidat tribes. By 'semi-nomads' he meant those Bedouin who spread with greater frequency and more widely either in their own territory or towards zones of sowing or pasturing where they remain for a long time on account of less prosperous conditions in their own territory, such as we find in the Magharba tribe and parts of the 'Awaqir, the Bara'asa, and the 'Abaidat tribes and in many of the more important client groups. By 'nomads' he meant Bedouin who, although they possess their own territory or recognized centre, emigrate for long periods to distant, and not always the same, objectives, and are almost always fractionized into small groups for reasons of watering and pasturing; or Bedouin who normally wander in desert territories, giving themselves exclusively to rearing camels. As examples of nomads in this sense he mentions the Aulad Shahin section of the 'Abaidat tribe and many units

---

[1] La Cirenaica—Geografica-Economica-Politica, edited by Olinto Marinelli, 1922–3.
[2] Le Popolazioni della Cirenaica, 1922–3, p. 444.

of the more independent client tribes. In other words, all the Bedouin of Cyrenaica are nomadic in some degree, some more and some less, and Col. De Agostini rightly stresses that whether they move much or little they all have the same characteristics when compared to peasants and townsmen.[1] They are all *bwadi*, as the Cyrenaican dialect has it, people of the tents, and they see themselves as a single people against the *hadur*, the citizens.

I have so far said nothing of the towns of Cyrenaica or of their inhabitants. They play a minor part in this story, which is about the Bedouin, but they cannot be entirely left out of it on account of their economic and political relations with the Bedouin, so I take this opportunity to give a brief account of them.[2]

Banghazi, which is supposed to be called after the saint Sidi Ghazi, buried in the town, is on the site of the classical Berenice. It is believed that after the disappearance of the Graeco-Roman community the site was unoccupied till the fifteenth century, when it was reoccupied by immigrants from the mercantile communities of the Tripolitanian coast, among whom Misuratans, both Muslims and Jews, preponderated in numbers and wealth. The Genoese Della Cella, who passed through the fly-infested town in 1817–18, in the time of the Caramanlis, says that it then contained about 5,000 inhabitants, at least half of whom were Jews.[3] Shaikh Muhammad 'Uthman al-Hashaishi, who was in the town in 1896, says that the greater part of the traders were immigrants from Sfax and the Island of Jerba—he was himself a Tunisian and often tended to exaggerate Tunisian influence—with some Greeks and a few Italians. 'As to the Turks, they do not give themselves to trade.' At this time Banghazi was a very simple, mostly mud-and-rubble, town, and the learned Shaikh makes a point of telling us that there were no posts or telegraphs, nor even a railway, save a line of three kilometres joining the official

---

[1] Ibid., pp. 32–3.

[2] The historical information is chiefly derived from Agostini, ibid., pp. 413–43.

[3] Paolo Della Cella, *Narrative of an Expedition from Tripoli in Barbary to the Western Frontier of Egypt in 1817*, 1822, pp. 194–5. (First published in 1819.) F. W. and H. W. Beechey (*Proceedings of the Expedition to explore the Northern Coast of Africa from Tripoly Eastward in 1821 and 1822*, 1828, p. 299) consider Della Cella's estimate too high. Theirs is 2,000.

residence of the Pasha to a garden; and that the town possessed only one machine for grinding corn.[1] The population increased considerably in the last decades of Turkish rule, reaching the figure of 16,500 in 1911.[2] In 1922 the population was 22,740, the great majority of whom were Arabs from the Maghrib, though some were immigrants into the town from the more sedentary Bedouin of the neighbourhood. It included also over 2,000 *qulaughla*, descendants of Turkish officials and troops and Arab women, and a large number of *shawashna*, descendants of Arab men and Negresses, with a sprinkling of *'abid*, full-blooded Negroes. There were also about 3,000 Jews and about 3,600 Europeans, almost all Italians. These elements, except for the Italians who left during the late war, are found in all the towns of Cyrenaica. There are also a few Cretans, the remnant of a small community exiled by the Italians.

Darna stands on the site of the Greek town of Darnis, from which the Arab name is presumably derived. It seems that it continued to be occupied throughout the Arab period, but was given new life through the settlement there of Muslim refugees from Spain at the end of the fifteenth century. According to tradition, towards the end of the seventeenth century the town was developed by a certain Muhammad Bey who organized irrigation and other public works there. The population was much increased by the settlement of merchants from the coastal towns of Tripolitania and of other countries of the Maghrib, either by direct migration or from Banghazi. When Della Cella visited the town in 1816 the population had been reduced by pestilence from 7,000 to 500.[3] In 1911 it was about 9,500[4] and in 1922 it was about 9,700 (not counting Italians) of whom 250 were Jews and the rest Muslims.

Al-Marj, the Italian Barce, was the site of the ancient city of Barke, famous in Greek times and to Arab historians of the first centuries after the Arab conquest of Cyrenaica. It fell into decay after the Hilalian invasion and was only a heap of ruins till 1842, when the Turkish administration built a fort there, a Sanusiya zawiya being constructed shortly afterwards. In 1922 the population, of very mixed origins, was 1,540. The other centres in Cyrenaica are no more than villages around admini-

---

[1] Op. cit., pp. 52 and 59.   [2] Coro, op. cit., p. 99.
[3] Op. cit., p. 177.   [4] Coro, op. cit., p. 102.

strative posts and contain not more than a few hundred persons. Shahhat and Tubruq had been Turkish posts before the Italians made them administrative centres. Taukra and Talmaitha had been Sanusiya lodges. Suluq and Qaminis were Italian creations. Marsa Susa (Apollonia) was first occupied by Cretan refugees during the Turco-Greek war of 1897. Ajadabiya, the town of which the Arab historian al-Bakri of the eleventh century spoke in such glowing terms, had ceased to be a settled centre until the Turks made it an administrative post. During the period of truce between the Sanusi and the Italians from 1917 to 1922 it became the seat of the Sanusi Amir, Sayyid Mahammad Idris, and afterwards an Italian administrative and commercial centre.

It has been noted that almost all the townsmen of Cyrenaica are immigrants from the west, from Morocco to Tripolitania, and the Bedouin regard them as foreigners and often with some distaste, especially the Tripolitanian immigrants. It is true that there is a small element of Bedouin origin in the towns, for the more stable and poorer Bedouin living near towns sometimes drift into them; but when they do so their descendants soon lose their links with the tents and their tribal status. The road to town life is a way along which there is no return, for the townsmen are not only foreigners, but their food, their speech, their dress, their manners, their interests, their loyalties, and in general their way of life and their sentiments, are different. The Bedouin visit the towns from time to time, but they do not feel at home in them, and they do not look at home in them either. In a town one can spot a Bedouin at a glance by his appearance, his step, his dignity, his naivety, and his loud voice, which sometimes startles the shopkeeper with whom he disputes a price.

The road to the towns is not only a way along which there is no return, but is a one-way track. A Bedouin can become a citizen, but a citizen can never become a Bedouin. He cannot live the life of the tents. Hence the Bedouin say that while it is always bad for a Bedouin girl to marry a townsman, it is possible for her to adapt herself to urban life, but it is out of the question for a Bedouin to marry a townsman's daughter, for it is impossible for her to become a daughter of the tents.

The *bwadi*, Bedouin, and the *hadur*, citizens, are separate communities. They are strangers to each other who meet but do not mix. There is a barrier between them and each distrusts the other. Nevertheless there is a measure of economic inter-dependence between them, and the tribes and the towns affect each other politically. In Turkish times the urban population, which, as we have seen, was small and contained a high pro-portion of Jews, was engaged in trade and domestic industries. The townsmen bought from the Bedouin animals, hides, wool, clarified butter, honey, beeswax, and ostrich feathers (ostriches were still hunted in the southern steppe in those days), and they supplied the Bedouin with those things he required but could not, or would not, make for himself: tea, sugar, rice, cloth, horseshoes, musket balls, flints, gunpowder, and earthenware. The urban craftsmen also made leather goods, manufactured salt from sea water, and conducted trade and exchange. Imports came by sea from Tripoli, Marseilles, London, Malta, Alexandria, and Crete, and overland from Alexandria.

But the townsmen of Cyrenaica never dominated the country as they dominate most of the Arab lands, where through usury, intimidation, monopoly of trade, and influence in the admini-stration and the courts they have reduced the countryman to the position of landless labourer or *métayage* serf. There was nothing in the Bedouin way of life which gave an opening to the usurer. Moreover, the towns had no monopoly of trade for, if necessary, the Bedouin could, since they were self-supporting in necessities, either go without urban supplies or obtain them overland from Egypt, as they showed during their war with the Italians. Consequently there were no rich landowning families living in the towns at the expense of the country-side, no aghas, beys, and pashas; and an educated middle class hardly existed outside the small official circle and lacked both wealth and influence. In general it may be said that in Cyrenaica the towns were not parasites on the country, but had their proper func-tions as trading centres and suppliers of the needs of the Bedouin population. The markets were free, not tied to town societies.

Nor could the Bedouin be coerced by force or law. The tribes were largely inaccessible and they were stronger than the towns, even with the administration behind them. The Bedouin were not afraid of the Turkish Administration, which sat very lightly on their shoulders, and they did not use the courts. The

Turkish Administration was centred in the towns but operated, as will be explained later, through the contacts of its local officials, who were generally Arabs of the country, with the leading tribal Shaikhs, with whom they made friends. These officials were townsmen or sons of Bedouin who had received an urban education and they acted as links between the citizen communities and the Bedouin. Through Bedouin relations with town merchants and officials what was happening in the world outside Cyrenaica percolated to the most distant tents. Another channel of political and cultural infiltration was the network of Sanusiya lodges. The Shaikh of the Sanusiya lodge at Banghazi was regarded as the ambassador of the head of the Order to the Governor of Cyrenaica and he was chosen for qualities which fitted him for this role. He was consulted by the Governor on matters in which the tribes were involved, and through him and the Brothers of the lodges of the towns news of the outside world reached the Head of the Order in the distant oasis of Kufra and the Heads of the local lodges, whose relations with the Bedouin in their localities were intimate. Thus, as will be seen, the Bedouin had a general idea of what the revolution of the 'Young Turks' meant and were aware of the impending crisis long before the Italian attack on their country was delivered. But though maintaining communications with the towns, neither the tribal Shaikhs nor the Sanusiya allowed themselves to be subordinated to them or identified themselves with urban interests. The Bedouin Shaikh did not, like the Syrian landowner, feel any need to have a town house, and the Sanusiya ever remained a country and Bedouin Order and directed its affairs from the desert.

Town and country kept apart, with the towns dependent on the country and not the country on the towns, because there was in Cyrenaica no client peasantry bound by debt, need of protection, and trade monopoly to the towns. The Bedouin did not settle on the land where they would be an easy prey to the usurer, overseer, and tax collector. Those who were defeated in the great tribal wars of the past and in the inter-tribal and inter-sectional fighting of more recent times migrated to Egypt and settled there as *fallahin*, and not in Cyrenaica. In Cyrenaica there is not the spur of adverse climatic conditions or the lash of land shortage to drive them to depart from their ancient

Arabian ways. In Egypt necessity has slowly subjugated the exiles to the peasant yoke. They long resisted but, like the Bedouin nomads coming from the Sinai Peninsula, had in the end to submit or perish. The absence of a substantial peasantry in Cyrenaica is one of the characteristics which most distinguish it from the Arab societies of Palestine, Syria, Iraq, Egypt, and the Maghrib. The peasant can be dominated. He is fixed to the earth and can be made to surrender it and till it for others. The Cyrenaican Bedouin is fixed to no place and cannot be forced to sell his birthright by bad seasons or intimidation. This has meant that there have not been in Cyrenaica any social enclaves attached to the towns through which the towns and administrative centres could lord it over the Bedouin. Outside the towns all is Bedouin and the Turkish Administration, and afterwards the Italian Administration, found that they could not get a grip on the Bedouin of Cyrenaica as they could on the peasantry of Tripolitania.

Nevertheless the towns and the Turkish, and later the Italian, Administration in them affected the tribal system by acting as a pull on those tribal segments which lived nearest to them, so that the tribes which lay between the towns and the steppe were attracted towards one or other of these poles. The political structure of Cyrenaica as a whole exercised in this way a significant influence on the segmentary tribal system.

IV

The Bedouin who became followers of the Sanusiya Order and whose country and way of life I have described are divided into tribes and tribal sections owning different tracts of the country. This tribal system existed in Cyrenaica long before the Grand Sanusi preached there and it continued to exist after his grandson Sayyid Muhammad Idris had fled the country and the Sanusiya Order had been abolished and its lodges destroyed by the Italians. It is the fundamental structure of Bedouin society which the Sulaimid tribes brought with them from Arabia.

The Bedouin of Cyrenaica are Arabs. The Arabian tribes who conquered the country and settled in it mixed with the indigenous Berbers, as is evident in their physical features to-

day, but even ethnically the Bedouin are more Arabian than
the people of Egypt, the Sudan, and Tripolitania, while
culturally they are as completely Arab as any people in the
world, proud Tamim and Quraish not excepted. In essentials
their language is that of the Hilalian invasion of the eleventh
century and no foreign language competes with it. The Berber-
speakers are a handful in the distant oasis of Aujila, and even
there they are bilingual, and the insignificant fractions of Jews
and Cretans in the towns speak Arabic, the Cretans being
Muslims as well. The Italian immigrants left the country of
their own accord during the late war. Thus the obstacles to
complete Arabization in the Maghrib (Tripolitania, Tunisia,
Algeria, and Morocco), a Berber culture, large Jewish colonies,
and European colonization are to-day all absent in Cyrenaica. In all essential matters also the Bedouin of Cyrenaica
are like Bedouin tribesmen elsewhere in the Arab world: they
have the same tented, pastoral, way of life, the same social
organization, the same laws and customs and manners, and the
same values.

The people of Cyrenaica are linked to the classical Arab
world of the east, to Egypt and the Jazirat al-'Arab (Arabia,
Palestine, Iraq, and Syria) rather than to the Maghrib; to the
sacred towns of Islam and to Umayyad Damascus, 'Abbasid
Baghdad, and Fatimid Cairo. More particularly they are linked
to Egypt, with which their country has had political ties from
the earliest times, and which is their natural market. The
desert comes down to the sea at the Gulf of Sirte and separates
Cyrenaica from Tripolitania and these two countries have
always gone each its own way. Cyrenaica was linked to Graeco-
Egypt, Tripolitania to Phoenician Carthage. Cyrenaica went
with Byzantium, Tripolitania with Rome. Indeed, as Despois
says: 'The Greater Syrtis is without dispute one of the most
decided frontiers, natural and human, to be found anywhere in
the world.'[1]

During the last few decades this separation has been brought
into relief again by the rise of the Sanusiya Order, for whereas
almost to a man the Cyrenaicans follow the Order politically,
the Tripolitanians, except for the Bedouin tribes, have shown a
lively animosity towards it. Moreover tribal ties between the

[1] Op. cit., p. 45.

two countries are weak. On the other hand, Cyrenaican tribes and tribal sections, notably the Aulad 'Ali tribe, speaking the same dialect and with the same customs as their cousins still in Cyrenaica, stretch unbroken from al-Sallum to Alexandria, and are also numerous in the Bahaira province of Egypt and in the Fayum. The Cyrenaican Arabs form to-day numerically by far the most important Bedouin element in Egypt, and apart from those who have remained tented there, there are many who have settled on the land.

In its general outline the history of the Arab conquest of Cyrenaica is well known. 'Amr ibn al-'As, during the Caliphate of 'Umar, conquered Syria and Egypt and in 643 overran Cyrenaica, then occupied by Berber tribes and under the nominal rule of Byzantium. He met with little resistance, and within seventy years the whole of North Africa, from Sinai to the Atlantic, was in Muslim hands. It seems, however, that the original conquerors only settled as garrisons in the coastal towns, and neither controlled the hinterland nor had any considerable ethnic influence on its Berber peoples. Bedouin settlement on a big scale and the complete Arabization of the indigenous Berber population took place from 1050 or 1051 in the famous Hilalian migration.

The Bani Sulaim and the Bani Hilal came originally from Nadj. They are of Mudarid stock, the Bani Sulaim being the senior branch. They passed into Upper Egypt as a result of the check to the Carmathian movement in Arabia, in which they were involved, and settled there; but they were inclined to be troublesome in a country little suited to their traditional way of life, so during the reign of the Fatimid Caliph al-Mustansir, his Vizier encouraged them to reconquer Tripoli and Tunis from the Berbers, who had again asserted their independence. Arab historians have compared their migration to that of locusts or wolves. The Bani Hilal passed westwards into Tripolitania and Tunisia, where many Bedouin tribes claim descent from them to-day. The Bani Sulaim mostly settled in Cyrenaica. It must be added that the nobility and the historical exploits of their forbears are for the most part unknown to the Bedouin of Cyrenaica.

The present-day descendants of the Bani Sulaim are spread from Egypt to Tunisia. Those of Cyrenaica are divided into two main branches, the Jibarna and the Harabi. The Jibarna tribes are 'Awaqir, Magharba (some list the 'Araibat section of this tribe separately), 'Abid, and 'Arafa. The Harabi tribes are 'Abaidat, Hasa, '*Ailat* Fayid, Bara'asa, and Darsa. These tribes are shown on the diagram below, which presents them as tribes and not in the genealogical fiction of proper names. Strictly speaking, the Bara'asa should not appear on this chart since it is only one section of this tribe, the Aulad Hamad, who are true Harabi. However, it has become customary to class them as Harabi.

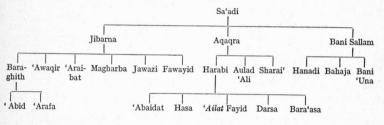

Attention is drawn to other names on this chart. The Aulad 'Ali, who have a fraternal relationship to the Harabi, about a century and a half ago lived in eastern Cyrenaica, but were compelled to migrate to Egypt by pressure from the Harabi, who received support from the Caramanli rulers of Tripoli. To-day they occupy the Mediterranean littoral from al-Sallum to Alexandria. Another branch of the Aqaqra, the Sharai', who migrated to Egypt, have become *fallahin* and are now found only as scattered families. When the Aulad 'Ali entered Egypt they found the Hanadi in possession of part of their present-day territory and drove them out of it. These Hanadi are now settled in the Sharqiya Province of Egypt. As will be noted from the chart, they belong to the Bani Sallam branch of the *Sa'adi* family of tribes. The Hanadi had previously dispossessed their brothers the Bani 'Una and this tribe is now completely absorbed in the *fallahin* population of Lower Egypt. A third fraternal branch of the Bani Sallam, the Bahaja, were also expelled from the Bahaira and are now settled in the Sharqiya and Gharbiya Provinces of Egypt. Of the Jibarna group, the Fawayid used to occupy the part of the plateau and plain now occupied by the Hasa, the Bara'asa, and the 'Abid. They were driven out of their country early in the nineteenth century, at the same time as the Jawazi, by a combination of the 'Awaqir, the Magharba, and the Bara'asa, assisted by the Caramanli rulers of Tripoli, and are now settled in the provinces of Fayum, Bani Suef, Bahaira, and Minya in Egypt. The Jawazi used to live in the country now occupied by the 'Awaqir, and they now mostly live in Minya Province of Egypt and in the Fayum. Another struggle which greatly altered the tribal distribution in Cyrenaica was two wars, the last about 1832, of the Magharba and 'Awaqir, aided by their Jibarna kinsmen the 'Abid and 'Arafa, against the tribes which occupied the *barqa* and the remnants of which now range the littoral of the western Sirtica. These tribes are known as *al-'Arab al-Gharb*, the Western Arabs.

So, in 1800 the Harabi and Jibarna tribes, which are now in undisputed control of all Cyrenaica outside the towns, occupied only part of the country, mostly the central, and the most northerly reaches of the western, plateau. The Jibarna were cut off from the southern steppe by the Fawayid and Jawazi, the whole of the *barqa* was occupied by *al-'Arab al-Gharb*, and the eastern part of the plateau by the Aulad 'Ali. The wars by which they drove out their rivals were long and savagely fought and many incidents in them still form part of Bedouin tradition.

As a result of these tribal wars the descendants of the Bani Sulaim invaders of Cyrenaica and the Maghrib thus began to return eastwards with a quota of Berber blood about the end of the seventeenth century and pushed out the tribes they found dwelling in the Western Desert of Egypt and pressed them into the Delta, where they were absorbed by the *fallahin*. The first intruders from the west were pushed to the Nile by stronger tribes coming behind them and these by yet stronger. They pushed one another like trucks on a siding. The Hanadi pushed out the Bani 'Una and the Aulad 'Ali pushed out the Hanadi, being themselves pushed on from behind by the 'Abaidat and other Harabi tribes. Besides the migration of whole tribes from Cyrenaica into Egypt there has taken place an exodus of many tribal sections and fragments, owing to intertribal fighting, until to-day there is not a Cyrenaican tribe, or even large section, which has not some of its members in Egypt, often whole lineages. The Bedouin of Cyrenaica know their kinsmen in Egypt and sometimes when the price of sheep is low in the Egyptian markets they leave their animals with them to sell on

their behalf when prices rise. There are said to be 30,000
'Harabi' alone, excluding the Bara'asa, in Egypt, most of them
in the Fayum, while the Aulad 'Ali and their client aggregates
number nearly 40,000.[1]

V

The Arabs of Cyrenaica distinguish between those tribes which
are *Sa'adi* and those which are *Marabtin*. The *Sa'adi* tribes are
so called after Sa'ada of the Bani Sulaim, their ancestress. They
are those nine tribes who hold the country by right of conquest:
the 'Abaidat, the Hasa, the *'Ailat* Fayid, the Aulad Hamad
(Bara'asa), the Darsa, the 'Abid, the 'Arafa, the 'Awaqir, and
the Magharba. The *Marabtin* tribes use the earth and water by
grace of the *Sa'adi* tribes of whom they are to a greater or lesser
degree clients. Savarese says that their status in Turkish times
lay between that of clients of ancient Roman law and that of
serfs of the glebe in western Europe in the Middle Ages.[2] The
Sanusiya did much to lessen the difference in status between
free and client tribes in Cyrenaica and to-day the larger groups
of *Marabtin*, although they may in theory live on *Sa'adi* land,
do in fact live independently and pay no fees to the owners of
the land. Sometimes violent disputes, and even wars, have
broken out between free tribes and their clients, such as the
famous battles between the 'Awaqir and the Shahaibat. Moreover, one has only to note that the predominance of the leading
sections of some free tribes is due to the support of powerful
client fractions to realize that, though the clients may be
considered not to have the full status of a noble Arab tribe, the
relationship between them and the owners of the country is often
one of mutual dependence. Thus the leading section of the
powerful Bara'asa tribe is the *'Ailat* Hadduth which in De
Agostini's lists numbers 2,520 persons, of whom only 630 are
true Bara'asa, the remainder being clients; and the leading
section of the 'Awaqir, the *'Ailat* Suliman, counts 1,200 clients
out of a total of 1,940. Where the relationship is one of mutual
dependence the two tribes are expected to help each other in
the payment of blood-money.

The client tribes are of different categories to which corre-

---

[1] G. W. Murray, *Sons of Ishmael*, 1935, pp. 277 and 296.
[2] Op. cit., p. 56.

spond different social statuses. Some are classed as *Marabtin bil baraka*, 'client tribes with the blessing' or *Marabtin al-Fatha*, 'client tribes of the prayer', and they often claim to be Sharifs. These 'sacred' tribes, such as the Aulad al-Shaikh and most of

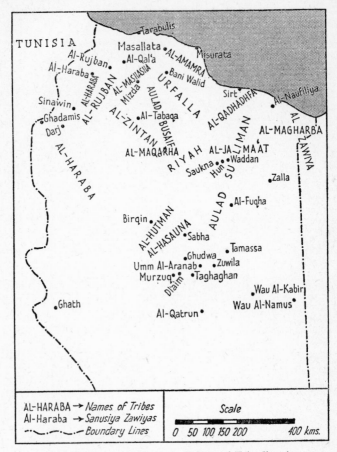

The Chief Sanusi Bedouin Tribes of Tripolitania.

the Masamir and Farjan, live among the *Sa'adi* as equals in virtue of the prestige they derive from their descent, or supposed descent, from saints, though the free tribes do not regard them as quite like themselves. Their ancestors are almost invariably believed to have come from the west, Morocco, Algeria, Tunisia, or Tripolitania. This move of pious men to the east began in the middle of the thirteenth century and has lasted to the present day. It is intimately bound up with the pilgrimage to the sacred towns of Islam. Round these pious men and round their tombs gathered for sanctuary the simple and oppressed, and from these and from the children of the holy men have sprung the *Marabtin bil baraka* tribes. The other client tribes have no sacred associations and are known as *Marabtin al-sadqan* because they pay *sadaqa*, a fee, to a free tribe for protection and for the privilege of using the earth and water. Some small broken-up fragments of this category on the plateau, such as the 'Awwama, Alauna, Hasanna, and some of the Qat'an and Sa'it, even to-day have a very inferior social position and are forced to make payments to, and to perform services for, the free tribes among whom they live. Other tribes of this second category live, as already mentioned, on territory which is to all intents and purposes their own and have long since ceased to pay a fee. This is especially the case to the east, in 'Abaidat tribal territory, where such client tribes as the Minifa, Qat'an, Taraki, and Huta live with independent status. In the west also the Fawakhir and Zuwaya are too powerful and warlike to accept overlordship. Also, the more nomadic groups in Cyrenaica are mostly client tribes and, like all nomads, resent any control or authority. Whatever the free tribes may say about them, they regard themselves as independent.

The provenance of the *Sa'adi* tribes and of some of the *Marabtin* tribes is shown together with the distribution of the Sanusiya lodges on the map facing page 35, and the approximate numbers of these tribes, and of a few others not shown on the map, are listed below.

Sa'adi				al-Zuwaya	.	.	.	3,700
al-'Abaidat	.	.	30,450	al-Shwa'ir	.	.	.	3,400
al-'Awaqir	.	.	27,500	al-Fawakhir	.	.	.	3,300
al-Bara'asa	.	.	21,000	al-Sa'it	.	.	.	2,900
al-Darsa	.	.	18,850	al-Majabra	.	.	.	2,500
al-Magharba	.	.	13,000	al-Minifa	.	.	.	2,500
al-'Arafa	.	.	9,300	al-Masamir	.	.	.	2,400
al-'Abid	.	.	6,850	al-Awajila	.	.	.	2,300
al-Hasa	.	.	6,500	Aulad al-Shaikh	.	.	1,650
'Ailat Fayid	.	.	100	al-'Aqail	.	.	.	1,400
				al-Shahaibat	.	.	.	1,350
Marabtin				al-Sarahna	.	.	.	1,250
al-Qat'an	.	.	5,850	al-Qabail	.	.	.	1,150
al-'Awwama	.	.	3,800	al-Huta	.	.	.	1,150

The figures for the free tribes include attached client groups, for the principal of which estimates are also given separately. The figures are taken from Col. De Agostini's monograph. The provenance of the chief Bedouin tribes of Tripolitania and of the fringes of Fazzan who are Sanusi, or sympathetic to the Sanusiya, is shown, likewise in relation to the distribution of Sanusiya lodges, on the map on page 52.

VI

Although there were in the past intertribal wars and feuds which have lasted into the present time, and in spite of the difference in status between free and client tribes, there were laws of the tents which gave every Bedouin the freedom of the whole country, and there was much coming and going between the tribes and exchange of hospitality, especially in the grazing grounds where sections with distinct territories on the plateau shared common pasturage to the south of it, and where the necessities of Bedouin life, watering at wells in transit, the crossing of another tribe's territory on the way to markets, the pursuit of straying camels, and the need to sow where rain fell, imposed a recognition of individual rights without regard to tribal affiliations or social status. Had it not been so, the Grand Sanusi could not have built on the tribal system his inclusive organization, for there would have been no foundations in culture, social structure, and sentiment, on which to build.

My inclinations as an anthropologist are to discuss at some length the tribal and kinship systems and the life of the tents, but I refrain from giving more than a bare outline of the tribal system, and I neglect altogether kinship and the life of the tents, because, however interesting detail about these matters might be to the ethnologist, a knowledge of them is, I think, unnecessary for an understanding of the development of the Sanusiya Order in Cyrenaica. I discuss the structure of the Cyrenaican tribe therefore only in so far as it is relevant to this general theme.[1]

Use of the term 'tribe' in Cyrenaica, even if it be restricted to the big free tribes, is always to some extent arbitrary for the political structure is highly segmentary. Nevertheless, though

[1] For a more general account see Savarese, op. cit., Pt. II, *passim*.

sections of a tribe may be opposed to one another they regard themselves as an undivided group in opposition to neighbouring tribes, and are so regarded by their neighbours. Thus a Qalbati is only a Qalbati in Hasa country. In 'Abaidat or Bara'asa country he is a Hasi. Likewise a Darsi or an 'Abidi in contrast to members of other tribes regards the whole of the Darsa or the 'Abid as his people, his tribal brothers.

Each tribe in this commonly accepted sense has its *watan*, its homeland, its soil, its arable, its pastures, and its wells; and each has its camel-brand which is also carved on the tomb-stones of its dead. The tribal lands are vested in the tribe, which has residual rights in them. They cannot, therefore, be alienated to other tribes without the consent of the whole tribe. A tribe is conceived of as a huge family descended from a common ancestor, from whom the tribe generally takes its name. Hence its segments can be figured either as a series of political sections or as genealogical branches of a clan.

A tribe is divided into several, generally two or three, primary divisions, or sub-tribes, which own well-defined portions of the tribal territory, in most cases running in strips unbroken by intrusive elements. These primary divisions are of the same pattern as the tribe of which they form part. Each division has its *watan*, which its members own and defend collectively. They believe that they are descended from a common ancestor, who is generally a son of the ancestor of the tribe. Primary tribal divisions split into secondary divisions, and secondary divisions into tertiary divisions, and so on. Each of the smaller divisions is a replica of the larger ones and has the same preferential and exclusive rights in its lands, an encroachment on which by another division will lead to fighting. Each has within the tribal brand its special lineage markings. The members of each division also consider that they are descended from a common ancestor who, in his turn, is descended from the ancestor of the larger division of which they form a section. The further the sub-division the more the resultant groups take on the complexion of kinship aggregates, rather than of political aggregates.

These kinship aggregates or extended family groups are the basic units of tribal life. They are called *biyut* (sing. *bait*). The tribe may be the residual owner of land and water but the *biyut* are the owners in use. Their members live in the same stretch of tribal territory, move during the rains to the same grazing grounds, use the same wells during the dry season, and cultivate adjacent strips of arable. The members of a *bait* have a lively sense of solidarity, and this is most evident in fighting and feuds. It is their common duty to avenge a slain kinsman and they share the *diya*, indemnity, should they accept it in the place of a life. They are jointly responsible for a wrong any one of them may commit. The smaller *biyut* are often identical with camps, usually from five to ten tents, in grazing grounds, and several closely related *biyut* camp near together in the vicinity of springs and wells in the summer, their combined camps then amounting sometimes to over a hundred tents.

What has been said above about tribal structure applies only to the free tribes and the larger client tribes living on their own land. The client tribes which are split up and scattered throughout Cyrenaica are not tribes in a political, but only in an ethnic, sense. It will be found that in any of the main tribes stranger groups, sometimes of client origin, have attached themselves to the clan dominant in the tribal area and through some fiction, myth, or fraud, have grafted their branch of descent on to the genealogical tree of this clan. The Bedouin use the word *laf* to describe this process and they say that kinship established in this way may become as strong as kinship of blood.

The structure of a tribe is expressed in terms of the lineage system of the clan dominant in its territory, the tribal segments being associated with branches of descent from the ancestor of this clan. The primary tribal sections are identified with lineages descended from some of this ancestor's descendants in the male line; the secondary tribal sections are identified with lineages descended from more of his descendants farther down the line of descent; and so on till the smallest territorial segments and the smallest lineages are reached. Thus a lineage considered as a branch of a clan consists of all those persons who trace their descent through the male line to a common ancestor, but it can also be, and in speech often is, conceived of politically as an agnatic group of this kind together with stranger and *Marabtin* accretions which occupy its territory and make common cause with it in disputes with other tribes or segments of the same tribe.

A simple example is given in illustration of tribal segmentation and of the consistency between lineages of a clan and segments of a tribe. In explanation of it a few words must first be said about the terms *qabila*, *'aila*, and *bait*. *Qabila* is the word generally used to denote a tribe or primary tribal division.

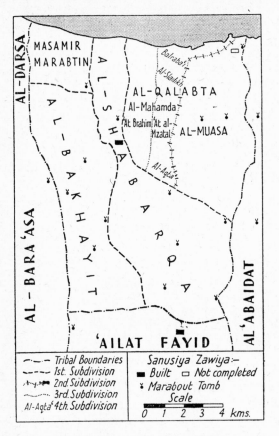

The Divisions of the Hasa Tribe.

'Ailat are the lineages into which a clan is divided and hence the sections of a tribe of various sizes in which these lineages are found and after which they take their names. *Biyut* are small lineages, or extended families, with a depth of five or six generations from the present day to their founders. It must be noted, however, that all these terms are relative and are used in a more or less comprehensive sense according to the context.

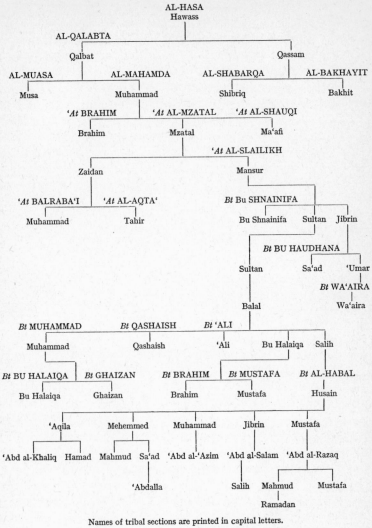

Names of tribal sections are printed in capital letters.
'*At* = '*Ailat*.
Bt = *Bait*.

If reference be made to the accompanying map and genealogical chart it will be seen that the Hasa tribe is made up of
three primary sections, the Qalabta, the Shabarqa, and the
Bakhayit, distributed in strips running from north to south,
which are very typical and give to each section equal condi-

tions of soil, water, and grazing. We trace the segmentation of the Qalabta alone and see that it has two divisions, the Muasa and the Mahamda. We follow the line of Muhammad alone and note that it splits into three lineages, '*Ailat* Brahim, '*Ailat* al-Mzatal, and '*Ailat* al-Shauqi (there is dispute, arising from quarrels over land, about the legitimacy of this branch). From Mzatal descend the three minor '*ailat*, al-Slailikh, al-Aqta', and Balraba'i. Following only the first line we note that '*Ailat* al-Shlailikh then divides into the various *biyut* shown on the chart, al-Habal, Mustafa, Brahim, &c., the male membership of only one of which, *bait* al-Habal, is presented in the genealogy. Where the name of an '*aila* or *bait* is different from that of its founder, it almost invariably means that the founder's nick-name has been used, the Cyrenaican Bedouin having a partiality for nicknames.

Each section of a tribe, from the smallest to the largest, has its Shaikh or Shaikhs. The tribal system, typical of segmentary structures everywhere, is a system of balanced opposition between tribes and tribal sections from the largest to the smallest divisions, and there cannot therefore be any single authority in a tribe. Authority is distributed at every point of the tribal structure and political leadership is limited to situations in which a tribe or a segment of it acts corporately. With a tribe this only happens in war or in dealings with an outside authority which for its own purposes recognizes the tribe as an administrative unit. There cannot, obviously, be any absolute authority vested in a single Shaikh of a tribe when the fundamental principle of tribal structure is opposition between its segments, and in such segmentary systems there is no state and no government as we understand these institutions; and criminal law is absent and civil law exists only in a very rudimentary form. Consequently the exact status of a Shaikh can only be defined in terms of a complicated network of kinship ties and structural relations. It is only necessary here to emphasize that his social position is unformalized and that he must in no sense be regarded as a ruler or administrator. Bedouin respect their Shaikhs, but they do not regard them as superiors. Rather their influence and wealth are considered as capital to be drawn on for the benefit of whoever is in need of them. So long as a Shaikhly family can keep their prestige, derived from the strength of their section, their wealth, their traditional place in Bedouin society, and the character of their leading members, so long only are they regarded as Shaikhs of whatever the grade may be.

In recording his impressions of the Aulad 'Ali tribe the generous and unfortunate Pacho gives an excellent picture of the Bedouin Shaikh's position in tribal society. He says that it is difficult to discover any government in their society, which might be called aristocratic, though it is such in form rather than in substance. The precarious authority of the Shaikhs rests not on force but on the renown and esteem they enjoy in the tribe. He adds that at the time of his visit it had become customary, after Muhammad 'Ali Pasha had broken the tribe, for the Shaikhs to get their titles confirmed by the Pasha of Egypt but that when they returned to their camps with the robes of honour bestowed on them by the Pasha of Egypt, these garments, far from adding to their prestige and making them objects of regard, excited derision and aversion unless the backing of the tribe had preceded the approval of the Pasha.[1]

The Italian lawyer Savarese has also written an illuminating description of the status of a Cyrenaican Bedouin Shaikh. Each *bait* and each *'aila* has its Shaikh, chosen for his age and wisdom or for his prowess, though the Shaikhship is generally hereditary in certain families. A Shaikh receives obedience and respect from his dependants but ought to be rich because the demands of hospitality are considerable. He takes a leading part in the settlement of disputes and must have the tact necessary to maintain the unity of the group in opposition to other groups of the same order. He represents his group in relations with these other groups and in the larger group of which it forms part. In matters in which his group as a whole is concerned he takes the advice of the Shaikhs of its divisions. He commands the men of the group in war and he collects the tribute due from the group to the Government. Nevertheless, a Bedouin Shaikh, however large the group he represents, lives and dresses like his fellow Bedouin, though, being rich, his tent may be larger than most and he has more horses and they are more richly appointed.

[1] J. R. Pacho, *Relation d'un Voyage dans la Marmarique, la Cyrénaïque et les Oasis d'Audjelah et de Maradèh*, 1827, p. 67.

He also has more wives than other Bedouin and is usually more cultured and intelligent.[1]

The most important of the Shaikhly families of the country, those which represented large tribal divisions vis-à-vis the Turkish Government, the Sanusiya, others sections of their tribe, adjacent tribes, and attached client groups, lost much of their influence with the loss of their stock and the exile of some of their more prominent members during the second Italo-Sanusi war. The authority of these traditional Shaikhly lineages was also undermined by Italian policies, first of recognizing and paying salaries to so many Shaikhs, some of whom were persons of little importance, that the office of Shaikh lost much of its virtue in the eyes of the people, and afterwards of ignoring the Shaikhs altogether. The better known of these Shaikhly families are the house of Bu Bakr bu Hadduth among the Bara'asa, the house of Lataiwish among the Magharba, the house of 'Abdalla among the 'Abaidat, the houses of Kizzih and 'Abbar among the 'Awaqir, the house of Asbali among the 'Arafa, the houses of Suwaikir and 'Ilwani among the 'Abid, the house of Bu Khatara bu Halaiqa among the Hasa, and, in the Sirtica, the most famous house of all, that of Saif al-Nasir among the highly nomadic Aulad Suliman.

[1] Op. cit., Pt. II, pp. 39–40.

CHAPTER III

THE SANUSIYA AND THE TRIBES

I

WHEN the Grand Sanusi came to preach in Cyrenaica he found the kind of society I have outlined: a congeries of tribes without law or effective government, for the Turks had little control over the interior, but with like values and habits and a community of life which crossed tribal boundaries. The Bedouin to whom he preached were simple people living the austere and monotonous life of the tents, with that savage character which has been so often portrayed, but also with those noble qualities which have seldom failed to evoke admiration from those who have lived among them. They were profoundly ignorant about the outside world and also—which is what touched the heart of the Grand Sanusi—about the faith of their fathers, and to this matter I must now return, since the Sanusiya was a missionary Order and can only be understood as such.

Though the Bedouin professed Islam before the Grand Sanusi influenced them by his teaching, they were almost totally ignorant of its doctrinal content, rites, or ritual and moral duties, and it is safe to assume that they did not obey its precepts. It is safe to assume this because even to-day, after a century of Sanusiya instruction, the Bedouin perform their religious duties in a very perfunctory way, if at all, and when Muslim law is at variance with tribal custom they follow tribal custom. In saying that they are lax, I do not suggest that they are not very sincere, Muslims. They are proud of being Muslims and consider themselves greatly superior to Christians, while they are contemptuous of Jews. Nevertheless, though they would not belittle, the Cyrenaican Bedouin feel no embarrassment at neglecting, the duties obligatory on every Muslim. The Confession of Faith is known to all and implicitly accepted by all. It imposes no irksome restrictions or tiresome duties. But they almost completely neglect—I speak of the more nomadic sections whom I know best, but it is probably true of most Cyrenaican Bedouin—their daily prayers, a duty which is absolutely obligatory and sinful to omit. I very much doubt whether many of the Bedouin know how to pray in the pre-scribed manner. As I have mentioned earlier, the Bedouin used to give alms to their zawiyas and in doing so they carried out one of the five major duties of a Muslim, but they regarded these alms as charity rather than legal dues. I have never met an ordinary Bedouin who had been to Mecca, or who even con-templated going there. Nevertheless, however lax they may be in other things, all Cyrenaican Bedouin keep the fast of Ramadan, and in this annual fast is summed up for them, more than in anything else, the obligations and privileges of Islam and its unity and strength. Moreover, although they are negligent Muslims themselves they respect piety in others. Brothers of the Sanusiya Order and religious men in general ought to pray regularly. That is their business and it is very necessary for the well-being of the community and worthy of liberal support, but the Bedouin is an unlettered man, a shepherd, and a warrior, and he has his own affairs to see to. Perhaps the Bedouin make up for their shortcomings by their enthusiasm for the *jihad*, holy war against unbelievers. They consider that they have fulfilled their obligation under this head in ample measure by their long and courageous fight, formally declared a holy war by the Caliph of Islam, against the Italians, the French, and the British. A Bedouin once said to me when I remarked how rarely I had seen Bedouin at prayer: '*nasum wa najhad*', '(but) we fast and we wage holy war'.

It must also be said that it would be an error to suppose that Islam had not, long before the time of the Grand Sanusi, strongly affected the character and custom of the Sulaimid Bedouin. This question, which is far from simple, need not be discussed in the present account and it is only necessary to note that the Bedouin assume that their customs are Muslim customs. It would also be a questionable judgement to assert that the Bedouin of Cyrenaica are not religious because they do not pay the same attention to outward ritual as do townspeople and peasants, for piety and holiness, as we have often been admonished, are not the same. The Bedouin certainly have a profound faith in God and trust in the destiny He has prepared for them and this faith and trust enhance that superb dignity which often contrasts so strikingly with their poverty and rags and what Paolo Della Cella describes as their 'excessive and habitual filth'.[1]

It is important that it should be understood that the Bedouin of Cyrenaica were Muslim, at any rate by allegiance if not by instruction, before the Grand Sanusi propagated the faith among them, because otherwise it would be difficult to account for their ready acceptance of his guidance. He was not appealing to a pagan people to embrace Islam, but to a Muslim people to show in their lives the faith they professed. It was his achievement to have given their religion organized form and direction, and by so doing to have exercised a persistent and transformative influence on their morals; for if the Bedouin neglect religious duties to-day and are by peasant and urban standards ignorant, loud, and lawless, it can be imagined that they were troublesome indeed before the Grand Sanusi and Sayyid al-Mahdi had taught them something of the duties of their faith and had softened the harshness of their customs. That the Sanusiya made a big difference to their way of life cannot be doubted. Shaikh Muhammad 'Uthman tells us of the Bedouin of Cyrenaica that 'They are very good-natured and of a cheerful disposition. They have a profound reverence for the Shaikh Sidi al-Mahdi, and they fear God and His Prophet. One is in perfect security among them; a stranger, an explorer, has he even loads of gold or silver, has nothing to fear from them.' He also says, and for the same reason, that there were peace and security for caravans in the Wadai and in those parts of the Sahara where the Sanusiya was established; and he adds that Sayyid al-Mahdi had achieved these remarkable results by the exercise of spiritual authority only, and not by force, 'as an Amir or Sultan would have done'. As for the citizens of Banghazi, of whom the Tunisian traveller had a very poor opinion, he says that they were proud, inhospitable, and lazy, and would still have been plunged in ignorance and without a vestige of civilization or of religious education 'if the goodness of God had not sent them the Sanusiya fraternity, which contributed much to their moral regeneration'.[2] Even Italian authors have to admit that the Sanusiya did much for the people

[1] Op. cit., p. 109.
[2] Op. cit., pp. 52, 59, 62, and 116–17.

of Cyrenaica.[1] The Bedouin remember with gratitude, as I have often heard them declare, the moral and cultural benefits brought to them by the Order. If they have fallen from the low religious and literary standards to which the Sanusiya raised a fraction of them it is due to the virtual extinction of its teaching office during their long struggle with the Italians.

II

The Bedouin the Grand Sanusi found in Cyrenaica were not only Muslims but also inveterate devotees of saints, the *Marabtin* (sing. *Marabat*) or Marabouts, as they are called in European accounts of North Africa, and the Grand Sanusi was in the long tradition of these holy men. Therefore, although I have touched on the matter in Chapter I, I need not excuse myself for treating it again in its Cyrenaican context, for Bedouin attachment to the Sanusiya springs from their personal devotion to the Grand Sanusi and his family, and not the other way round, and the Grand Sanusi derived his sanctity, and thereby his power, from the fact that he was a Marabout. The Bedouin are familiar with saints and ignorant of Orders. To them the Grand Sanusi was a saint and wonderworker, and a man with *baraka*, an ample measure of God's grace which flowed through him to ordinary folk; but there was nothing extraordinary about him. They knew his kind of old. When he died his tomb became a shrine, the largest and richest in Cyrenaica it is true, but only one among very many, dating from the Companions of the Prophet Muhammad, through the Martyrs who were killed fighting for the faith in Cyrenaica, to the pious and learned men of yesterday and the day before. His successors, by their kinship with him, and in virtue of their spiritual legacy from him, became heirs to his *baraka*; and so, to a lesser degree, have the heirs of the other religious teachers who came to Cyrenaica from the west, who died and were buried there, and whose descendants are the *Marabtin bil baraka* lineages of to-day. The authority the Grand Sanusi had over the Bedouin of Arabia and North Africa can be parallelled by the careers of many holy

---

[1] Giuseppe Macaluso, *Turchi, Senussi e Italiani in Libia*, 1930, p. 32; Giglio, op. cit., p. 22; and Arcangelo Ghisleri (quoting Andrea Pedretti), *Tripolitania e Cirenaica dal Mediterraneo al Sahara*, 1912, p. 132.

men in North Africa whose families still retain much wealth and influence. It was this Marabout status of the Grand Sanusi in the eyes of the Bedouin which won him their respect: it was the organization of the Sanusiya Order, an organization the earlier Marabouts did not have, which enabled him to turn this respect into a theocracy.

There is more than one explanation of the origin of the word *'Marabat'*. That generally accepted is that it derives from the root RBT, to bind, and hence from *'ribat'*, a fortified convent, inhabited by warrior-monks, found on the marches of Islam in its early days of expansion by arms. The word later became attached to the tribes which settled in Andalousia under the leadership of the Saharan tribe of the Sanhaja and was corrupted into the European 'Almoravides'. After the fall of the Sanhaja dynasty in the twelfth century part of the *Marabtin* tribes fell back into central and southern Morocco, whence many individuals moved eastwards. Some settled in Cyrenaica, generally on their return from the pilgrimage to Mecca, and their fanaticism, asceticism, ability to read and write, and thaumaturgic powers, impressed the simple Bedouin, who accepted them as holy men and magicians and used them to write charms, to perform religious rites, and to act as mediators in intertribal disputes. Sometimes, as we have seen, these men founded lineages which, dwelling under the shadow of their saintly forbears, became nuclei of social agglomerations which have developed in course of time into tribal groups, thus taking the shape of the tribal society in which they lived. The word *'Marabtin'* thus came to mean holy men (and their tombs) and then, in addition, tribes tracing their descent, or supposed descent, from these holy men and also, finally, in Cyrenaica, tribes who are clients of the great *Sa'adi* tribes which own the earth and water.

Some of the better known of the Cyrenaican saints, but by no means all, have gleaming white cupolas, supported by four walls, erected over their tombs, and inside the walls is a *tub*, a wooden box, over the grave, and this is covered with coloured cloth on which are inscribed passages from the Koran. Inside also are often a few pages from sacred books, occasionally a few small coins given by the local Bedouin, and any property, such as tents or ploughs, the Bedouin have wished to deposit in a safe place when on seasonal moves. Often a shrine, sometimes the shrine of a very famous saint, is no more than a wall of stones, with perhaps a stick, with pieces of cloth tied to it, erected over the grave, and this is the usual form in the steppe grazing-grounds. There are generally cemeteries around the tombs.

All these shrines are visited by the Bedouin from time to time, when they are passing by or when they have some request to make of the holy man. Many of them are cult centres, an annual ceremony, one of the chief events of the Bedouin year, being held at them; and when they are near the border between tribes, or between tribal sections, this is an occasion for intertribal, or intersectional, gatherings. There is no saint whose tomb is much visited by the Bedouin who has not performed miracles, some of them very remarkable miracles, and there is probably none who has not at some time or other cured the sick or given an heir.

The tombs of these holy men, Sidi this, Sidi that, and Sidi the other, are found in profusion over the whole of inhabited Cyrenaica. The historically best known are those of Sidi Rafa', one of the Companions of the Prophet, near al-Zawiya al-Baida on the plateau, of Sidi 'Abdalla, one of the Prophet's standard-bearers, in the oasis of Aujila, and of the founder of the Sanusiya Order, Sidi Muhammad bin 'Ali al-Sanusi, at Jaghbub oasis. The shrines belong to the tribes and tribal sections in whose earth the Marabouts are buried and the Marabouts are looked upon as tribal and sub-tribal patrons. Like the Sanusiya Order, they have become part of tribal life.

I have earlier reproduced Col. De Agostini's map of the Hasa tribe to serve as an example of the territorial distribution of lineages. The same map serves to illustrate the distribution of shrines in a tribal territory. It can be seen from this map, which shows only the best-known Marabout tombs, that all the different sections of the tribe have their shrines, and I would draw attention to an interesting feature of the distribution which I have also noted in other tribal areas: how often these sacred spots are near a tribal boundary, or near the boundary between one tribal section and another. This may not be pure chance, for the Marabouts in their lifetimes were regarded as standing outside the tribal system, to which indeed, being foreigners from the west, they did not belong, and their chief political role was to act as mediators between tribes and between one tribal section and another. Even to-day their tombs are regarded as neutral points, as it were, and are often the place chosen for a meeting between the Shaikhs of one tribe, or tribal section, and those of an adjacent tribe, or section, when some matter has to be settled between them. It has sometimes happened also that when two tribes have disputed the ownership of territory, they have settled the dispute by allotting it to a Marabout, which means to his descendants, so that one then finds a *Marabtin* strip between two *Sa'adi* tribes or tribal sections. One of the best examples of this is the strip of country owned by the Aulad al-Shaikh tribe between the 'Awaqir and the 'Abid and 'Arafa tribal domains. In the same way tribes made gifts of disputed wells to dead saints. Where a *Marabtin* tribe has grown out of a Marabout family they will be found living in the area around their tombs. Thus the Aulad al-Shaikh territory spreads out from Sidi Mahiyus, part of the Masamir live near Sidi Nuh, the Mshaitat live around Sidi al-Mshaiti, and the Qat'an live near Sidi Hashim and Sidi Suliman al-Tair.

So, long centuries before the Grand Sanusi began his mission in Cyrenaica, the Bedouin were used to the sight of an *'alim*, a learned man—for anyone who can read and write is a learned man to the Bedouin—coming from the west to heal their children and beasts, break droughts, write talismans, and teach them the beliefs and law of Islam. Such a man was also a *muhakkam*, one who arbitrated in their disputes and said the *fatiha* at their settlements and undertakings to make them binding. He could arbitrate among them because he was not of them. He was not like them a tented son of the steppe, though his descendants may have learned to live as such, but a *Marabat*, a man who follows religion and not the rains. The Bedouin of Cyrenaica owe much to these holy men, for, ignorant and superstitious though they may have been, they taught the tribesmen to respect learning and religion and kept those twin lights burning, even if dimly, through centuries. The Bedouin do not forget them, or to say a prayer for them, when they pass their tombs; and they have given the freedom of their earth and water to their descendants. Without these forerunners the Grand Sanusi could not have planted his Order in the country. It is planted in their bones.

Marabouts of the kind I have described were still coming to Cyrenaica from the west up to the time when the Grand Sanusi began his preaching in the country. Two of them whom he found there, already living among the Bedouin, the one on the western and the other on the eastern part of the plateau, teaching them and settling their disputes, became his followers: Sidi Ahmad bin 'Abdalla al-Sakkuri, a late arrival from the west whose descendants became Shaikhs of the zawiya of al-Marj, and Sidi al-Martadi Farkash, of an old *Marabtin* family of Cyrenaica, whose descendants became Shaikhs of the lodges at Umm al-Razam, Bishara, and Martuba. But the great majority of the Grand Sanusi's helpers were men who had come with him from the west, chiefly from Algeria. Other *Ikhwan* families, mostly of the Khattabi lineage, of which the Sanusi family are a branch, came later, also from Algeria, in the time of Sayyid al-Mahdi. To the Bedouin they were all Marabouts and when they had in their lifetimes a reputation for piety or learning their tombs in the Sanusiya lodges in which they resided became places of cult like those of their forerunners all over Cyrenaica. But unlike the earlier Marabouts these Sanusiya Brothers were not only holy men. They were also members of a fraternity, of an organization. The Sanusiya Order was thus not only heir to the accumulated capital of the Marabouts, but was able to exploit it as a corporation. It incorporated a number of isolated cults into a single wider cult, fractionized, it is true, by tribal particularisms, but, all the same, brought under a common organization. Each lodge of the Order was a cult centre, but it was something more: it was part of a general cult directed through the lodges towards the Head of the Order. The tribes of Cyrenaica became through the Order linked from above in a common, if loose, organization under a single, sacred, Head. This was possible only because a tribal system already existed uniting the different tribes, in spite of their feuds and enmities, into a society which, though lacking political unity, rested on common sentiments, a common way of life, and a common lineage structure.

What gave stability to this new relationship between the Bedouin tribes and the Sanusiya Order, turning the sacred Head into a secular leader and the religious organization into a government, and changed a loose federation of tribes into a nation, was common hostility to outside interference, an ingredient supplied in measured quantities by the Turks and copiously by the Italians.

III

The rudiments of Islam which the Grand Sanusi found in Cyrenaica made his teachings acceptable, delivered as they were without embellishments, to the Bedouin of the country, and the Marabout tradition which he also found there made him personally acceptable to them. His chief difficulty must have been the rivalries between tribe and tribe and between tribal section and tribal section down to the smallest sections. This difficulty was overcome by transferring the centre of the Order to desert oases, where it could not become identified with any particular tribe, and by distributing its lodges impartially throughout the tribal territories.

Of the forty-five zawiyas belonging to the tribes of Cyrenaica proper (including al-Naufiliya and excluding the Kufra lodges) probably twenty-one were founded before 1860 or during the lifetime of the Grand Sanusi, twenty-two during the lifetime of Sayyid al-Mahdi, and two when Sayyid Ahmad al-Sharif was Head of the Order.

A high proportion of the lodges of the Order in the time of the Grand Sanusi were along the line of oases on the 29th parallel, for to the lodges of the Cyrenaican oases on that line must be added those in the oases of the Sirtica, Zalla, Saukna, Hun, and Waddan, all founded round about 1855, and probably that in al-Fuqha also. Lodges were early planted in the oases partly on account of their importance as caravanserai and trading centres, partly because the oases-folk were more tractable than the Bedouin, and partly because the stability of these centres gave greater opportunity for corporate religious life. The Sanusiya certainly made a deeper religious impression on the peoples of the oases than on the Bedouin.

It will have been noticed also how few of the Sanusiya lodges were founded in the towns of North Africa. There are no lodges in the towns of Egypt and though the Order counts many followers in the towns of Cyrenaica and is politically dominant in them it has only one zawiya in each, Banghazi, Darna, and al-Marj ; and that at Banghazi, the capital of the country, was only founded about 1870. The Sanusiya lodge in Tripoli town was not built till 1882. It must, however, be remembered that in Turkish times Banghazi and Darna were little more than villages and al-Marj only a military post and that, as already explained, their inhabitants were foreigners, either Jews or immigrants from Tripolitanian towns who were generally affiliated already to other Orders. Moreover, the Turkish administration functioned from these centres, and that alone would have prevented the Grand Sanusi from making them the headquarters of his mission. There could not be two governments in one large village, especially as the Grand Sanusi disapproved of the Turks and they were suspicious of him. Also the presence of the Turkish Government in the towns ensured order and some, even if very small, opportunities for education and religious instruction and services, and Sayyid Muhammad bin 'Ali al-Sanusi had settled in Cyrenaica with the express purpose of reviving the faith and raising the culture of the totally illiterate and almost heathen Bedouin, whose contact with the towns was negligible. The social functions carried out by the Sanusiya lodges in Cyrenaica were more consistent with settlement among wild tribesmen than among peaceful citizens. Propaganda of the faith, educational work, cultivation of gardens, settlement of disputes, provision of shelter, hospitality, and security to travellers, and of refuge for the pursued, the weak, and the oppressed are all functions especially appropriate to tribal and barbarous conditions of life.

The Order was based on the tribes and not on the towns. The lodges were founded by tribes or tribal sections and the tribes or their sections regarded them as tribal institutions. Al-Qasur zawiya was not just a lodge of the Order in 'Abid tribal territory. It was the 'Abid zawiya; just as al-Marj was the 'Arafa zawiya, Shahhat the Hasa zawiya, and so on. The tribal system and the Sanusiya organization interpenetrated. The Sanusiya gave to the tribes a national symbol and the tribes participated in it through their lodges. It was the combination of a common organization with representation that allowed for tribal allegiances and rivalries which provided the Order with sure foundations.

So much was the Sanusiya organization based on the tribal system that the distribution of the lodges may be said to have reflected tribal segmentation, mirroring lines of cleavage between tribes and between tribal sections. The Sanusiya organization was fractionized along these fissures. The distribution of lodges among the 8 *Sa'adi* tribes was Hasa, 1; 'Ailat Fayid, 1; Bara'asa, 1 (a second lodge, al-Nayyan, was little more than a grain store attached to al-Zawiya al-Baida); 'Abid, 1; 'Arafa, 1; Magharba, 2; 'Awaqir, 6; Darsa, 9; and 'Abaidat, 14. There were 17 lodges among the Aulad 'Ali tribe in Egypt and for the Aulad Suliman with their attached tribes in the Sirtica only one, Sirt, if we exclude the lodges in the Sirtican oases. This uneven distribution may be related in part to the location of trade routes, harbours, springs, concentration of summer wells, and so forth, but it was undoubtedly due chiefly to variations in tribal cohesion. The more cohesive tribes had a single lodge, or, in the case of the Magharba, 2 lodges. The very cantonized Darsa tribe, whose lack of solidarity was largely due to their very broken country and the oecological self-sufficiency of their sections, each of which was more or less stable in its own territory, had no less than 9 lodges. The ethnically heterogeneous, widely dispersed, and structurally confused 'Awaqir tribe had 6 lodges, and the 'Abaidat tribe, which showed even less unity of sentiment and action, had 9 lodges. The most broken up tribe of all, the tribe in which the sections were most intermixed, and the tribe which displayed the minimum of political cohesion, was the Aulad 'Ali of Egypt, which had 17 lodges.

Among the Hasa, who possessed only the Shahhat lodge, in the territory of the Shabarqa section, though on the edge of the territory of the Qalabta section, rivalry between these two sections led to the foundation of a lodge at Marsa Susa, where the Order still claims the endowments, but a sense of tribal unity in the end prevailed and the project was abandoned. Likewise in the leading Tamia section of the Bara'asa tribe the rivalry between its two principal sub-sections, the Hadduth, in whose territory was the al-Baida lodge, and the Jilghaf, led to the Jilghaf marking out with a low wall the site of a new zawiya in the *silk* al-Hamama in the southern steppe country; but, here again, the lodge was never built. The location of al-Qatafiya and al-Naufiliya corresponded to a traditional jealousy between the Shamakh and the Ra'idat sections of the Magharba tribe. In the oasis of Jalu, where there was not the same tribal solidarity as in the neighbouring oases of Aujila and al-Jikharra, the two lodges were almost next door to each other. This was because the oasis was split into two opposed villages, each occupying about half of it with a strip of waste ground in between. A similar lack of unity in the Egyptian oasis of Siwa accounts for the building of several Sanusiya lodges there.

IV

Starting from the foundation of al-Zawiya al-Baida in 1843 the Order spread itself throughout Cyrenaica until it embraced in its network of lodges the entire tribal system of the country. It seeded itself, as it were, in the crevasses between tribes and between tribal sections, and its points of growth were thus also the points of convergence in tribal and lineage structure.

A tribal zawiya seems generally to have been founded in the following manner. A tribe or tribal section saw with envy that a neighbouring tribe or section had a zawiya. They sent a deputation to the Head of the Order and asked him for a Shaikh to teach their children, cater for their religious needs, settle their disputes, and so forth. The Head of the Order granted them their request and sent them a Shaikh chosen from among the learned and pious men who surrounded him at Jaghbub. The Shaikh probably took with him one or two companions, *Ikhwan*, Brothers of the Order, to help him start the new lodge which the tribesmen built in the most favoured spot in their territory. Simple structures though these zawiyas were, they took many years to complete, being added to when further accommodation was required, in the leisurely Arab way. Most of them were built on Graeco-Roman foundations so that the tribesmen who constructed them found stone ready to hand.

Through the kindness of Shaikh Muhammad al-Tayyib al-Ashhab I have seen the letter sent in 1855 by al-Sayyid Muhammad Ibn 'Ali al-Sanusi al-Khattabi al-Hasani al-Idrisi to his virtuous sons, some of the Shaikhs of the Sdaidi section of the 'Awaqir tribe, about the building of the zawiya of Msus. He says that he is sending to them Brothers to construct the buildings and that he has instructed them to build an annex which he can use as a resthouse when he visits the zawiya, though this is not to be built till the zawiya is completed. There will be builders and carpenters among the Brothers and all that is required of the tribal Shaikhs is selection of the site and supervision of the work. He points out to them that the work is for their benefit, in that they and their sons will receive in the zawiya an education, especially in the Koran and in the laws of Islam, and will be able to worship there. The Grand Sanusi then cites passages from the Koran and the *Hadith* commending religious benefactions. Finally he prays God to assist those engaged in the building and those who have made themselves responsible for the upkeep of the zawiya. God helps those who help others. A man reaps what he sows.

Some of the Cyrenaican lodges were larger than others but they all had the same features, a straggling warren of stone buildings comprising a mosque, schoolrooms, guest-rooms, apartments for the Shaikh of the zawiya and his family, rooms for teachers and pupils, and houses for the Brothers, clients, and servants, and their families. Many had small gardens near-by and the local cemetery was usually adjacent to a lodge. Jaghbub, where several hundred persons lived, was the largest of such communities. The ruins of Dariyana and al-'Azziyyat are also extensive and must have housed several hundred persons, but the average lodge probably housed only some fifty to a hundred persons, including wives and children, though there were often *Marabtin* families attached to the zawiya living nearby, sometimes in caves dating from classical times. The importance of a lodge was not to be estimated so much by the number of its occupants as by its tribal position and the number of its Bedouin adherents.

The Shaikh of a new zawiya would point out to the local tribesmen that he and his companions had no means of supporting themselves or of maintaining the zawiya. The various sections nearby then gave to the lodge the lands adjoining it, this estate surrounding a lodge being known as its *haram*. On the plateau the lodges were generously endowed with arable, in the steppe with wells, and in the oases with date-palms and springs. Later, further gifts of arable, wells, springs, and date-palms, or part use of these, would sometimes be made, especially when there was a dispute between two sections about ownership of property and neither would give way to the other, for they might then settle the matter by surrendering their claims to the zawiya.[1] Another way in which a lodge obtained rights in land was by asking permission of its owners to sow it. Constant repetition of this favour eventually gave the zawiya rights of use in it in perpetuity.

The tribesmen also assisted the Shaikh of the lodge in the cultivation of the lands, though most of the work was done by

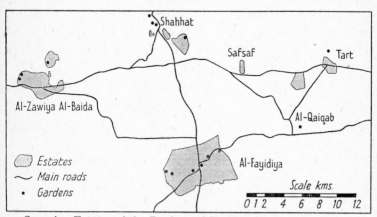

Sanusiya Estates of the Zawiyas of Shahhat, Tart, al-Fayidiya, and al-Zawiya al-Baida.

the zawiya community itself. At sowing time the Shaikh would pitch his tent near the area to be cultivated and prepare a communal meal, taking with him some sacks of rice for the purpose. The local Bedouin then came with their draught animals and sowed and ploughed for a couple of days on behalf of the zawiya. The same procedure took place at harvest time. Besides gifts of land and voluntary service in cultivating, the Bedouin were expected to pay a tithe to the lodge at harvest time and after lambing. No doubt many of them paid annual dues but it is unlikely that any strict record was kept or that payment could have been enforced had they been averse to making it.

That it was expected that the Bedouin might promise services more readily than perform them is suggested by an interesting document, dated 1307 A.H., found by the Italians at the

[1] Savarese, op. cit., p. 193.

Taukra zawiya and given in an Italian translation by Judge Colucci.[1] In it the tribal sections of the Baraghtha, Tursh, Dinal, and Shilmani place themselves under obligation, through the signatories to the deed, to pay the zawiya of Taukra alms on flocks and crops, to supply camels to carry supplies to Jaghbub, and to help the zawiya in sowing, building, excavations, and other works. Subject to the penalty of paying double alms they will not, without the permission of the Shaikh of the zawiya, render like services to other zawiyas. They promise also to defend the zawiya and to respect those who live in it, or who are its guests, and agree that those who fail to do so may be punished in body or in estate. Each will be for the zawiya and the zawiya for each. God is greater than any man. Those who are obedient will be recompensed by Him. Peace be to those who follow the right path.

The estates of the Sanusiya Order were *waqf* (called in Cyrenaica *habus*), inalienable endowments made in love of God by tribal sections and sometimes by individuals. They belonged to the various lodges to which they were donated, with the Order as a whole as residuary, and not to the family of the Grand Sanusi or to the Shaikhs of the lodges.[2] It was understood that when Bedouin donated tracts of country round a lodge they could continue to pasture and sow on any land not being used by the resident Brothers and to use the wells when there was sufficient water in them. The Shaikh of a zawiya was the legal administrator of its properties. The Head of the Order had no direct say in the administration of the estates, and in all probability only knew roughly of their extent. The revenues of one lodge could not be used for the upkeep of another, but any surplus over the expenses of a lodge were paid into a central pool. The members of the Sanusi family and the teachers and administrative officials of the Order lived in the distant oases of Jaghbub and Kufra, which produced little but dates, and had to be supplied from the lodges of the coastal region. Supplies were sent by caravan partly in local produce, such as skins, wool, grain, butter, honey, and meat, and partly in money or imported goods: rice, tea, sugar, and cloth. These gifts were

---

[1] Op. cit., pp. 434–5.

[2] Fernando Valenzi, 'La Senussia in Cirenaica ed il suo Patrimonio', *Rivista delle Colonie Italiane*, 1932, pp. 432–3.

sadaqa, freewill gifts, though if a lodge did not send them its Shaikh was reminded of his obligations. The lodges dealt with certain trading houses at Banghazi, giving them import orders against future sales of local produce.

This practice worked well enough during the lifetime of the founder and his sons but, as so often happens in Islamic Orders, later descendants began to demand individual shares in the wealth of the Order. While Sayyid Ahmad al-Sharif was its third Head it began to be the custom, a few years before the Italian invasion, to earmark the surplus revenues of particular lodges for particular members of the Sanusi family, and these members became regarded as patrons of the lodges which supplied them and responsible for their supervision. The territories in which the Order was dominant began to fall into spheres of influence controlled by individual members of the family, the allocation of spheres tending to be determined by the maternal kinship of various members with *Ikhwan* families occupying lodges in them. Sayyid Muhammad 'Abid and his brother Sayyid 'Ali al-Khattab had a lien on the *barqa al-baida* and Fazzan, where their maternal relatives the Ashhab family were influential Shaikhs of lodges; Sayyid Safi al-Din on the *barqa al-hamra*, where his maternal kinsmen the Mahajib family were predominant; Sayyid Muhammad Hilal on the Marmarica where his maternal kinsmen of the Sharifian Tursh lineage had considerable influence; and Sayyid Idris and his brother Sayyid al-Rida on the Cyrenaican plateau, where they had maternal ties with the important Bu Saif and Ghumari families. Sayyid Ahmad al-Sharif had a lien on Tripolitania, where lived his maternal kinsmen the powerful Fawatir tribe of Zlitin territory.

The endowments of the Order in Cyrenaica ran into thousands of hectares.[1] Several lodges had each more than 1,000 hectares attached to them. The fourteen lodges whose lands were technically registered in 1919 by a mixed Italo-Sanusi commission possessed more than 50,000 hectares. The total lands of the Order may well have been more than 200,000 hectares, or somewhere in the neighbourhood of 500,000 acres. Much of the land was of use only for grazing, but much was valuable agricultural country on the plateau. Wherever there were

---

[1] An *Ettaro* is 10,000 sq. metres or 2·471 acres.

springs and gardens there were properties of the Order, for such sites were particularly suitable for settlements of its Brothers since, unlike the Bedouin, they were sedentary and house-dwellers. In the semi-desert the Order owned, or part-owned, many of the best wells. In the oases of the 29th parallel and in the Archipelago of Kufra it owned extensive gardens and shares in springs and many thousands of date-palms. As it was a country and Bedouin Order its urban properties were inconsiderable: a few houses, mostly used as shops, in Banghazi, Darna, and al-Marj.

Anyone who studies the distribution of the Sanusiya lodges in Cyrenaica will observe that they were placed where he might expect them to have been placed on a politico-economic plan. A very large number were, as I have mentioned, built on Graeco-Roman foundations, and they were constructed on important caravan routes, on small inlets in the coast to command schooner trade, and in strong defensive positions. They were distributed to cover all the more important tribal aggregates, and the principal lodges were built at the centres of tribal life, as is especially evident among the southern nomads, who concentrate in summer time at such points as al-'Azziyat, al-Makhili, al-Nayyan, al-Qatafiya, and al-Naufiliya. In other words, where the Greeks and Romans and Turks found it convenient or essential to build villages and posts was where the Sanusiya established its lodges. Later the Italians used many of the same sites for their administrative and colonist settlements.

On assessments made by the Italians in the early days of their occupation, in 1913 and in 1919, for twenty Cyrenaican lodges of the Order it can be reckoned that their total annual revenues were about 150,000 Lire. On this basis, as those assessed were representative, a rough estimate of the total revenue of all the lodges in Cyrenaica would be about L. 400,000 or 10,000 Pounds Sterling at the 1919 rate of exchange. Of the lodges for which assessments were made, those with the largest revenues were al-'Azziyyat, al-Qasur (L. 15,000), Msus (L. 20,000), and al-Tailimum (L. 20,000). The surpluses sent to the Headquarters of the Order were estimated for only eight of the zawiyas, and in these eight cases the surplus amounted to rather under a third of the total revenues. Gen. Rodolfo Graziani states that the total annual revenue of the lodges of the Order, excluding those at Jaghbub and Kufra, was calculated at more than 200,000 Lire.[1]

The Italian figures appear to include all sources of revenue, agricultural produce, increase in stock, and the gifts received in beasts, cereals, honey, skins, mats, carpets, and butter. At the time there could have been no adequate assessment and an estimate of revenue in money is an inappropriate measure in what was for the most part a subsistence economy. The zawiya community lived partly by its own labour, largely that of servants and slaves, assisted, as explained, by the Bedouin of the vicinity at seed-time and harvest. The produce of its cultivations and gardens and of its flocks and herds was supplemented by contributions in kind from the Bedouin. In theory such contributions were an annual tithe, but in practice it is more likely that the Bedouin brought presents of beasts, butter, honey, &c., to the zawiya when they happened to visit it, or when its Shaikh let it be known that he was in need of something; and that now and again there was a general whip-round for a caravan to Jaghbub or Kufra. That is the Bedouin way of doing things.

Bedouin are hard-headed people and they expect a return for their labour and gifts. The neighbouring tribesmen considered that they were adequately rewarded for their support of their zawiya by the services it rendered, for, like the Christian monasteries of Europe in the Dark Ages, Sanusiya lodges served many purposes besides catering for religious needs. They were schools, caravanserai, commercial centres, social centres, forts, courts of law, banks, store houses, poor houses, sanctuary, and burial grounds, besides being channels through which ran a generous stream of God's blessing. They were centres of culture and security in a wild country and amid a fierce people, and they were stable points in a country where all else was constantly on the move. A Bedouin camp might be anywhere. A zawiya was fixed to the earth and its community with it. But the chief benefits the lodges conferred on the Bedouin were, as the Grand Sanusi told them in the letter quoted earlier, that they and their children might learn from scholarly and pious men the faith and precepts of Islam, that they might have the

[1] *Cirenaica Pacificata*, 1932, p. 125.

opportunity to worship in a mosque, and that by charity to their lodges they might earn recompense hereafter.

Each lodge had its Shaikh, who represented the Head of the Order. He arbitrated between the Bedouin, led the tribesmen to holy war, acted as intermediary between the tribe or section and the Turkish administration, dispensed hospitality to travellers, supervised the collection of tithe, directed cultivation of grain and care of stock, dispatched surplus revenues to the Headquarters of the Order, acted as prayer-leader on Fridays, and assisted in preaching and teaching. There were besides a number of other functionaries among the Brothers: the Shaikh's deputy, the *imam* to lead the daily prayers and to teach the Koran and canon law, the *mu'allim* to teach reading, writing, and arithmetic in the zawiya school, and perhaps a special *muadhdhin* to call the faithful to prayer, though any of the Brothers could do that.

V

In principle, as we have noted, the lands attached to lodges belonged, like the lodges themselves, to the Order, and more particularly to the lodge to which they were donated, and not to any particular individual or family. In practice certain Shaikhly families tended to gain an hereditary interest in them. What happened in the early days of the Order was that a Shaikh was sent by its Head to found a lodge and when it was established he was translated to a fresh missionary field. Shaikhs of lodges were in this way moved fairly frequently at first, but it later became the practice to leave a Shaikh in charge till his death and then to nominate his successor from among his kinsmen, with the approval of the tribe and on the advice of Shaikhs of neighbouring lodges. What mostly seems to have happened was that the tribal sections concerned asked for a son or brother of the last Shaikh to be appointed director of their lodge and the Head of the Order confirmed their choice. As one Darsi tribesman put it: 'The Shaikh of our zawiya must be a man favoured by the hearts of the people.' In course of time the tendency for the Shaikhship of a lodge to be regarded as hereditary became very marked, it being understood that if there was a suitable candidate from the family already established in the lodge he would be appointed, a view with which the later Heads of the

Order concurred. Thus we find charge of a zawiya continuing in the hands of a single family to the point at which Muhammad Yahiya bin al-Sanusi bin 'Umar al-Ashhab was appointed by Sayyid Ahmad al-Sharif to succeed his father as Shaikh of Msus at the age of sixteen. Some of these families sent their roots so deep that not only did they obtain what amounted to hereditary rights to a particular lodge, but controlled several lodges. Such were the influential families of Ghumari, Kalili, Farkash, and Ashhab, and the Khattabi families.

Hence we find to-day that many of the lodges are in hereditary charge of a family of Shaikhs who consider that they have a pre-emptive claim to its directorship and to enjoyment of its revenues, a claim backed by tribal opinion and by the acquiescence of the present Head of the Order. Thus the Dardafi family may be said to own the Shahhat lodge, the Isma'ili family to own the Fayidiya lodge, the 'Ammur family to own the Qafanta lodge, and so on. So much is this the case that disputes now sometimes arise, as in 1942 at Qafanta and Mirad Mas'ud, between members of a family about which of its members should succeed to the directorship of a lodge and control of its revenues.

This development is not surprising. Poor communications and the troubled times since 1911 have encouraged local autonomy in the Sanusiya organization. The Shaikh of a lodge brought up his family in it and his sons had no other home than the lodge and no other friends than the Bedouin around it and the families of Shaikhs in nearby lodges. Tribesmen dislike change and prefer to have for the Shaikhs of their lodges members of families they know and who share their local interests. But the tendency towards hereditary succession is also related to the fundamental lineage structure of the tribes among whom the lodges are distributed, for it is noticeable that whereas hereditary succession became customary in the Bedouin, or tribal, lodges, it has been by comparison lacking in the urban lodges of Banghazi and Darna and in those oases where tribal structure has become obscured by village life. This would seem to suggest that *Ikhwan* families tend the more easily to become stabilized as lines of hereditary Shaikhs the more closely they are associated with tribal structure. It is precisely in the most powerful, numerous, and integrated tribal sections that we find hereditary transmission of Shaikhship of lodges most accentuated, such as the Bara'asa-Tamia section (al-Zawiya al-Baida), the 'Awaqir-Sdaidi section (Msus zawiya), and the 'Abaidat-Ghaith section (Tart zawiya). In the same way the earlier Marabouts became, as has been noted, founders of lineages which were on the pattern of the branches of the Bedouin clans among whom they lived, and attached to them.

Also it must be remembered that the lodges were tribal institutions built by the local Bedouin so that they might participate in the *baraka* of Sayyid Muhammad bin 'Ali al-Sanusi. They participated in it through the Shaikhs of their zawiyas who received their *baraka* direct from the hands of the Grand Sanusi himself, or from the hands of son Sayyid al-Mahdi, and passed it on to their sons. This *baraka* belonged to the tribe, or tribal section, which built a lodge just as the *shaukha*, the secular Shaikhship of the tribe, or tribal section, belonged to it and had to be kept in it. In both the continuity of family succession had to be maintained, unless there were good reasons for acting otherwise. Thus each tribal section emphasized its autonomy in its hereditary line of religious Shaikhs, through whom the *baraka* of the founder of the Order was transmitted to them, whilst proclaiming its membership of a tribal federation with common allegiance to the Head of the Order.

As I have pointed out when speaking of the sacred *Marabtin* tribes of Cyrenaica, it was customary for the descendants of a Marabout to reside near his tomb. I have further mentioned that the Shaikh of a Sanusiya lodge, who is also called a *Marabat* by the Bedouin, might, if he had during life a reputation for piety, rather easily gained in Islam, be venerated as a saint when he was dead and his tomb become a shrine. This is another reason why Shaikhly families have tended to become hereditary directors of lodges.

Just as almost all the Marabouts of Cyrenaica were foreigners from the west, so were almost all the Shaikhs of the Sanusiya lodges. The Dardafi and Isma'ili families came from Tripolitania, the Ghumari family from Morocco, the 'Ammur, Bu Jibali, and Khattab families came from Algeria, and so on. As a class they enjoyed, and still enjoy, a reputation for sanctity among the Bedouin on account of their knowledge of the Koran and of reading and writing, and of their strict performance of religious duties. This reputation was doubtless enhanced by their foreign origin, for the Bedouin of Cyrenaica were accustomed to look to the west for piety.

At one time many, perhaps all, the Shaikhs of lodges were fairly well educated in such subjects as theology, canon law, and commentaries on sacred texts. To-day most of these alumni of Jaghbub University are dead and their successors, brought up in the bitter years since 1911, are for the most part very ignorant, some being almost as illiterate as the Bedouin themselves. The Bedouin regard them with a curious mixture of respect and condescension. They look up to them as learned and pious men who possess *baraka*, they kiss their hands, they call them '*Sidi*', and they listen respectfully to their admonishments and arbitraments. At the same time they look down on them for not being tribesmen and Bedouin, children of the tents. The Bedouin harmonize these conflicting attitudes by saying that a *Marabat* is a different kind of person from a Bedouin and cannot be expected to behave in the same way or to have the same outlook. He has been brought up to read books, pray, wash, and to do other things the Bedouin finds unnecessary in his own life. He has not been reared in the roving life of the tents nor learned the shepherd's art. Since they regard the *Ikhwan* as a different kind of people, the Bedouin do not intermarry with them nor with the Sanusi family, who belong to the same category. The *Ikhwan* families marry among themselves. The Sanusi family marry the daughters of *Ikhwan*, but do not give their daughters to persons outside their own kin.

The importance of the *Ikhwan* families in the history of the development of the Sanusiya is evidently very great. From the foundation of al-Zawiya al-Baida in 1843 to the appearance of Sayyid Ahmad al-Sharif in Cyrenaica in 1912 the Heads of the Order were absent from the country, either in Arabia or in distant oases, and its direct influence on the tribes was exercised by the Shaikhs of its lodges in their midst. Their ritual position within the tribal system combined with their structural position outside it enabled them to settle disputes and to unite and lead the various sections which had sponsored their lodges when the Order required their support. It was they who roused the

Sudanese against the French in 1902 and, as we will see, it was they who roused the Bedouin of Cyrenaica and of large parts of Tripolitania and Fazzan against the Italians in 1911; and it was they who attempted, unsuccessfully, to rouse the Bedouin of Egypt against the British in 1915. It was, above all, their propaganda and personal example in the field which made the struggle against Italy a national war and a religious crusade. To-day they have been broken by death, exile, and expropriation, and are poor and ignorant, but in the heyday of their power the Turks rightly estimated their influence and were careful not to encroach on their prerogatives.

VI

The thesis I have maintained in the foregoing pages, that the Sanusiya kept its cohesion and developed into a political organization largely because it was identified with the tribal system of the Bedouin, is supported by the lack of cohesion, common direction, and political influence of the other Islamic Orders in Libya, which won adherents only in the towns of Cyrenaica and among the citizens and peasants of Tripolitania, and in neither country found support among the Bedouin. I mention these other Orders for this reason, and also because a reference to them, however brief, places the Sanusiya in a more general setting as only one among many Darwish Orders. These other Orders are, however, described barely, since the part they have played in the political history of Cyrenaica is negligible.

The following Orders besides the Sanusiya are represented in Cyrenaica: Qadiriya, Rifa'iya, 'Arusiya, 'Isawiya, Tayyibiya, 'Azuziya, Madaniya, and Sa'adiya. The Qadiriya and the Rifa'iya are the only two classical Orders with lodges in the country, though the others eventually trace their descent from classical sources by those tortuous ramifications so confusing to the student of Islamic fraternities.

The distribution of the lodges of these Orders in Cyrenaica at the present time is shown in the table opposite. A knowledge of the history of the Orders is not necessary for an understanding of the history of the Sanusiya in Cyrenaica and is therefore omitted. It is necessary only to know that they all entered Cyrenaica from the west, both those, the majority,

LODGES OF ORDERS OTHER THAN THE SANUSIYA IN CYRENAICA IN 1942

Townships	'Arusiya	'Isawiya	Rifa'iya	Qadiriya	Madaniya	Sa'adiya	Tayyibiya	'Azuziya	Total
Banghazi	11	5	2	2	—	1	—	1	22
Darna	4	5	1	1	1	—	2	—	14
Al-Marj	1	1	—	—	1	1	—	—	3
Ajadabiya	1	1	—	—	1	—	—	—	3
Marsa Susa	1	1	—	—	—	—	—	—	2
Tubruq	1	1	—	—	—	—	—	—	2
Talmaitha	—	1	—	—	—	—	—	—	1
Taukra	1	—	—	—	—	—	—	—	1
Burdi Suliman	1	1	—	—	—	—	—	—	2
Suluq	1	—	—	—	—	—	—	—	1
Bedouin									
Aulad al-Shaikh	1	—	—	—	—	—	—	—	1
TOTALS	23	16	3	3	2	2	2	1	52

(The lodge at Marsa Susa listed as 'Isawiya is shared by this Order and the Rifa'iya. Under *Bedouin* is listed the only lodge outside towns at the present time. The lodgeless 'Azuziya community at Banghazi is included.)

which have a Maghribi origin and those which were founded in Iraq. Egyptian Orders are not represented in Cyrenaica. These facts are explained when it is pointed out that the Orders found in Cyrenaica to-day were introduced by urban immigrants from the west who settled in Banghazi and Darna as traders and artisans. Whence follows the most important feature of the non-Sanusiya Orders, their urban character. With the exception of the Madaniya and a single lodge of the 'Arusiya, these Orders are represented only in the towns. Occasionally one of their lodges was built with aid from local tribesmen, as the 'Arusiya lodges at al-Marj and Tubruq, but such examples are rare and in no way invalidate the statement that the Sanusiya alone has considerable following among the Bedouin. The adherents of the single 'Arusiya lodge at Bu Zaid are Bedouin of the Aulad al-Shaikh, immigrants from Tripolitania who regard themselves as direct descendants of Sidi 'Abd al-Salam, the founder of the Order whose rite they follow. The only competitor of the Sanusiya among the Bedouin was the Madaniya, which still retains its hold on the Fawakhir of the *barqa*, a tribe ill disposed towards any authority, and a few *Marabtin* fragments elsewhere, though these Bedouin now follow Sanusiya leadership in other than purely religious matters. There was at one time tension between the two Orders, complicated by tribal rivalries in the *barqa*, but it has now been for the greater part resolved. Apart from the opposition of the Sanusiya, the loss of influence of the Madaniya was hastened by its too close attachment to the fortunes of the declining Ottoman Caliphate, dissensions between the descendants of its founder, and a split in the Order itself.

The Sanusiya has always shown marked tolerance towards other Orders and it must, moreover, be noted that there are no doctrinal differences between the Orders, that members of different Orders worship together in the same mosques, and that sometimes a man is a member of several orders at the same time. We have seen that the Grand Sanusi in his early period joined a number of different Orders and our Tunisian friend Shaikh Muhammad 'Uthman seems to have made a hobby of joining them.[1] Furthermore, the founders of all the Orders are revered as saints by the common people everywhere, regardless

[1] Op. cit., pp. 64–6 and 251.

of their affiliations. Hence the Sanusiya does not oppose the other Orders in the towns on a religious plane, although it does not approve of those which are convulsionary, and they do not compete with it politically. It is only in the interior that the Order will not permit a rival, because competition for the allegiance of the Bedouin must be political. Italian efforts to play off these Orders against the Sanusiya were founded on ignorance of the nature of an Islamic *tariqa* and seem to have been ineffectual.

Since almost all the non-Sanusiya lodges are urban it follows that the history of the growth and spread of the Orders is part of the general history of the growth and spread of the urban centres of Cyrenaica. Some of the older lodges in Benghazi and Darna are over 150 years old, but most of them and all those in the smaller administrative centres date from late Turkish times or were built during the Italian occupation. An urban lodge is generally a small, very simple, structure and its members seldom total more than 50 to 100. It may be regarded as a kind of club, founded for religious exercises, for the performance of good works, and for social insurance. It also serves as a resthouse for travelling members of the Order and as a *malja*, a place of refuge for the poor and the sick. Few of the lodges are endowed, and most are very poor.

I do not wish to underestimate the social and, in the broadest sense, political importance of the urban Orders in Cyrenaica. They provide the only spontaneous and co-operative associations in the towns and thus fill a gap for ordinary people both in the town society and in a religion which pays little attention either to corporeal works or, outside the mosques, to corporate worship. Outside the lodges of the Orders there were in Turkish times no associations dispensing charity or giving education, and worship in the mosques within the wide society of Islam does not provide the intimacy and colour men need in acts of common devotion. The lodges give to their members a double attachment and a double security, membership of a welfare association, which gives them a feeling of material security, and membership of a devotional group, which gives them a feeling of spiritual security. Also, in spite of their lack of numbers and organization, the urban lodges are links in chains which, running through Islamic countries and cutting across natural and political boundaries, help to keep the Islamic world together against the impact of western civilization and imperialism. A member of the Qadiriya or Rifaʻiya Orders can wander from lodge to lodge from China to the Atlantic. A member of the Madaniya is received as a brother if he goes to Maknas, Istanbul, or Mecca. An ʻIsawi or ʻArusi finds lodges of his Order all over North Africa, obeying the same rules, bearing the same banner, using the same books of devotion, performing the same ritual, and bound by a common brotherhood. These Orders, therefore, are not unimportant in shaping and propagating a common opinion and feeling among Muslims about any question of the day which affects Islam.

But in a narrower political sense they have little importance, even in the urban centres. They are too weak and poor to act as cells in a movement of a political kind, for they show, as René Brunel says of the ʻIsawiya, 'lack of unity of direction' and 'absolute lack of cohesion'[1] In Cyrenaica the Sanusiya alone has been capable of becoming a political movement and hence of all the Orders alone aroused the suspicion of Istanbul and the hostility of Rome. We may inquire, therefore, what it is which has distinguished the Sanusiya from the other Orders in the country. As we have noted earlier, the fakiristic exhibitions of some of the Orders, so dear to the common man in the towns, were uncongenial, even repellent, to the Bedouin, who, in any case, had no affection for the townsmen and for things emanating from the towns. Also the Bedouin, socially and morally secure in their tribal and kinship systems, felt no need for further associations. Their need was for some authority lying outside their segmentary tribal system which could compose intertribal and intersectional disputes and bind the tribes and tribal sections together within an organization and under a common symbol. Hence, while the urban lodges were clubs—and this was the status of the Sanusiya lodges in the towns as much as it was that of the lodges of the other Orders—the Sanusiya lodges in the country-side were political, administrative, and economic, as well as religious and educational, centres. The urban lodges followed the social pattern in urban communities generally. Corporate life was narrowed to small quarters, single streets, a few houses, outside which people belonged, it is true, to a

---

[1] *Essai sur la Confrérie religieuse des ʻAîssâoua au Maroc*, 1926, p. 53.

residential community but felt no strong obligation to one another nor the need for common action. Religious Orders in such communities tend to become fractionized along the lines of social cleavage into sub-urban and sub-sub-urban lodges, each serving a few families in its vicinity and leading its own life with its own following and resources independently of the others. Social life in the towns is amorphous. There is no structure corresponding to the tribal system. The Sanusiya became dominant because it shunned the towns and sought its converts among the Bedouin and built its centres within the tribes. The Sanusiya Brotherhood was founded on a Bedouin brotherhood.

It is of great interest to note that the Sanusiya held a place in relation to other Orders in western Arabia like to that which it held in Cyrenaica. The learned Dutch Arabist, Snouck Hurgronje, who spent a year in western Arabia in 1884 and 1885, states that in the towns the Order 'has remained to this day highly honoured, but by no means overtopping its sister orders. For the districts of the Hejaz, inhabited by Harbis and other Beduins, it possesses however the highest significance, for its practical mission has succeeded in bringing to a great extent under its leadership the sons of the desert who are refractory to all authority and are far removed from the official Islam.'[1]

[1] C. Snouck Hurgronje, *Mekka in the latter Part of the 19th Century*, 1931, pp. 55–6. (First published in 1888–9.)

CHAPTER IV

THE TURKISH ADMINISTRATION

I

UNTIL 1912, when Turkey surrendered Libya to Italy, Tripolitania and Cyrenaica were part of the Ottoman Empire and it was under Turkish hegemony that the Sanusiya Order was born and grew to maturity. The Turkish administration was an important influence in its development and must be reviewed.

I have seen the relics of the Ottoman Empire, men and places, in most lands of the Levant and North Africa and have admired the economy with which it bestowed peace upon the Arab world for close on 400 years. The Turks well understood that the successful practice of the art of administration depends not only on attention to some things but no less on inattention to others. They did not confuse government with bureaucratic interference in the name of moral regeneration. A general condemnation of Turkish rule has, however, been so long fashionable that I can scarcely hope to alter so widely accepted a judgement. I can do no more than make a passing gesture of respect to one of the characters in this Cyrenaican story, the Turk.

We have only such bare hints of what happened in Cyrenaica after the Hilalian invasion as Arab historians give us. At the downfall of the Mamluk dynasty in Egypt in 1517 Cyrenaica went with that country to the Turks, and its history under Ottoman rule from the sixteenth to the nineteenth century is almost entirely a blank. One may say with some confidence, however, that the Bedouin were little affected by Turkish rule. Those nearest to the coastal towns were doubtless compelled to pay taxes from time to time, but the tribes as a whole must have continued to lead their ancient way of life and to settle their own affairs among themselves. In 1711 a rebellion at Tripoli against the Sultan's authority led to the emergence of a local Janissary dynasty, the Caramanlis, who for a time exercised control over Cyrenaica also. It was during the period of their rule that Paolo Della Cella accompanied a military expedition sent by the Pasha of Tripoli to Darna. He records how the Bedouin whose country was traversed by the expedition were compelled to pay taxes and furnish supplies, and how forty-five of the Shaikhs of the Jawazi tribe were treacherously murdered and many of their followers massacred.[1] Generally, however, it may be said that Cyrenaica has no history, other than Bedouin traditions of inter-tribal wars, from 1051 to 1835, in which year the Turks regained control of Libya from the Caramanlis. On their return they instituted a more systematic administration than had been exercised during their earlier occupation.

The Turks returned to Cyrenaica about the time the Grand Sanusi first visited the country and eight years after their reoccupation he founded his first zawiya on the plateau. As the Sanusiya Order gained the confidence of the Bedouin and became accepted as their spokesmen, it was necessary for the Ottoman authorities to take it into consideration in their dealings with the tribes of the interior. The Order made it possible for the different tribes to express themselves politically as a unit for the first time in their relations with the outside world. The tribes provided the Order with a social system, and the Order gave to that system a political organization at a time when it was beginning to be brought into more direct contact with political forces outside tribal society.

The Sanusiya is known to have been given a Charter about 1856 by Sultan 'Abd al-Majid I. His firman was brought from Istanbul by Sidi 'Abd al-Rahim al-Maghbub, later Shaikh of the Sanusiya zawiya at Banghazi, who had been sent to Istanbul for the purpose and had the utmost difficulty, as was often the case with visitors to the Ottoman capital, in obtaining an audience with the Sultan. Whatever other privileges the firman conferred on the Order—I have not seen the document—it certainly exempted its properties from taxation and permitted it to collect a religious tithe from its followers. A second firman was issued later by Sultan 'Abd al-Majid's brother, Sultan 'Abd al-'Aziz, and was brought from Istanbul to the Governor of Tripoli by Sidi Abu al-Qasim al-'Isawi, 'Abd al-Rahim's successor in the Banghazi lodge. There is in the Land Registry at Banghazi a letter from the Governor of Tripoli to the Governor of Banghazi giving the essence of this firman. It confirms the privileges granted by the earlier firman and adds to them that

---

[1] Op. cit., *passim* and p. 220 seq.

of the right of sanctuary within the precincts of the lodges of the Order. It is complimentary and written in the fulsome language of such documents.[1]

Nevertheless, the Turks were under no illusion. They did not believe that the Sanusi loved them, but they knew that if it came to a decision the Order and the Bedouin would support them against any of the Christian Powers of Europe. This is evident from the correspondence found in the archives of Tripoli by the Italians when they captured the town in 1911.[2] Shaikh Muhammad 'Uthman, writing in 1896, says frankly that the Turks were ill disposed towards the Sanusiya and would have liked to have taken Sayyid al-Mahdi to Istanbul and there given him a palace, the Turkish equivalent for *résidence forcée*, as they had done with Abu al-Huda, the Head of the Rifa'iya Order, and Shaikh Dafir, the Head of the Madaniya Order; and he adds that the Sayyid, on his side, had no liking for the Turks. When the Shaikh was in Banghazi the Shaikh of the Sanusiya lodge there was dismissed from his post by the Sayyid because he had allowed himself to be corrupted by the Turkish Authorities.[3]

The Ottoman Government was not much concerned about the exact juridical status of the Sanusiya Order, a question which greatly exercised Italian writers at a later date when this had become an important issue in their dealings with the Order. There were hundreds of Bedouin tribes and dozens of religious Orders in the Ottoman Empire and the Turks were matter-of-fact people who wisely left such questions alone. In the mosques under the Order's control the name of the Sultan was proclaimed at Friday prayers, but this means very little. Doubtless the Grand Sanusi and his successors took the view that the Caliphate had been usurped by the Ottoman Sultans—they could hardly have taken any other view—but it had long been in Ottoman hands and Turkey was the only independent Muslim Power capable of protecting Muslim interests. In practice also they accepted the secular authority of the Sultan as ruler of the Ottoman Empire.

[1] Salim bin 'Amir, op. cit., May 1944.
[2] Published in 1912 with the title *Relazione fra Turchi e Senussi. Documenti rinvenuti nell' Archivio di Tripoli* (Ufficio Politico Militare). Quoted by Macaluso, op. cit.
[3] Op. cit., pp. 65–6 and 106.

The local Turkish officials were content for the most part to sit in the towns, many of them no doubt regretting that they had ever been sent to Cyrenaica, where their salaries were low and often in arrears, and to let the Sanusiya control the interior so long as taxes were paid and no overt act was committed against the Sultan's authority which might bring them to the notice of the Court; and the Central Government for its part was quite prepared to forget that Cyrenaica formed part of the Sultan's dominions so long as there was peace there and it sent annual tribute to Istanbul. The Turks were indifferent otherwise to what happened in Libya, which was a poor province, particularly the Cyrenaican part of it, where their administration was even less efficient than in Tripolitania, where it was happy-go-lucky enough. They had quite enough troubles elsewhere without alienating to no purpose a powerful Islamic Order and the warlike Bedouin who supported it. They therefore left the Sanusiya to perform many of the functions of government in the interior—education, justice, the maintenance of security, and even to some extent the collection of taxes, though in the matter of tribute there were difficulties, for Bedouin do not willingly pay taxes to anyone, and since they already paid a tithe to the Sanusiya, with a grace which contrasted with their reluctance to pay taxes to the Turkish Administration, they were disinclined to pay twice. When any question arose which required direct contact between the Head of the Order and the local Governor it was established through the Shaikh of the lodge at Banghazi, or a special messenger was sent from Jaghbub or Kufra to the Turkish Governor at Banghazi, or he sent a messenger to the Head of the Order in his oasis seat. From time to time the Central Government sent an envoy to the Head of the Order with gifts and instructions to report on what was going on in the Sahara, and on such occasions he was received handsomely and returned with the blessings of the *Shaikh al-Tariqa* on the Sultan. Sometimes, as we have seen, the Head of the Order sent a deputation to Istanbul.

The payment of taxes and the maintenance of peace and communications, the only two functions of government the Turkish officials bothered their heads about, were intimately connected. Minor quarrels among the Bedouin themselves little interested them, but armed resistance to taxation was certain to earn them a reprimand on the double count of decrease in revenue and lack of security. It was essential, therefore, to get the Bedouin to pay their taxes without making too much trouble about doing so. To this end the Turkish administrative organization was largely directed. In 1879 the *Vilayet* of Banghazi was, in matters of civil administration, finally separated from that of Tripoli and in 1888 became an autonomous *sanjaq* directly dependent on Istanbul. It was governed by a *mutasarrif* nominated by, and directly responsible to, the Central Government. On him depended all the officials of the Administration, though the chief among them were appointed by the Imperial Government. The senior officials were usually Turks. The country was divided for administrative purposes into a number of districts, each under a *qaimaqam*, except that of Banghazi, which came directly under the Governor himself; and all except the Aujila-Jalu and Kufra districts were further divided into sub-districts under mudirs. These districts and sub-districts followed tribal divisions and subdivisions as any administration in Cyrenaica must do, since the tribes and their sections are the fundamental social departments of the country. Hence sections of a nomadic tribe might be residing at any time in a sub-district different to that to which they were administratively attached, and even in a different district.

In his direction of the affairs of the administration, finances, and police, the Governor was assisted by an administrative council composed of the chief accountant, the secretary, the qadi, the mufti, and four elected members from the local population. Each *qaimaqam*, nominated by the Imperial Government, had an administrative council similarly composed. The mudirs, nominated by the Imperial Government on the proposal of the Governor, had no council established by statute but co-opted tribal Shaikhs when they wanted their advice or co-operation. In the towns there was a representative, called *mukhtar*, elected by the property-owning citizens for each ward, and at Banghazi and Darna there were urban councils of a simple kind.

It was the mudir in charge of a sub-district who had direct dealings with the Bedouin tribes and the lodges of the Sanusiya Order. In 1911, just before the Italian invasion, there were six districts including Kufra, which came nominally under the

Turkish administration in 1910, and the Banghazi district, which came directly under the Governor of Cyrenaica for administration. Attached to each district were the sub-districts shown in the list below,[1] in which the tribes attached to each sub-district are also given. The Bara'asa came under Banghazi, although they lived well to the east, for political reasons, the tribe being exceptionally rebellious.[2]

Districts	Sub-districts	Tribes
Banghazi (directly dependent on the Governor)	Suluq Qaminis Barsis Sidi Khalifa	'Awaqir
al-Marj	Slanta al-Marj al-Haniya	Bara'asa 'Arafa and 'Abid Darsa
Darna	al-Sallum Tubruq al-Banba al-Qubba	'Abaidat
	Shahhat	Hasa
Ajadabiya	Marsa Braiqa	Magharba
Aujila and Jalu	—	Awajila and Majabra
Kufra	—	—

The administration was very slapdash by European standards. Indeed, Shaikh Muhammad 'Uthman says darkly: 'There is at Banghazi no organization, political, administrative, or financial. I say no more about this matter: it will be understood why.'[3] This was, of course, an exaggeration, for however simple the administration may have been, and perhaps for that reason, it worked—with a good deal of grumbling it is true, but without undue conflict. Revenue was collected and would have exceeded the cost of the very cheap administration of the country if the proceeds of some taxes had not been sent to Istanbul. Much of this revenue came from import and export duties, but the bulk of it was derived from taxes on herds and a tenth of the harvest in kind, the collection of which was in the hands of the mudirs. It was the task of these mudirs, who were generally literate

[1] *Notizie relative al Sangiacato della Cirenaica e alle Mudirie dipendenti dal Mutassarifato di Bengasi* (Ufficio Politico Militare), 1913.

[2] Fabrizio Serra, *Italia e Senussia*, 1933, p. 17; idem in *La Cirenaica*, 1922–3, p. 182.

[3] Op. cit., pp. 59–60.

Arabs, to assess and collect taxes, to maintain security, and to control the few police allotted to them. In this task they expected co-operation from the local Shaikhs of the tribal sections and the Shaikhs of the Sanusiya lodges.

It is remarkable that the Bedouin paid any taxes at all, for the mudirs had not sufficient force at their command, nor had the Governor at Banghazi, to compel the Bedouin to pay if they were determined not to do so. The mudir of Slanta had only 50 to 60 soldiers in his sub-district and the Bara'asa whom he administered could have annihilated this force with ease, as could the 'Awaqir the 50 soldiers and the handful of police stationed at Suluq. That taxes were collected at all, and all the more that they were collected without constant disturbance, is to be accounted for partly by the recognition by the Shaikhs of the tribal sections, with whom the mudirs were careful to keep on good personal terms, that there was a moral obligation to pay them; but there were also sanctions if they were not paid. If the Shaikh of a tribal section did not collect the taxes due from that section, he was held responsible and action could be taken against him personally. The mudir, accompanied by a small armed force, went a round of the tribal sections attached to his sub-district each year, generally in springtime, and sent out other tax-collecting parties in other directions. Sometimes special tax commissions appointed by the Governor also toured the country. A favourite device was for such parties to quarter themselves in the camp of a recalcitrant Shaikh and to reside there as his guests, for the soldiers and police carried few provisions, till the tax was paid. The Shaikhs, on the other hand, were made partners in the undertaking by, besides investment with an official robe and status, receiving a percentage of the taxes collected, the mudir himself also taking a percentage. Moreover, each Shaikh whose section paid the tax was determined that the other sections should not escape paying as well. A Shaikh was able to divide up the assessment on his section among the minor Shaikhs, and the minor Shaikhs among yet smaller ones. It was in the interest of each Shaikh to see that the smaller ones did not escape their share and leave him with the responsibility for a deficit. Responsibility was in this way passed down the tribal structure. On the whole the system worked well and the Turkish officials and the Bedouin did not get on badly together. Each understood the other. Also there was much elasticity in the taxes which appealed to the Bedouin, who prefer to pay a heavy tax one year and lightly or not at all another year, rather than to pay a regular and inevitable tax. The assessments were seldom revised and often had little relation to the capacity of a tribal section to pay. The result was that taxes were always in arrears and in some years, or for some sections, remitted altogether. Those sections nearest the Turkish posts paid the more easily because they were the more vulnerable. Some of the more nomadic Bedouin escaped payment altogether, or at any rate for years at a stretch. It is, I think, safe to assume that the taxes actually collected over a number of years were light. Otherwise the Bedouin would not have paid them.

Perhaps the chief reason why taxes were collected without constant rebellion was the support given to the administration in this matter by the Sanusiya. The Turks held the coastal towns and a few inland posts outside which their direct control of the country was restricted to those Bedouin who lived a fairly stable life in the immediate vicinity of these centres. The rest of the country was left to the Sanusiya and its own devices, though, as we have seen, the Turks sent occasional patrols into the interior. Sporadically, without much enthusiasm or perseverance, the Administration at one time tried to extend its effective control into the hinterland by nominating to official posts, and giving arms and money to, selected tribal chiefs, such as the Shaikhly families of Hadduth, Lataiwish, and Saif al-Nasir. Bu Bakr bin Hadduth of the Bara'asa was made *qaimaqam* of al-Qaiqab, where he had a castle; 'Ali Lataiwish of the Magharba was made *qaimaqam* of Sirt, where he, also, had a castle; and the fierce old warrior chieftain of the Aulad Suliman, Saif al-Nasir, was made mudir of Bu Njaim. This procedure resulted in brigandage rather than in good administration and was in the main discarded. Instead the mudirs worked directly through the Shaikhs of the tribal sections and, especially when dealing with intertribal and intersectional affairs, through the Shaikhs of the Sanusiya zawiyas. Some of the older notables of Banghazi have told me that the Pasha, as the Governor was often called, would never have succeeded in collecting taxes among the Bedouin had it not been for the co-operation of the

Heads of the Sanusiya lodges, who often accompanied the mudirs and tax commissions to the Shaikhs of the tribal sections attached to their lodges. It was to the common interest of the Turkish Administration and of the Sanusiya that there should be order, security, justice, and trade in the country, and they co-operated to maintain them.

The Turkish officials did their utmost to remain on good terms with the Sanusiya Shaikhs and to this end, and doubtless also because they found no difficulty in accepting, as educated men, its exalted teachings, some of them affiliated themselves to the Order. Membership of it gave them prestige in the eyes of the Bedouin as great, if not greater, than their official status gave them. Likewise the more prosperous merchants who had dealings with the Bedouin tribes or sent caravans to the Sahara and Sudan found it advisable to be received into the Order. It is for this reason that in all the towns of Libya we find a small body of the richer and more cultured citizens ascribed to the Order, while the common people belong to other or no Orders.[1]

But though the administration of Cyrenaica might be called at this period a Turco-Sanusi condominium there was an undercurrent of jealousy on both sides which occasionally gave rise to open conflict. A sure occasion was any effort on the part of the Administration to tax the Sanusiya estates. Although these had been exempted from taxation by the Sultan's firman, the local administration made rare and unsuccessful efforts to exact taxation on them. When in 1908 they tried to tax the crops of the Sanusiya holdings a tribal meeting, attended by 150 Shaikhs headed by 'Umar bu Rqaia of the Darsa tribe, met at the zawiya of al-Haniya and decided not to pay any more tribute to the Turkish Government till it revoked the tax. The Government then dropped the matter, though the trouble continued till 1910. Earlier, the Governor Ahmad Pasha Zuhadi (1904-5), acting on instructions from Istanbul, had tried to impose a tax on the crops of tribesmen and zawiyas alike. The Bedouin round al-Marj had thereupon attacked a Turkish detachment charged with collecting the tax and sent them back to Banghazi stripped of everything they possessed. The outcome was that the Governor was relieved of his office.

[1] Capt. Emilio Canevari, *Zauie ed Ichuan Senussiti della Tripolitania*, 1917, *passim*.

The Sanusiya thus used the Turks to buttress its position in its dealings with the tribes, and combined with the tribes to resist any encroachments on its prerogatives by the Turkish Government. It was in the interests of both Administration and Order that the tribes should not get out of hand, and it was in the interests of tribes and Order that the Administration should not become too powerful. The Sanusiya acquired from its central position between the other two parties a pre-eminence in the interior which led to the tribal system becoming already in Turkish times a proto-state with an embryonic government of its own. The tribes first began to see themselves as a nation through the Sanusiya's relations with the Turkish Administration. They were all 'Sanusi' *vis-à-vis* the Administration.

Ultimately it was the tribes who called the tune to both the Turkish Government and the Sanusiya Order. It would have taken a well-equipped army to have subdued them had they made a united revolt, and the Governor had only a meagre force at his disposal and could have had little hope of receiving much assistance from Istanbul. The Order had only moral weapons and though the tribal Shaikhs received its instructions with respect and every sign of acquiescence they did not necessarily act on them. Both Administration and Order were therefore compelled to compromise in their dealings with the tribes, who were, as Bedouin always are, at heart opposed to any interference and restriction. A typical situation of the latter days of Turkish rule was that described to me by the Banghazi notable 'Umar al-Kakhiya, at one time a member of the Ottoman House of Representatives. He was sent by the Governor of Cyrenaica to make agreements with the tribes in the eastern and western wings of the country by which they should refrain from cutting the Government's telegraph wires, a Bedouin habit which was later to irritate the Italian authorities and during the late war British Signals. I mention two further incidents in illustration of Turco-Bedouin relations. About 1895 forty members of the Tamiya section of the Bara'asa tribe jointly killed a tax-collector, a certain 'Abd al-Rahman al-Katib, for, among other affronts, having taxed the client tribes directly instead of through their *Sa'adi* overlords. They then fled to the Marmarica, from where they treated with the Turkish Authorities for a settlement by payment of 13,000 Riyal, or thirteen times the usual blood money, to the dead man's son. In 1898 the Darsa and Bara'asa threatened to prevent the Turkish Government from cutting cypress trees on their tribal lands for telegraph poles, although the trees were in law State property, and the matter had to be settled by negotiation, the Turks agreeing to pay for the trees on condition that the Bedouin helped in the cutting of them.[1] Turks and Bedouin managed in this kind of way to accept the presence of the other in a spirit of mutual tolerance. Just as the Sanusiya did not ask the Bedouin to change their way of life, but only to lead better lives, so the Turkish officials did not ask them to change their way of life, but only to pay taxes and, within reason, to keep the peace. In general we can agree with Professor Gregory's summary of the position when he wrote in 1909: 'The Turks apparently know how far they can go in interference with the Arabs, and during recent years have on more than one occasion altered their policy to avoid conflict with the natives.'[2]

II

The momentous events which took place in Turkey in 1908 made little difference to the political situation in Cyrenaica. In that year the 'Young Turks' gained control in Turkey and in the following year deposed the Sultan 'Abd al-Hamid II, who was succeeded by Muhammad the Fifth. The declaration of 'Liberty, Equality, Fraternity, and Justice' was coldly received by the Arab population of Banghazi, and the attempt by a section of the Turkish officials to create in the town a local branch of the Committee of 'Union and Progress' met with the strongest opposition. The two Cyrenaican delegates elected to the Parliament at Istanbul in the elections which followed the new constitution were both candidates of the party opposed to 'Young Turk' policy. Both in Tripolitania and in Cyrenaica the Arabs, citizens and Bedouin, were outraged by the revolutionary and rationalist leanings of the 'Young Turks', who aimed at the destruction of the Caliphate and of the religious Orders which

---

[1] Savarese, op. cit., pp. 162–3.

[2] J. W. Gregory (and others), *Report on the Work of the Commission sent out by the Jewish Territorial Organization under the Auspices of the Governor-General of Tripoli to examine the Territory proposed for the Purpose of a Jewish Settlement in Cyrenaica*, 1909, p. 13. See also Coro, op. cit., p. 19; Giglio, op. cit., p. 36; and Ismail Chemali, *Gli Abitanti della Tripolitania*, 1916, p. 39.

were one of its main supports. In the place of the cosmopolitan empire of the Ottoman Caliphs they wished to substitute a pan-Ottoman empire under the leadership of Turkey and to the cultural, religious, and political disadvantage of the Arab peoples. The Arabs everywhere reacted against these fanatics.

These events are interesting in that they show that the Arabs were not only conservative but also had a strong affection for the old Caliphate Order. They are of further importance in this account in that they were partly responsible for misleading Italian observers about the true state of affairs in Cyrenaica. Some members of what may be called the Arab party, as opposed to the committee of 'Union and Progress' which took on the complexion of a Turkish party opposed to Arab interests, approached the Italian Consul at Banghazi for diplomatic support. The Consul used the circumstances to make pro-Italian propaganda in the town and to extend it to the country-side by distributing gifts among some of the Bedouin Shaikhs. These urban quarrels and the precise form they took on this occasion, by seeming to drive a deeper wedge between Turk and Arab, combined with the usual Bedouin grumblings which had so recently led to unrest to mislead the Italians into believing that they would receive urban Arab, and even Sanusi Bedouin, support when they launched the attack they were preparing, or that these elements would at least remain neutral. They made errors both of judgement and of policy. They failed to allow for the quarrels endemic to any urban Arab society and for the fact that Bedouin are everywhere and at all times against government. They accepted at their face value the exaggerated and distorted reports of unrest in the interior by informants who seem to have been the corrupt riff-raff commonly employed by intelligence services. At the same time they failed to take advantage of what cleavages there were before the Turks, faced with a desperate hazard, closed them, for, as we will see in later chapters, Italian propaganda that they were entering Cyrenaica to free the Arabs from the Turkish yoke in the event convinced no one. The Arabs did not feel themselves to be under a yoke. Urban Arab and Sanusi Bedouin might view the Turkish Administration with irritation and suspicion, but before the storm wider loyalties to Islam and the Sultan held them. The urban Arabs sided with the

Turks and as soon as news of hostilities reached the interior the Shaikhs of the Sanusiya lodges and the Shaikhs of the tribes flocked amid general enthusiasm to the Turkish standard.

It was evident to both Turks and Arabs what was afoot, and the threat of Italian invasion, coming on top of the French advance in the Sahara, brought the Ottoman Government and the Sanusiya Order closer together in common adversity. The Ottoman Empire was threatened with the loss of its African possessions and the Sanusiya with the loss of independence and the rule of infidels. Istanbul and Kufra began to send out feelers towards each other. The Sanusiya had till this time refused to allow the Turkish flag to fly over Jaghbub and Kufra, or to permit a Turkish representative to reside in those oases, though efforts had been made to persuade them to do so, a flag even being dispatched to Kufra for the purpose by the hands of 'Umar al-Kakhiya in 1908. Sayyid Ahmad al-Sharif and his advisers were now anxious to proclaim Ottoman sovereignty in the Sahara, so long as they were not directly interfered with, because the Turkish flag might be expected to protect Kufra against French attack. Also, having no diplomatic status in world affairs, they were not able to make official representations against French aggression in the Chancelleries of Europe except through the Ottoman Court. In 1910, therefore, Sayyid Ahmad al-Sharif agreed to receive a Turkish *qaimaqam* at Kufra, on condition that he was a Sanusi, and to fly the Turkish flag there. Murad Fuad Bey, the Governor at Banghazi, sent him Kailani Lataiwish, a member of the leading family of the Sanusi tribe of the Magharba. The Banghazi notable Husain Pasha Bsaikri told me that later, in 1911, after the Italians had landed in Cyrenaica, the Turkish administration sent their first, and only, mudir to Jaghbub. He was also a leading Sanusi tribal Shaikh, al-Husain bin Abu Bakr bu Hadduth al-Bara'asi. He raised in the sacred village for the first, and last, time the Turkish flag and posted a few police there. He remained at his post till Enver Pasha's visit to the oasis in 1912 when, on account of the agreement reached between Enver and Sayyid Ahmad al-Sharif, he was withdrawn.

In return for these concessions the Turks sent troops, though little more than a token force, to Tibesti in 1910 and to Borku in the following year. In 1912 they were mostly withdrawn on account of the Italian invasion of Tripolitania. Realizing that they were helpless without Sanusiya support not only in the Sahara but also in Libya, since they would not be able without command of the sea to reinforce their garrisons there, the Turks showed themselves anxious to win over Sayyid Ahmad al-Sharif by also conferring on him new privileges. In 1910 the Governor of Banghazi proposed to make him a monthly grant of 4,000 Piastres, and the Governor of Tripoli sent a telegram in cipher to his representatives in various parts of Tripolitania asking them whether they thought the Sanusiya Order powerful enough to warrant additional privileges, which was apparently the view of Istanbul. His representatives, judging by its lesser influence in Tripolitania, where it never gained the unanimous support it received in Cyrenaica, reported that in their opinion the political importance of the Order had been exaggerated.[1]

Such of these events as were known to Italian observers shortly before and in the early stages of their war with Turkey led them to false conclusions because the complexity of Arab sentiments was not appreciated. The structure of Bedouin society is such that whatever the size of the group a man considers himself to belong to in any situation, he is in virtue of his loyalty to it opposed to other groups of like order in the tribal structure. He is loyal to his *bait* against other *biyut*, to his *'aila* against other *'ailat*, and to his *qabila* against other *qabail*. Nevertheless, he has a strong feeling of communion with all the Bedouin of his country, regardless of their tribal affiliations, in common opposition to the towns. But Bedouin and citizen are both Arab and they made common cause against the Turks, especially when the activities of the 'Young Turks' forced Turk and Arab into rival camps. But even Arab and Turk shared wider loyalties in their regard—unequal, it is true, but still shared—for the Sultanate and for Islam and they reacted in spontaneous accord against threats from Christian Powers, the French advance in the Sahara and the Italian invasion of Libya. Against Christians and Europeans Arabs and Turks were no longer Arabs and Turks but Muslims, just as against the Turks Bedouin and citizens were no longer Bedouin and citizens but Arabs, and against the towns tribesmen were no longer members of different tribes but a Bedouin community.

[1] Macaluso, op. cit., pp. 88–90, and Serra, op. cit., p. 37.

CHAPTER V

THE FIRST ITALO-SANUSI WAR (1911–17)

I

I HAVE given an account of the conditions in which the Sanusiya took root in Cyrenaica and of the circumstances which favoured its growth. I now describe how its Bedouin followers, under its leadership, resisted Italian aggression during two wars, from 1911 to 1917 and from 1923 to 1932, and finally lost their independence and suffered Italian domination until relieved by British arms in 1942. It will be seen how the long struggle accentuated the political functions of the Sanusiya in a manner I indicate forthwith.

For segmentary structures of the kind we find among the Bedouin of Cyrenaica to develop rudimentary governmental, or statal, organs it would seem necessary that for a long period of time all the segments of the society should find themselves in common opposition to some outside force. It is not merely that such opposition fuses the segments in corporate action. A new form of political structure which includes the enemy comes into existence and necessitates a new orientation of political values. In a segmentary system each segment sees itself as a unity in opposition to an opposed segment of the same size and kind; so when all the segments come into a corporate relation of opposition to some political group outside them which has a different kind of political structure and belongs to a different political system they tend to see themselves as a unity *vis-à-vis* this group and as a unity on the same structural model as itself. The small Bedouin society of Cyrenaica in this way slowly took on the political form of the European countries into the orbit of which it was drawn. It could only enter into structural relations with the states of Europe on the model of the European state.

When the Italians invaded the country and the Turks made peace the tribes continued their resistance in the name of the Sanusiya. In their social system tribe was balanced against tribe and tribal section against tribal section. It was the Sanusiya which gave to all the tribes and their sections a common symbol which stood for their common interests. Faced with amorphous, but seemingly ineradicable, opposition from the Bedouin the Italians more and more directed their hostility to the Sanusiya Order as a tangible head to the resistance which could be destroyed. Failing to crush opposition they were forced to come to terms with it, but they could not come to terms with a tribal system—only with an organization and through a person, the Head of the Order, who could speak for that organization and for the tribes which it represented. Both in fighting the tribes and in trying to come to terms with them, the Italians thus threw the Sanusiya organization into political relief, and the *tariqa*, the religious Order, began to speak of itself as a *hakuma*, government. The peace negotiations, therefore, centred round a contradiction. The Italians attempted to exact recognition of sovereignty and this implied recognition of the right of the Head of the Order to surrender sovereignty, which he could do only if he were in a position analogous to that of the Head of the Italian State, a status the Italians would not concede. Nevertheless they were compelled, in order to establish relations with the tribes, to grant the Head of the Order the title of Amir, and implicitly to recognize him as not only the Shaikh of a religious Order, but the Head of a political organization. As will be seen, the dilemma led to much equivocation and finally to a second Italo-Sanusi war. In this second war the Sanusiya was entirely destroyed as an organization, political, economic, and religious. It persisted nevertheless as a sentiment, and the Head of the Order in exile in Egypt still retained the allegiance of the Bedouin who saw in his freedom the hope of their own.

When the last European war broke out and Cyrenaica became a battlefield of first importance it was in the interests of each side to ensure that the local population would be favourable to it. The Italians, having destroyed the Order, the one organization through which they might have made effective propaganda among the Bedouin, were confronted in the country with an unimpressionable mass of sullen resentment which could in no way be influenced to their advantage. The British, on the other hand, who sought to rouse the Bedouin to renewed rebellion, at any rate up to the point at which they gave what assistance to British arms they were capable of, had a ready means of influencing them to this end in the exiled Head of the Order and many influential Shaikhs of tribes who recognized his authority. But the British Government, which in the past had consistently refused to admit that Sayyid Muhammad Idris was more than the Head of a religious Order, were in the new circumstances compelled to accept his offer of help as coming from a person who could act in a political sense and for the whole population of Cyrenaica. The Sayyid had, therefore, to be recognized as an Amir and to be permitted to recruit his own army under the Sanusiya flag. The Bedouin of Cyrenaica could only take part in a world struggle between states as a unit within their structure, as a political unit of the same order as the other allied countries, which were autonomous states acting through their own governments in their relations with the British Government and Armed Forces. The recognition of Sayyid Muhammad Idris as a political leader was easier for the British in that in war national sentiment is at a high pitch and those engaged in the struggle are particularly sensitive to national aspirations and sympathetic towards them. They are then anxious to placate national movements in their own empires and to encourage those in the empires of their opponents. To the British all the people of Cyrenaica were Sanusi and they so spoke of themselves in their dealings with British troops, and not as members of particular tribes or as citizens of particular towns. Through the long years of struggle Bedouin and townsmen alike had come to identify their interests with those of the Sanusiya Order, and to see in the Order the symbol of their particularist aspirations. 'Sanusi' had become a word which could be translated 'Cyrenaican'. It had ceased to have a religious content and had acquired a purely political one.

II

This is a history of the Sanusi of Cyrenaica and not of Italy so that there is no need to record the domestic and international circumstances in which Italy went to war with Turkey. Nor is it necessary to narrate the reasons the Italians gave for their declaration of war. Italy had certain historic claims to a sphere of influence in Libya and her strategic interests in the coast of Africa opposite her shores are obvious. It is easy to understand

Italian feelings about Libya. They 'knew it was no Eden' and they occupied it 'simply in order to be able to breathe freely in the Mediterranean—to avoid being stifled amidst the possessions and naval bases of France and Great Britain'.[1]

Although the Italians declared war with the minimum of both provocation and warning it was generally known to the Turkish Authorities at Istanbul, Tripoli, and Banghazi, as well as to the Arabs of Libya, that an invasion was being prepared and could not for long be deferred. The Italians had for some years pressed for facilities and concessions in Libya and it became increasingly clear that their importunities must eventually furnish an occasion of war. The Ottoman Government resisted them as far as it could. Where it could not directly refuse them it temporized and, when forced by diplomatic pressure to give way, sought by subterfuges to nullify any concessions it had granted. The Italians had been particularly anxious to acquire land in Libya, both for individuals and for the *Banca di Roma* and other corporations. When compelled to allow Italians to buy land the Turks used their influence with the Arabs to encourage them to refuse to sell.

But although war was known to be inevitable, and even imminent, the Turkish Authorities, in their happy-go-lucky way, did little to prepare for it. At the last moment, indeed, they made some small efforts to send reinforcements in men and arms to their Libyan garrisons, efforts the Italians made the occasion of their ultimatum of 26 September 1911; but this was offset by the earlier dispatch of the bulk of the Tripolitanian forces to deal with a revolt in the Yaman and by the transfer of the Governor of Tripolitania, Ibrahim Pasha, who was a good military leader. The Turks were also at the time engaged in suppressing an insurrection in Albania, and the Balkans were in a ferment which was to lead in the following year to the first Balkan War. Apart from these troubles, once war had been declared the Turks were able only meagrely to supply or reinforce their garrisons because from the beginning the Italians had an overwhelming superiority at sea.

When war broke out the Turks had an establishment of about 5,000 men in Tripolitania and about 2,000 men in Cyrenaica, but the garrisons were well below strength and badly

[1] Ambrosini, *I problemi del Mediterraneo*, 1937, p. 23.

equipped. Coro says that at the end of May 1911 they had, not counting officers, 3,010 men in Tripolitania and 1,200 men in Cyrenaica.[1] The Italian expeditionary force consisted of 34,000 men, 6,300 horses, 1,050 wagons (*carri*), 48 field guns, and 24 mountain guns; and the Italians counted on being able to ship to Africa all the reserves and modern equipment that might be required were resistance to prove stronger than was expected. At the height of the campaign, when Italy entered the Great War, she had about 60,000 troops in Libya. It looked therefore as though the Turks had no chance of putting up more than a token resistance, and the Italians certainly expected a walk-over and were surprised, then alarmed, at the resistance they had to overcome. They were dilatory and over-cautious after their main landing at Tripoli, hanging about in the town instead of pushing on into the interior before the Turks had time to organize resistance and attract Arab volunteers. In Cyrenaica also they delayed too long their advance into the interior and gave the Bedouin time to come to the assistance of the Turks and for some adventurous young Turkish officers, among them men who were later to make names for themselves in world history, to reach the field from Turkey. The Italians also under-estimated the skill and pluck of the Turkish soldiers and they misjudged—the worst of their miscalculations—the attitude of the Arab population of Libya to the war. They believed that the Arabs were so irate with the Turks that they would not assist them and might even turn against them. Indeed, so confident were the Italians of Bedouin support that, according to local statements, they were themselves supplying them with arms in Cyrenaica for some months before the outbreak of war.

Looking back it is easy to see that another blunder was made in taking it for granted that the Sanusiya Order was hostile to the Turks to the point of being willing to remain outside the dispute or even to co-operate with a Christian Power to be rid of them. If the Head of the Order—'*Il famoso papa nero*', as the Italian press, most inappropriately, used to call him—wanted to create for himself an independent kingdom in North Africa, as it was supposed that he did, it seemed likely that he would have been glad to see the Turks driven out of Libya. But, apart from the fact that the Sanusiya and the Ottoman

[1] Coro, op. cit., p. 121.

Governors had generally, in spite of occasional disagreements, managed to rub along together in a spirit of live and let live, it is difficult to understand how the Italians could have imagined that the Sanusiya Shaikhs would have preferred them to the Turks who, after all, were Muslims, if not very good ones, and sometimes personal friends as well; especially in view of the low opinion the Arabs of the Near East generally had formed of Italians in comparison with other Europeans. Also, if they had hoped for help or neutrality from the tribes and the Sanusiya, and they undoubtedly did hope for it, one might have expected that they would have prepared for it by making direct contact earlier with the persons of chief influence among the parties. That they did not do so may be attributed in part to over-confidence and in part to over-estimation of the assurances of such crafty citizens of Banghazi as 'Uthman al-'Anaizi and 'Umar al-Kakhiya. Mansur al-Kakhiya was indeed sent in 1912 to Kufra to bribe Sayyid Ahmad, without result, and there were some further vague semi-official efforts made in 1913 and 1914 to get into touch with the head of the Order, but they also came to nothing.

III

War was declared on Turkey on 29 September 1911 and opened with the bombardment of Darna town on the following day and of Tripoli town a few days later. During October the Italians occupied Tripoli, Tubruq, Darna, Banghazi, and Khums. The disembarkation at Banghazi was against a rough sea and stiff opposition. After this initial resistance the Turkish garrison withdrew to the interior, as did their garrisons in the other coastal towns of Libya, since they could be shelled from Italian warships without being able to reply, their few coastal guns having a very restricted range. The garrison made Banina, about 12 km. to the east of Banghazi, their headquarters and here they were quickly joined by contingents of all the Bedouin tribes of western Cyrenaica with the Shaikhs of the Sanusiya lodges at their head. The Turkish garrison had from the beginning been in consultation with Shaikh Ahmad al-'Isawi, the Sanusiya representative at Banghazi and the Head of its zawiya there; and he wrote to all the Shaikhs of the tribal lodges in the neighbourhood asking them to recruit volunteers for war.[1] In doing so he was, according to local information, acting on instructions received from Sayyid Ahmad al-Sharif who, though he was in distant Kufra, seems to have been well aware, as indeed was everyone concerned, of Italian intentions. The tribal bands, following the Sanusiya Shaikhs, poured into Banina and put heart into the small Turkish garrison. Strengthened daily by tribal reinforcements the Turco-Arab force on the Banghazi front was able to contain the Italians in the town till 'Aziz Bey al-Masri (later Inspector-General of the Egyptian Army) arrived to direct operations. The Turkish garrison at Darna, which had also retired behind the town, was reinforced in the same way by the tribes of eastern Cyrenaica, roused and led by the Shaikhs of the tribal lodges of the Sanusiya in that part of the country. When Enver Bey (later Turkish Minister for War) arrived by camel from Egypt he took charge of the Darna sector, where he was assisted by Mustafa Kamal (Ata Turk, later the first President of the Turkish Republic). A third camp was established in the Marmarica near Tubruq under command of another young Turkish officer, Adham Pasha al-Halabi. Here also the Turkish garrison was joined by the local tribes and the Shaikhs of their lodges. The Turkish Commanders always took the Shaikhs of the tribes and lodges into consultation.

Without these tribal reinforcements the Turks certainly could not have continued for long to resist. As it was, resistance not only became possible, but the whole character of the war changed, both in Cyrenaica and in Tripolitania, where the Bedouin also flocked to the Turkish standards. It ceased to be a war in which a foreign power was trying to seize its colonies from a tired empire, and became a colonial war in the traditional sense of a European power attempting to deprive a native people of their liberty and their land. In Cyrenaica it became, in fact, more and more an Italo-Sanusi, rather than an Italo-Turkish, war and ended as a simple struggle of the Bedouin of Cyrenaica under Sanusiya leadership for freedom from a foreign yoke.

Enthusiastic though they were, the Bedouin who poured into the Turkish camps were in no sense soldiers. Full of spirit, courageous to the point of recklessness, their one aim was to

[1] Muhammad al-Akhdar al-'Isawi, *Rafu' al-Sitar*, pp. 13–18.

charge the enemy, who was armed with the most modern equipment and generally entrenched. They charged on horseback, firing wildly, wherever they might come across him, without any regard to danger, terrain, or odds. The Turkish officers had great difficulty in the early days of the campaign in restraining these impetuous cavaliers, but Turkish tact, the example of the disciplined Turkish troops, and the disastrous results of their own impetuosity soon taught them to act with greater caution, though not the patience necessary in the professional soldier. Realizing that the war might be protracted, Enver tried to make the Bedouin volunteers feel that they were as much part of the army of resistance as the Turkish regulars and to give them some military training, in however random a fashion. He chose 300 young Bedouin of the principal families of tribal Shaikhs from among the volunteers and gave them training at his camp at al-Zahir al-Ahmar, some 20 km. to the south-west of Darna. They were given arms and uniforms sent from Turkey, were housed in Turkish army tents, and received Turkish pay. This small Bedouin contingent, trained under Turkish regular officers and N.C.O.'s, took part in the fighting in 1912 and proved to be a valuable adjunct to the slender Turkish forces. When trained some of them were put in charge of the training of the *Mahafiziya*, the Bedouin irregulars, of whom there were about 2,000 at Enver's camp. Besides the irregulars, who resided on and off at the Turkish camp, all the Bedouin for many miles round could be relied on to join in the fray whenever the Italians ventured to move from entrenched and fortified positions. Most of the Bedouin were armed, but their rifles were of a very old make, mostly old one-round Greek pieces. When Enver received his irregular and scanty supplies from Turkey he distributed a small number of Turkish rifles among them. Later they equipped themselves with Italian rifles taken in fights, and they had a ready source of ammunition in every Italian column. The irregulars occasionally received largesse from Enver but for the most part paid themselves in loot.

Enver looked yet farther ahead. In June 1912 he selected 365 boys, mostly from among the sons of the Bedouin Shaikhs, and sent them to Istanbul to be educated for posts in the Cyrenaican army and administration. The first thirty to be commissioned were later sent to al-Sallum to join Sayyid Ahmad al-Sharif before the outbreak of war in Europe in 1914. Six months later another seven were sent to Cyrenaica but were captured *en route* by a French warship. Many of these lads later distinguished themselves in Asia Minor in the wars there which followed the 1914–1918 war in Europe, and remained in Turkey for good.

IV

The Italian plan in Cyrenaica was to advance simultaneously from Banghazi in the west and Darna in the east, gripping the central plateau between pincer columns and bringing the enemy to decisive engagements. In the Banghazi zone a column advanced on 28 November 1911 on the suburbs of Sidi Khalifa and al-Kwaifiya. But the Italian forces in and around Banghazi still only had superiority within the range of their naval guns. They were on the defensive and the Turco-Arab force at Banina had the initiative. On 12 March 1912 the Turco-Arabs made a big general attack on Banghazi. This was a blunder which cost them dear. The official Italian account says that they left about 1,000 corpses on the field; but it must be said here, and in reference to all reports of enemy forces and casualties quoted elsewhere in this book, that Italian figures must be treated with reserve. The occupation of Banghazi was now extended to about 8 km. around the town and fortified on that arc. While the Italians sat behind these fortifications at Banghazi with the Turco-Arab force besieging them from Banina, the progress made in the Darna sector was even more disappointing. The town is backed almost immediately by the plateau to which access is difficult owing to the steepness of the incline. Finding the terrain too difficult for an offensive, the Italians remained in the town, with the country around it in undisputed control of their enemies. The fighting which took place on the periphery of the Italian defences was a struggle for control of the Wadi Darna, which supplies the town with most of its water. On the night of 11 to 12 February, Enver Bey launched an attack on the town, but failed to take it, and by July a new girdle of defensive works had been thrown around it, within which the Italians continued to be besieged by the Turco-Arabs, estimated at 8,000 to 12,000 armed men. On 17 September took place a severe fight at Ras al-Laban in which the Italians lost 10 officers and 174 men dead and wounded and their enemy 1,135 dead. Further fights, more in the nature of skirmishes than battles, took place from time to time as the Italians tried to occupy various strong-points to protect the town and control the wadi. In the Tubruq sector fighting was limited to occasional Turco-Arab demonstrations in small numbers against the Italian working parties engaged in fortifying points outside the port to protect it against attack from the land side.

In the first days of September 1912 Gen. Caneva, who had hitherto commanded operations in the whole of Libya, was replaced and the command was divided, Gen. Ragni taking over in Tripolitania and Gen. Briccola in Cyrenaica. To these two Generals was entrusted the advance into the interior, but before they were able to put their plans into operation, Turkey made peace with Italy on 17 October 1912.

The Turks were about to become involved in the first Balkan war, and also were well aware that the Powers of Europe would not interfere on their behalf, but regarded the Italian invasion of Libya with sour benevolence. Had they been able to reinforce their garrisons in Libya, they might have continued the war, but without command of the sea this could only have been done through Egypt, and it was so well understood that England would not permit transit of troops through Egypt that the Turks did not embarrass the Khedive by asking for the favour. In these circumstances Turkey entered into negotiations. A *modus procedendi* was established between Italy and Turkey on 15 October 1912 by which it was agreed that the Sultan should give with his firman full and entire autonomy to Cyrenaica and Tripolitania, entrusting the protection of Ottoman interests in the two provinces to his representative, the *naib al-sultan*, and that the King of Italy should afterwards by Royal Decree regulate the conditions of the new autonomy on the basis of Italian sovereignty and define the status of the Sultan's representative. This preliminary understanding formed part of the formal Treaty of Losanna (Ouchy) of 17 October 1912. By it Turkey promised to withdraw all armed forces from Libya, in return for which undertaking, and when it had been accomplished, the Italians agreed to hand back to Turkey the Dodecanese Islands they had occupied during the war. The

Sultan duly issued his firman while the Italians published a
Royal Decree reaffirming their sovereignty over Libya, already
declared annexed by a Royal Decree in November 1911.

The treaty appears to have been carelessly drafted. What it
amounted to was this: the Italians wanted the Turks to withdraw their meagre forces and equipment from Libya, when it
was hoped that the Arab population would at once submit, and
in return for this they were prepared to make what they thought
would be a purely nominal concession by permitting the Arabs
to continue to recognize the Sultan as their Caliph. and to have
relations with him as such through his representative at
Tripoli; while the Turks wanted to escape from the predica-
ment of having to defend a part of their empire they could not
reach, without the inevitable loss of prestige the Sultan would
suffer were he formally to surrender part of the *Dar al-Islam* to
a Christian Power. The Italian politicians had promised their
people a quick victory without much expenditure in lives and
money and were prepared to sign any agreement which could
be presented as such, without giving much consideration to the
implications of what they were signing. Turkish diplomacy was
true to form. The Sultan hoped that if he inserted some dubious
clauses in the agreement, the situation in Europe might, before
they could be clarified, deteriorate to the point at which the
Italians would find themselves involved elsewhere than in
Libya, and he would find himself with allies; as indeed it
happened. In the meanwhile, till such a desirable event were
to take place, the Arabs might, with some unofficial encouragement, be prepared to carry on resistance in Libya by themselves;
as indeed they were.

The terms of the treaty contained a fundamental ambiguity.
The Sultan's representative was to combine the functions of
a kind of consul in charge of Ottoman affairs with those of a
liaison between the Caliph and his Libyan followers. His precise
status and powers were never determined, but it was evident
that the Sultan had gone out by the front door only to return
by the back. Moreover, under the treaty he had the right to
nominate the Grand Qadi of Tripoli and hence to maintain
control over the whole religious organization of the provinces
in which the Italians claimed sovereignty, and with religious
control went political authority, for Muslim qadis are political

as well as religious functionaries. The Italians seem to have been under the impression that they could exclude the Sultan's secular authority while admitting the Caliph's spiritual authority in Libya. This was a singular error, because the functions of the Caliph of Islam were not of a sacerdotal order at all, but entirely political. Hence, as Macaluso justly observes, by the Treaty of Losanna 'sovereignty in Libya was divided for some years between Italy and Turkey'.[1]

The Turks withdrew their forces from Tripolitania under the terms of the treaty and opposition in that country was soon overcome, except for sporadic resistance in the *qibla*, the Sirtica, and Fazzan, in which parts Sanusiya influence was strong. The peace made very little difference to the military situation in Cyrenaica, partly because the Turkish garrisons remained behind to provide a disciplined core to the tribal resistance, and partly because the Bedouin tribes, who gave bulk to the resistance, had in the Sanusiya Order a common organization and leadership lacking in Tripolitania, where every tribe and every prominent tribal Shaikh acted independently and internal dissensions showed themselves as soon as the integrating presence of the Turkish army was withdrawn.

The Turkish soldiers who remained in Cyrenaica were drawn from every part of the Ottoman Empire—Albanians, Kurds, Syrians, Iraqis, Circassians, Anatolians, Macedonians, and Thracians—and were practically mercenaries who lived by the sword. Slovenly though they were, they were fine fighters and frugal as well, being content to campaign on rice, potatoes, bread, and an occasional helping of meat; and in Enver Bey they had an inspiring leader. Enver, being a regular soldier, was, however, anxious to return to Turkey to take part in the fighting in the Balkans. Before departing for the Bulgarian front and handing over his command in Cyrenaica to 'Aziz al-Masri he paid a visit to Sayyid Ahmad al-Sharif at Jaghbub, making a remarkable trip to the oasis in the only motor-car the Turco-Arab forces possessed. According to local statements the Sayyid, who had arrived at Jaghbub from Kufra in September 1912, had already declared that he would not be partner to a peace, so he required no persuading when Enver asked him in the name of the Sultan Muhammad V to carry on the struggle

[1] Giuseppe Macaluso, *Fascismo e Colonie*, 1930, p. 7.

as the Sultan's representative. If the Head of the Sanusiya
Order could have been mistaken in the early stages of the war
for no more than a benevolent spectator whose real attitude
was unknown, the illusion was now dispelled. After Enver's
visit to Jaghbub all official correspondence and documents from
the Headquarters of the Order were stamped 'al-Hakuma al-
Sanusiya', the Sanusiya Government. The Order now claimed
the status of a government of a semi-autonomous State and as
such it led the resistance to Italian arms.

The small Turkish garrisons thus had behind them all the
Bedouin of the country—the townsmen were sympathetic, but
soft and of little account one way or the other—and behind the
Bedouin the Sanusiya Order. They were fortified also by the
knowledge that behind the Sanusiya was the moral backing of
the whole Arab and Muslim world, and even of peoples who were
neither Arab nor Muslim. Throughout the Near East in particular, but also everywhere in the world where coloured peoples
were articulate, the struggle was seen to have a deeper significance than a mere transfer of territories from Turkey to Italy,
or the mere acquisition of another bit, one of the few remaining
bits, of Africa by a European Power. Like a great octopus,
Europe had stretched out its tentacles to seize and exploit the
whole of Africa and Asia. The tentacle which now held Tripolitania and Cyrenaica in its grip belonged to the same beast
which held half the world in its clutches. It was not the future
of a handful of Bedouin which was being decided, but the future
of Europe.

The Muslim world could do little to help their fellow Muslims,
but they showed their indignation. The Arab and Muslim press
railed against the Italians. The Bedouin boys sent by Enver
from Cyrenaica to be educated in Turkey were everywhere on
their journey received with acclamation as the sons of the
brave Libyan mujahidin, the fighters for the faith. A Sanusi
mission to Istanbul to do homage to the Caliph, though not
received by him for diplomatic reasons, found plenty of support, especially in 'Young Turk' circles. Committees to collect
funds for the war were formed in Egypt, Turkey, Syria, the
Hijaz, and other parts of the Near East. An Egyptian Red
Crescent Society was formed to look after the Libyan sick and
wounded. A British Red Crescent Society was also founded in

1912 for the same purpose by British sympathizers with the Arab cause and Indian Muslims.

V

On 13 April 1913 Gen. d'Alessandro attacked the Turco-Arab camp at Banina and after 10 hours' heavy fighting took it by assault, killing 200 men and capturing about 50 prisoners and much equipment. The Turco-Arabs from this time onwards abandoned any further attempt to hold a line and organized resistance gave way to the kind of guerrilla warfare the country, inferiority in numbers and arms, and lack of military training of the Arabs indicated as the most appropriate tactics. The Italians were therefore able to advance rapidly in column in the grand style and to defeat Arab bands wherever they met them by superiority in numbers and fire power. They occupied Bu Mariyam, al-Abyar, Taukra, al-Baniya, and Jardis al-'Abid. While this column, the 2nd Division under Gen. d'Alessandro, was advancing on Jardis al-'Abid a second column, the 4th Division under Gen. Tassoni, disembarked at Talmaitha after a sharp engagement, and from there advanced on al-Marj and took the village. The two Divisions then met at Jardis al-'Abid. From there the 4th Division moved eastwards and in mid-May took without much opposition Marawa, Slanta, Shahhat, Marsa Susa, and other points. The ease with which they were able to march through the country and the way in which the Bedouin bands nine times out of ten gave way to them on the field, made the Italians take too optimistic a view of the campaign. They had yet to learn that marching from point to point and occupying the points does not make any great impression on an enemy for whom places have little significance, and that it is one thing to force Bedouin bands to give ground and quite a different thing to conquer a hardy and elusive people scattered over a wild and rugged country. The whole country was up in arms and the general will to resistance was now strengthened by the arrival on the field of Sayyid Ahmad al-Sharif from Jaghbub and a Turco-Arab victory shortly afterwards, an event the Bedouin naturally attributed to the Sayyid's *baraka*. This victory was in the Darna sector.

After the fighting in the autumn on the periphery of the town there had been little activity on this front till late in the spring of 1913. The Turco-Arab camp was at Sidi 'Aziz, where they had some thousands of men, mostly tribal volunteers, and a few cannon and machine-guns. The Darna command decided to destroy this force in order to link up with the Tassoni column driving towards the town from the west. On 16 May 1913 the Italians launched an attack with some 5,000 men, three batteries of field guns, and a machine-gun section, under Gen. Mambretti. The fighting went against the Italians who lost their nerve and fled in disorder, losing 10 officers and 60 men besides 400 wounded, missing, or taken prisoner. They also lost a battery of guns and much equipment. The battle of Sidi al-Qarba', or of the *yaum al-juma'*, the Friday, as the Bedouin generally speak of it, prevented the further advance eastwards of the Tassoni column and the planned pincer movement between this column and the Darna force. It also threw Sayyid Ahmad into relief as the head of the resistance. At this point the Turks began to fade into the background and the Sanusiya Order and its Head to take responsibility for the direction of resistance. The defeat of Friday also involved the Tassoni column in a series of indecisive actions conducted from their forts during the summer months, in which the Turco-Arabs had the initiative, though they usually suffered heavier casualties than the Italians through inferior fire power and drill. Nevertheless, Italian losses were not negligible, their heaviest casualties in a single engagement being 100 dead, including 6 officers, when one of their units was surprised at Safsaf. Meanwhile in western Cyrenaica Suluq and Qaminis were occupied. On the whole plateau what for a colonial war may be regarded as heavy fighting and large-scale engagements continued to take place throughout the late summer and the autumn of 1913: the Turco-Arab force in a fight at 'Ain bu Shimal, 10 km. to the south-west of 'Ain Mara, on 6 October, was said to have numbered as many as 3,000 men. The Italian success at 'Ain bu Shimal enabled them to effect a junction between their forces in the Shahhat and Darna zones. Under this pressure Sayyid Ahmad al-Sharif withdrew to the west, where he made Msus and its neighbourhood his headquarters from October 1913 till he moved to the Marmarica to take part in the closing scenes of the first Italo-Sanusi war.

By the end of 1913 the campaign had broken up into a series

of guerrilla fights and skirmishes, making it very difficult to describe its development. Some observations on the general nature of such fighting are made later in recounting the events of the second Italo-Sanusi war. The camps of the Turco-Arab forces at Banina, al-Tanji, Bu Shimal, and al-Madawar had been broken up and concerted resistance on the part of the Turkish regular forces had mostly ended, leaving the conduct of operations in the hands of the Bedouin, though the tattered Ottoman condottieri still took part in the fragmentary resistance. The war had become a true *guerra di partigiani* and in answer to its new pattern costly Italian columns began to give way to small mobile units, mostly composed of native troops, wandering through the country in all directions to destroy guerrilla bands, to punish the *tribù ribelli*, and to escort caravans. At the end of the year Gen. Ameglio became Governor of Cyrenaica and, as organized resistance was considered to have ceased, set about pacifying the country. For military purposes it was divided into three sections: an eastern sector, in which action was to be directed towards preventing contraband entering Cyrenaica from Egypt and to strike at the large enemy camp being formed in the Marmarica; a central sector in which the objective was to destroy the enemy camps at al-'Arqub and Slanta and to attempt a thrust beyond these to the Sanusi depot at al-Makhili, supply base for all the Turco-Arab camps in Cyrenaica; and a western sector, in which a drive was planned against the 'Awaqir and Magharba tribes, who kept up hostile activities from Ajadabiya and Msus. It was decided to begin these threefold operations at the end of February 1914, acting simultaneously in the three sectors, offensively in the zones of Banghazi, Shahhat, and Tubruq, and defensively in the zones of al-Marj and Darna.

During February there were many fights in the Shahhat zone. There was also fighting in the Banghazi zone, including two big battles, at Umm Shakhanab (Sanusi, 179 dead: Italians, 21 dead) and at al-Shlaidima (Sanusi, about 200 dead: Italians, 14 dead). Al-Zuwaitina was occupied and from there the village of Ajadabiya was entered without resistance and razed to the ground on 16 March 1914. The Italian force then retired to al-Zuwaitina and Ajadabiya was reoccupied by the Arabs and had to be retaken, this time by fighting (Sanusi, 130 dead). In the zone of al-Marj there was also heavy fighting. Here the Italians were on the defensive and the Arabs attacking in a way very costly to themselves. There was also fighting in the Darna zone.

The total result of these operations in all parts of the country was that by mid-July all the principal Turco-Arab camps in central and western Cyrenaica had been occupied: al-'Arqub, Marawa, Taknis, al-Shlaidima, and Ajadabiya. The Bedouin forces had been compelled to withdraw to south of the Wadi al-Farigh, to the southern slopes of the plateau, and to the Marmarica. They continued, nevertheless, especially from the southern slopes of the plateau, to conduct improvised attacks on caravans and advanced posts. It was therefore decided to expel them from their new refuges on these slopes, and with this end in view Italian columns penetrated into the desert-scrub country to the south of the plateau in pursuit of the enemy. The Bedouin bands withdrew eastwards under the pressure of these attacks and formed concentrations at Khawalan and in the Marmarica. They were being hard pressed and had to face at the same time enemies more lethal and demoralizing than Italian arms: plague, smallpox, typhus, and drought and locusts bringing famine in their train. The crops had failed for two years in succession in Cyrenaica and Tripolitania; and local markets were in the hands of the Italians. The only source of supplies open to the Bedouin were the Egyptian ports, chiefly al-Sallum, and the markets of the Delta, and from these points large, but insufficient, quantities of food, particularly flour, poured in a steady stream across the frontier.

Bedouin mortality was certainly high. Lo Bello reckoned that by the end of 1914 nearly two-thirds of the population of Cyrenaica had died, 300,000 in 1911 being reduced to 120,000 in 1915.[1] One must agree, however, with Mondaini,[2] that Lo Bello's figure is exaggerated, for the casualties were almost entirely among the Bedouin and had they been as high as he puts them the long resistance of the Bedouin against the Italians in the second Italo-Sanusi war would have been impossible. In spite of their heavy losses and the great hardships they had to endure they kept up the struggle in a succession of

---

[1] 'Le Vicende politico-militari dei primi dodici Anni di Occupazione Italiana in Cirenaica', *Rivista Coloniale*, 1925, p. 126.

[2] Op. cit., p. 374.

guerrilla encounters, especially on the central plateau—in the month of August alone Italian historians consider ten such encounters worth recording.

To crown their difficulties the Turkish Commander, 'Aziz Bey al-Masri, with most of his officers deserted them late in 1913 or very early in 1914. Sayyid Ahmad was a proud and headstrong man with whom it was not easy to co-operate and disagreements between him and 'Aziz Bey had increased to the point at which 'Aziz Bey felt it necessary to withdraw to Egypt, as indeed he was supposed to have done in 1912 under the Treaty of Losanna. 'Aziz Bey left without Sayyid Ahmad's knowledge or consent, taking with him most of the artillery. An attempt to intercept him on his way to Egypt by a party of the Minifa tribe was unsuccessful and costly to the Minifa.

This incident might have caused a final rupture between Arab and Turk, the Sanusiya and the Ottoman Government, if it had not been for the outbreak of the Great War in Europe. When Italy entered the war on the side of the Allies in May 1915, the British felt obliged to institute on behalf of their ally a blockade of the coast, and Sayyid Ahmad and his followers found themselves in a precarious position, and more than ever dependent on Turkish supplies. The Turks, having entered the war on the side of the Central Powers in November 1914, found themselves once again officially at war with Italy in July 1915 and no longer had to be circumspect in supplying the Sayyid with munitions, and their powerful German ally was now able to supply the means of transport by submarine. The Sayyid thus found himself in a dilemma. He had no wish to become embroiled in a world war, but he was not in the position to refuse the help Turkey and Germany were able to give him against the Italians at a time when it was increasingly difficult for him to obtain supplies from any other quarter, and when with a little extra help he had every chance of driving the intruder out of his country altogether. For the Italians were in a poor plight in both Tripolitania and Cyrenaica even before their entry into the European war increased their responsibilities.

After the Peace of Losanna and the withdrawal of the Turkish forces from Tripolitania the country, always disunited at the best of times, was easily overrun by Italian columns to its farthest confines. Col. Antonio Miani was able to march in triumph to Murzuq. It was a march through water, yielding to the weight of his column but closing behind it. The tide turned and the Italians were overwhelmed. The signal for a general rising was the massacre of an Italian caravan going from Mizda to Brak on 26 August 1914. Sayyid Muhammad 'Abid, the member of the Sanusi family in charge of the affairs of the Order in Fazzan, who had made tentative overtures to Col. Miani when he seemed to be carrying everything before him, now raised the tribes of Fazzan and southern Tripolitania behind him. Col. Miani had incautiously recruited Bedouin friendlies to accompany his expedition and these, as might have been expected, revolted at the same time. Meanwhile in the Sirtica the Sanusi tribes led by the Aulad Suliman and the Magharba were still undefeated and in arms, and had been joined by some of the more obstinate Sanusi and Bedouin elements from Tripolitania, including a considerable part of the Aulad bu Saif tribe. Here, in the summer of 1914, the genial Sayyid Safi -al-Din, Sayyid Ahmad al-Sharif's youngest brother, had taken command of the resistance in the name of the Sanusiya. The Sirtica offered excellent opportunities for keeping it going: inhospitable, without ports but allowing the disembarkation of supplies and reinforcements by Turco-German submarines, far alike from the centres of Tripolitania and Cyrenaica, and inhabited by tribes with a tradition of turbulent independence and devotion to the Sanusiya Order. Col. Miani, made over-confident by the ease with which he had marched through southern Tripolitania and Fazzan, advanced incautiously from Misurata into this barren land and was decisively defeated at Qasr bu Hadi on 29 April 1915. The treachery of his Misuratan friendlies under Ramadan al-Shtaiwi turned the defeat into a rout. The Italians lost, besides the rifles and ammunition with which the native and Italian units were armed, a reserve of 5,000 rifles, some millions of rounds of ammunition, several machine-guns, artillery with plenty of shells, the entire convoy of food supplies, and even the bank. After this victory Sayyid Safi al-Din marched into Old Tripolitania to put himself, in the name of the Sanusiya, at the head of the Arab resistance. He just failed to bring the whole country under the Sanusiya flag, not on account of Italian opposition, which was negligible, nor entirely on account of his own shortcomings, which were considerable, but chiefly because of the ancient feud between the Bedouin and interior party of Tripolitania to which most of the Sanusiya supporters belonged, and the urban and coastal party represented by Ramadan al-Shtaiwi, the self-made lord of Misurata. Ramadan defeated the Sayyid in an encounter near Bani Walid early in 1916 and, to avoid further bloodshed between the Arabs themselves, Sayyid Safi al-Din was ordered by his cousin Sayyid Muhammad Idris, by that time in charge of the affairs of the Order, to withdraw to the east. This defeat set the limit to Sanusiya political influence in Old Tripolitania at the Wadi Zamzam.

If in Tripolitania Italy had swallowed more than she could digest and was violently sick, in Cyrenaica what she had swallowed stuck in her throat. Although at the end of 1914 the Italians were on paper in control of the country as far as the Wadi al-Farigh and, on the plateau, the watershed, in fact they merely held posts in it and had very little authority outside these posts, which they supplied with difficulty and by an extravagant and cumbrous convoy system. Opposite the posts, harassing communications and keeping the garrisons on the alert day and night, were still unbeaten the Bedouin bands along what they called their *khatt al-nar*, their line of fire, a barrier which prevented any Italian contact with the tribes other than those few sections in the immediate vicinity of their forts. The Bedouin who had submitted, at any rate nominally, were the Baraghtha and a few other 'Awaqir between Banghazi and Suluq, the *Marabtin* Fawakhir and some of the Magharba near Ajadabiya, most of the Hasa tribe, a few Bara'asa sections near Shahhat, and the Darsa sections near al-Haniya. The rest of the country was unreservedly hostile.

While the Bedouin kept up ceaseless guerrilla activity around the Italian forts Italian difficulties were mounting as a by-product of the European war, although Italy had not yet entered it, and she found herself unable to give full attention to her Libyan venture. There was restlessness in the hinterland of Eritrea and it was thought that an incursion from Abyssinia was not impossible, so that Eritrean units intended for Cyrenaica had to be kept at home, and the Cyrenaican command was thus deprived of its best troops on whom, rather than on its national troops, it had come to rely more and more to do most of the fighting. In 1914 there were eight battalions of Eritreans in Libya. The collapse in Tripolitania coming on top of their other troubles caused a panic in Cyrenaica and the garrisons of the interior were hastily withdrawn between January and October 1915. Thus even before Italy, after much hesitation and bargaining, entered the European maelstrom her North African empire was already in collapse.

Giolitti, who had stood for non-intervention, lost office amid general execration in May 1915 and Italy declared war on Austria. In August 1916 she also, under pressure from her allies, declared war on Germany. The war was not a happy one for Italy. There was strong opposition to it in the country, opportunism in the ministries, military incompetence, desertion from the armed forces, and all-round defeatism and selfishness which led, after repeated military failure, to the disaster of Caporetto in October 1917. In the midst of these troubles Giolitti's successors were anxious to end the expensive and un-successful diversion in Libya, a desire which led, as will be seen in the next chapter, to the truce with the Sanusi of April 1917 known as the *modus vivendi* of 'Akrama (Acroma). The out-break of the second Turco-Italian war (1915–18) had some advantages from Italy's point of view. It enabled her to retain the Dodecanese Islands (Rhodes and eleven other small islands) and she had an excuse for rescinding the privileges the Sultan enjoyed in Libya under the Treaty of Losanna. Also, the British might be expected to be less tolerant of supplies reaching the Bedouin of Cyrenaica across the Egyptian frontier and through Egyptian ports, and by German and Turkish sub-marines. Nevertheless, its immediate result was an almost total evacuation of Tripolitania, where the Italians were able to hold only Tripoli town, a strip of coast to the west of it and Khums, and of Cyrenaica, where they held only the towns and villages near the coast and a few inland posts with which communica-tion from the coast was maintained precariously. Everywhere the Bedouin had the initiative and the Italian garrisons were demoralized and besieged. If Sayyid Ahmad al-Sharif had not now decided to launch an attack on the British outposts in the Western Desert of Egypt the final outcome might have been very different from what it was.

VI

Italian pressure on the Turco-Arab forces during 1914 had the effect of pushing the main concentration of their troops eastwards where they were farther from the Italian bases and gained additional protection from the proximity of the Egyptian frontier. The Italians wished to avoid complications with Egypt and England in which they might find themselves involved were they to operate along an ill-defined frontier, and it was partly for this reason that the large-scale operations planned for the Marmarica by Gen. Ameglio were not put into effect. By the end of 1915 there were concentrated at Masa'ad (Amseat), about 3 km. from al-Sallum, some 2,000 armed men in Sayyid Ahmad's camp. This concentration did not cause much uneasiness in British circles at Cairo, for the Sanusi had no quarrel with the British and in the past Sayyid Ahmad had expressed himself well disposed towards them and had compared them favourably to the French and Italians. In two interviews on the frontier with Bimbashi Royle of the Frontiers Administration in November 1914 he had given assurances, the honesty of which there was no reason to doubt, that the concentration was not aimed at disturbing the frontier but was solely directed against the Italians. Nevertheless, the British reinforced their troops in the Western Desert of Egypt.

During 1915 Turkish and German officers landed from submarines on the Marmarican coast, bringing with them arms and money and other supplies to Sayyid Ahmad's camp. Among the arrivals were the Turkish officers Nuri Bey, Enver Bey's brother, and Ja'afir Bey al-'Askari (later Prime Minister of Iraq) and the Tripolitanian Berber leader Suliman al-Baruni, a tempestuous person. Sayyid Ahmad came more under the influence of these men the more he found himself compelled to rely on them for supplies for his famished people and for direction of his motley army of Bedouin seasoned with the remnants of the Ottoman forces of 1911. It is proof of the sincerity of his assurances to the British that he resisted for so long the pressure they exerted on him to attack British advanced positions in the Western Desert and that when in the summer of 1915 he discovered a plot, on behalf of Turco-German interests, to force the issue by involving his forces in conflict with British frontier posts he arrested the ringleaders and sent them under guard to Jaghbub. Among the plotters were Suliman al-Baruni and the Sayyid's own brother Hilal, a miserable creature who had, as early as May 1913, approached the Italians in a letter denouncing Sayyid Ahmad and Mansur al-Kakhiya.[1]

Sayyid Ahmad's cousin, Sayyid Muhammad Idris, always spoken of by the Bedouin as Sayyid Idris (by which term I refer to him in future) or by the more intimate title of Sidi Idris, was strongly against any action which might bring the Sanusi into conflict with the British, and his counsels were a restraining influence on his impetuous kinsman. Sayyid Idris had in May 1914 gone on pilgrimage—his habit in moments of crisis—and had contacted the British political authorities in Cairo on his way to Mecca. On his return in February 1915 he had been received in a friendly manner by Lord Kitchener and the Residency staff in Cairo and had visited the British General Officer Commanding in Egypt. He seems to have made it clear to the British Authorities that his view of the situation did not entirely agree with that of his cousin, and from this time the British favoured his pretensions to the leadership of the Bedouin of Cyrenaica. At the end of the month he had left for al-Sallum in a coastguard steamer and had joined Sayyid Ahmad at Masa'ad.

In the end Sayyid Ahmad's heart had the better of his judgement. He was an old-fashioned Muslim and a very headstrong one. He had in July 1915, after the declaration of the second Turco-Italian war, been nominated, by a firman of the Sultan, Governor of Tripolitania and of the dependent regions, and he had promulgated locally the Caliph's *jihad* against infidels in general, into which category the British clearly came. He found it difficult, therefore, to refuse the Sultan's instructions to attack in the Western Desert to ease British pressure on the Turkish forces operating in Palestine to cut the Suez Canal. With all his courage and piety Sayyid Ahmad was vain, and doubtless wished to see himself in the heroic role flatterers depicted to his imagination. He may have been misled by them into supposing that the Aulad 'Ali tribe of Egypt would rise to support him. In the event the Aulad 'Ali who, though pre-

---

[1] Serra, op. cit., pp. 13 and 156 seq.

dominantly Sanusi, were an unwarlike people, were prevailed on by British representatives to remain quiet. Presumably also he was impressed by the stories interested persons told him of Germany's might and of her military successes. Many able politicians, diplomats, and generals in Europe, who had far better opportunity and far greater knowledge for judging the outcome than the Sayyid, were at this time convinced that the Central Powers would win the war. He was doubtless also misled by the little he had so far seen of European armies, small French Colonial columns of native troops and the dilatory and incompetent Italian military machine, into believing that war with the British in the Western Desert would be on the same scale.

These considerations apart, it may be doubted whether the Sayyid had any choice. The Turkish officers in his camp were his military advisers and the only persons who could supply and direct his forces. They persistently pressed him to action and urged the tribal and Sanusiya Shaikhs, over whom they had won much influence by their fighting qualities, their superior training and equipment, and the authority of their rank, to the same end. Those in favour of an attack on the British were supported by the strongest advocate, hunger. The Bedouin were reduced to desperation by famine, and an advance into Egypt seemed to offer an immediate satisfaction of their needs. In these circumstances they were likely to act as they thought fit, without waiting for instructions or paying much attention to any that might be given. A Bedouin horde is not a disciplined army and a leader of irregulars has often to be led by them. Whether, in the event, Sayyid Ahmad gave the order to attack the British posts or they were attacked without waiting for his direction is not entirely certain, but it is most likely that the attack was his responsibility. Already engaged in a desultory war with France in the Sudan and in a life and death struggle with Italy in Cyrenaica, he now, with quixotic abandon, attacked Great Britain in Egypt: a handful of Bedouin against three European Powers.

The campaign was short and decisive. In November 1915 Nuri Bey took al-Sallum by surprise, the small British garrison escaping by sea and three-quarters of the Egyptian troops going over to the enemy. He then advanced on Sidi al-Barrani and afterwards Marsa Matruh. The British made a counter-offensive in January 1916. Consistently beaten in a series of encounters, the forces of Sayyid Ahmad and Nuri Bey were finally routed at al-'Aqqaqir, to the west of Marsa Matruh, on 26 February 1916, by Gen. Peyton, an engagement in which Ja'afir Bey and his staff were captured. On 24 March al-Sallum was reoccupied. British armoured cars did great damage among the scattered Bedouin, 'shooting all loaded camels and men within reach'.[1] Seeing his men hopelessly routed and confused Sayyid Ahmad retired with a small bodyguard to Siwa oasis, then to al-Bahariya, Farafra, and finally al-Dakhla, in all of which oases in the Western Desert of Egypt there was a large Sanusi element. It is often said by writers, and the view seems to have been held by British Intelligence, though I do not know on what evidence, that he intended to link up with a revolt (November 1915) of 'Ali Dinar, the Sultan of Darfur in the Egyptian Sudan, though the Sultan had never been friendly towards the Sanusiya. It is quite possible that the Turks or the Sayyid, or both, had some such crazy plan. Anyhow, 'Ali Dinar's rising was crushed without difficulty and he was killed in the autumn of 1916.

After his defeat at the hands of the British, Sayyid Ahmad had at least the good sense to realize that his people were too exhausted to continue the struggle, that negotiations would have to be entered into, and that overtures from him were not likely to be acceptable to either the British or the Italians. He therefore, in the interests of his country and of his Order, handed over political and military control in Cyrenaica to Sayyid Idris. Sayyid Idris's brother, Sayyid al-Rida, was to assist him on the plateau and Sayyid Hilal in the Marmarica. Sayyid Safi al-Din was placed in charge of Sanusiya interests in the Sirtica, Sayyid Muhammad 'Abid in Fazzan and the *qibla*, and Sayyid 'Ali al-Khattab in the oases of Kufra. Sayyid Ahmad remained religious head of the Sanusiya *tariqa*.

It was, therefore, with Sayyid Ahmad's consent, indeed approval, that Sayyid Idris entered into negotiations with the British from Ajadabiya, whither he had repaired in the winter of 1915, before the attack in the Western Desert, to avoid being implicated in an action he could neither countenance nor stop.

---

[1] W. T. Massey, *The Desert Campaigns*, 1918, p. 150.

THE SAYYID AHMAD AL-SHARIF (MACALUSO)

Nuri Bey visited him at Ajadabiya and tried to win him back to the Turkish allegiance but failed to change his opinion. Such being the case, Nuri knew that resistance could no longer be kept up in Cyrenaica and set off for Tripolitania to try his luck there. Other Turkish officers and pro-Turkish elements, the irreconcilables, joined him, their departure being hastened by a new treachery on the part of Sayyid Hilal. This dissolute young man presented himself to the Italian authorities at Tubruq in March 1916, shortly before negotiations began between Sayyid Idris and the Anglo-Italian mission at al-Zuwaitina. He stated that he had come to ask for provisions for the starving Bedouin of the Marmarica, but he was also, as Canevari puts it, 'desirous of a life more in accordance with his aspirations'.[1] This was the first member of the Sanusi family the Italians had bagged and they were delighted to see him. At their suggestion he used his influence, both as a grandson of the Grand Sanusi and as a grandson of the Shaikh of an important Marmarican zawiya, to pacify the 'Abaidat tribe, who surrendered, largely as a result of his efforts and in return for food for their starving families, over 1,000 rifles to the Italians. The Italians also made use of his services to effect an uncontested entry into the port of al-Burdi Sulaiman in May 1916 and afterwards into Masa'ad, Sayyid Ahmad's old camp. His activities did Sayyid Idris a twofold harm, politically by weakening his military position and therefore his bargaining power while negotiations for peace were taking place, and morally by lowering the prestige of the Sanusi family in the eyes of the Bedouin by drunkenness and debauchery, for he led openly a scandalous life in the company of Italian officers.

The negotiations at al-Zuwaitina between the Anglo-Italian mission and Sayyid Idris broke down, partly because Sayyid Idris did not feel secure enough of his own position to agree to terms without first gaining the consent of Sayyid Ahmad. For this reason, and because they were anxious to end their military commitments in the Western Desert and could no longer countenance the occupation of Egyptian oases by enemy forces, the British dispatched a force from al-Kharja oasis to occupy al-Dakhla oasis on 17 October 1916. Sayyid Ahmad fled to al-Bahariya and thence to Siwa which, in its turn, was occupied

---

[1] Op. cit., p. 15.

by a British motor column early in 1917, while resumed negotiations were taking place between Sayyid Idris and the Anglo-
Italian Mission at 'Akrama. The occupation, sharply contested
in a day's fighting, was possibly designed in part to cure Sayyid
Idris of his lifelong malady of procrastination and to speed up
the negotiations.

Sayyid Ahmad fled once more, this time for good. He went
first to Jaghbub and thence through the oases of the 29th
parallel to the Sirtica. His intention was to continue the war
against Italy in Tripolitania, but Suliman al-Baruni and Nuri
Bey, with whom he was by this time also on bad terms, had
got there before him and linked up with Ramadan al-Shtaiwi,
the old enemy of the Sanusiya in Misurata. Warned off Tripolitanian ground by these men, Sayyid Ahmad came down from
the interior of the Sirtica to al-'Aqaila and from there took
passage in a submarine for Turkey in September 1918. The
Sayyid's departure was good-bye to many things: to British
arms, to Ottoman rule, to the Sanusiya empire, and to Sayyid
Ahmad al-Sharif al-Sanusi.

VII

The mechanized raid on Siwa oasis was the last action between
the British and the Sanusi. From the British point of view the
Sanusi war was a small incident in a great war. The Sanusi also,
curiously, regarded it as no more than an incident in their war
with Italy, though it proved for them to be a disastrous one.
But although it was of minor importance and was wholly successful, the British were glad to see the campaign brought to a
close. Casualties on their side had been negligible, but 35,000
Imperial troops—British, Australians, New Zealanders, Sikhs,
and South Africans—had been tied down to the Western
Desert of Egypt for many months when they were needed, and
badly needed, elsewhere; and the expense had been prodigious.
All the British wanted now was as quickly as possible to patch
up a truce which would make any further trouble along the
frontier unlikely and free their troops for other duties. All the
troops wanted was to get away from the scorching, freezing,
dust-blown desert of the Marmarica. I suppose that there was
not one among them who foresaw that 24 years later their sons
would be back—British, Australians, New Zealanders, Sikhs,

and South Africans, as before—in the land of asphodels; this time with the Sanusi as their friends.

But if the British were to return, the Turks departed once and for all. When Sayyid Ahmad left Cyrenaica for Tripolitania there were still in the former country the remnants of its original Turkish army, and though most of these made their way westwards some remained to continue Turco-German propaganda, and occasional submarines made their appearance on the coast to the same end. The Turkish cause still found much sympathy among the Arab population and might have persuaded the Bedouin to follow Sayyid Ahmad and the sinking star of the Ottoman Caliphate, rather than Sayyid Idris and their own interests, had not exhaustion reduced them to that point at which men think only of peace. As it was, Turkish interests were in no way considered, at Sayyid Idris's own request, in the discussions which led to a truce, and when, under the terms of the truce, the Sayyid was compelled to arrest Turkish officers and agents still in the country, the Bedouin for the most part readily accepted his action. It is to his credit that he did not hand over any of these persons to the British or Italians.

The ambivalent attitude of the Sanusiya Order to the Ottoman Sultanate was at last resolved by splitting the Headship of the Order between two individuals. In the person of Sayyid Ahmad the *Tariqa al-Sanusiya* still followed the Sultanate, but only as a religious order and without territorial attachments, while in the person of Sayyid Idris it put on pace in its development into an Arab Amirate of Cyrenaica. The elimination of Turkey from Cyrenaican affairs was a vital step in its transformation. European powers with interests in the country were forced now to deal with the only person capable of speaking for its Bedouin tribes collectively, Sayyid Muhammad Idris. The Order had achieved diplomatic status.

Sayyid Ahmad's departure marks the end of the Sanusiya empire as well as the end of the Ottoman Empire in North Africa. The Sanusiya reached the peak of its political expansion in 1902, the year in which Sayyid al-Mahdi died, and Sayyid Ahmad was heir to its declining fortunes. All his efforts to hold up the advance of the French were without avail and he saw one by one its Saharan provinces fall to them. By 1918 all that

was left to it in these regions was the isolated oasis of Kufra.
He had by his foolish attack on the British brought about the
destruction of the lodges of the Order and of its political
influence in the Western Desert of Egypt. Tripolitania had also
been lost to the Sanusiya, though it was by this time almost
entirely free from Italian domination. Ramadan al-Shtaiwi of
Misurata barred its way into Old Tripolitania. Fazzan was in a
state of anarchy. All that remained to the Order was its
original North African core—the tribes of Cyrenaica and its
Cyrenaican lodges—for in spite of all their defeats and miseries
the Bedouin of the country still remained loyal to the Order
whose interests were their own. The Italians were very far from
having conquered these Bedouin and the history of the Order
from the time of Sayyid Ahmad's departure is identical with
the history of their continued resistance to the Italians under
its leadership, first by diplomacy, then again by arms. With its
empire and its dependence on the Sultanate the Order lost also
its religious character and became, through its exclusive
identification with the interests of the people of Cyrenaica, an
almost purely political movement.

Although there were for many years rumours, greeted with
great enthusiasm by the Bedouin and with nervous appre-
hension by the Italians, of Sayyid Ahmad's impending return
to Cyrenaica he never again set foot on the African continent.
Born in 1873, Sayyid Ahmad al-Sharif was still in the early
forties when he left for Turkey. He was described at this time
as a man of medium height, stout, for an Arab on the dark side,
with a firm and determined face adorned with a small moustache,
close-cut whiskers on the upper jaw, and close-cut beard.[1] The
Sayyid was obstinate, impulsive in his judgements and impetuous in his actions, and he seems to have been proud,
quarrelsome, and fanatical. He was not prepared to compromise, and the British and Italians were in entire agreement
that no understanding could be reached with him. But he was
a pious Muslim and a brave and loyal man, tenacious of his
beliefs, stubborn in his upholding of them against overwhelming
odds, and dignified in their defeat. There was a certain wildness
in his schemes and recklessness in his execution of them which
compel admiration.

[1] Admiralty War Staff, Intelligence Division, 26 May 1915.

After his departure from North Africa, Sayyid Ahmad continued to lead an adventurous life. His wars against France, Italy, and Great Britain had made him a world figure, and in the eyes of Muslims one of the foremost fighters for Islam of his time. He was much sought after by the pan-Islamists of Istanbul, who wished to use his name in their propaganda directed to bringing Turks and Arabs more closely together. In April 1921 he was designated King of Iraq at the Assembly of Angora, but Faisal, backed by the British, had the advantage of him in this project. He and his name played a big part in persuading the Muslim minorities of Turkey to throw in their lot with Mustafa Kamal. After Mustafa Kamal's victories Sayyid Ahmad returned to Istanbul, where he tried to re-establish the Caliphate, a project for which Mustafa Kamal showed less enthusiasm. Early in 1922 we find him at Urfa making peace between the great Bedouin tribes of Shammar and 'Anaza. We then find him at Marsina trying to reunite Syria to Turkey. From there he went to live at Damascus. The French found his presence in Syria embarrassing and expelled him from the country in December 1924. Thence he went to the Hijaz, where he remained till his death at al-Madina on 10 March 1933. During the last years of his life he took less interest in politics. He seems to have won the personal respect of King Ibn Sa'ud, and he was called upon to settle local disputes, the most notable of his achievements as peacemaker being a settlement of the quarrel between the Amir Idris of 'Asir, the descendant of the Grand Sanusi's teacher at Mecca, and the Imam Yahiya of the Yaman, but he mainly lived in retirement among his books. He lived just long enough to see the Sanusi cause to all appearances as finally extinguished in Cyrenaica as it had been elsewhere.

CHAPTER VI

THE PERIOD OF THE ACCORDS (1917–23)

I

SAYYID Idris's approaches to the allied powers eventually led to the British High Commissioner in Egypt, Sir Henry McMahon, sending Col. Milo Talbot, a man of integrity and with a considerable knowledge of North African affairs, to represent his country in the negotiations. Col. Talbot, accompanied by his Egyptian secretary Ahmad Muhammad Hasanain (later the famous explorer of the Libyan Desert), left Alexandria on 25 May 1916 and after preliminary discussions at Rome joined the Italian delegates, Col. Villa and Com. Piacentini, at al-Zuwaitina; and there also awaited him the Idrisis of Luxor, descendants of that Sayyid Ahmad bin Idris al-Fasi who had been the Grand Sanusi's teacher at Mecca. They had been sent to Cyrenaica at Sayyid Idris's request to assist him in the negotiations. Sayyid Idris himself was camped some miles away in the interior with his counsellors and supporters.

Discussions between Italy and England about the Sanusi had begun in February 1915 and an understanding had been reached on 31 July 1916, adhered to by France in March 1917, by which each undertook not to sign an agreement with the Sanusi without the consent of the other and to recognize Sayyid Idris as Head of the Sanusiya Order. It was clearly stipulated that the Sayyid should not be afforded recognition as an autonomous ruler, though the possibility of allowing him, under the sovereignty of the occupying State, administrative autonomy of some of the oases might be examined. On this point the Italians had earlier shown themselves to be very sensitive and the British Government had felt it expedient to assure them that it did not favour Sayyid Ahmad's claims to independence, pointing out to them that the recognition of Sayyid Ahmad as a secular ruler would be harmful to England as well as to Italy since it would involve the British Government in awkward frontier questions in the Marmarica.[1] Col. Talbot's instructions

---

[1] Bruno Aglietti, 'La Confraternita Senussita', *Oriente Moderne*, Jan.–June, 1946, pp. 6–9.

in the negotiations state explicitly that Sayyid Idris was to be regarded as a spiritual leader and not as a temporal leader.

Sayyid Idris had his first meeting with the Allied Mission on 25 July 1916 and the three-cornered discussions were spread out over the months of August and September. Between the Sanusi and the British there were easy relations from the beginning. Sayyid Idris had made friends with the British in Cairo, trusted them, and desired that the trust might be mutual. The British, for their part, were far from unsympathetic towards the Sanusi, and those who had met him respected the sincerity of their leader. Col. Talbot, while remaining on excellent terms with the Italian delegates, kept the confidence of the Sayyid, although he had sometimes, on behalf of the Italians, to press him to accept demands of which he personally disapproved and which could in no way serve British interests. He found little difficulty in obtaining the release of the British crew of the *Coquet*, who had for some time been prisoners in Sanusi hands.

Italo-Sanusi relations were very different. Sayyid Idris disliked the Italians and he thoroughly distrusted their intentions. The Italians suspected that Sayyid Ahmad and Sayyid Idris were in collusion, though pretending to be at variance, and aimed only at obtaining a temporary truce which would ensure entry into the country of supplies destined for a renewal of the struggle later; and they were resentful of the British, who, they thought, intended to relieve themselves of an embarrassment at the expense of Italy. It was soon evident that there was little hope of a permanent settlement, so a *modus vivendi* was sought which would at least give both sides a chance to recuperate.

At the beginning of the discussions the Italians said that they could only continue them if their prisoners were released, but the Sayyid had no intention of giving them up without a *quid pro quo* and adopted his usual delaying tactics when faced with demands of this kind, pleading that he would first have to ask permission of Sayyid Ahmad who had taken the prisoners, since he could not give one set of instructions and his cousin contrary ones. As Sayyid Ahmad was still at al-Kharja oasis, consultation by camel-mail could be relied on to delay the issue for some weeks. However, largely owing to Col. Talbot, agreement on this point was achieved, only to be overruled by the Italian Government at Rome, which considered its terms humiliating, on the grounds that its delegates had not been empowered to sign it. They were recalled and replaced by Maj. Riccardi and Gen. Ameglio, who were to continue the negotiations from Banghazi. Sayyid Idris thought that he had been deliberately tricked and wanted to know whether any future engagements entered into with the Italians might be revoked in the same way. Col. Talbot was also irritated at Rome's action, since it was he who had persuaded the Sayyid to sign the agreement. Negotiations were thereupon broken off for some months and Col. Talbot and his staff returned in October to Cairo to report to the High Commissioner.

Interference of this kind from Rome and Banghazi was one of the difficulties which beset the negotiations. Another difficulty was Sayyid Idris's diplomatic technique, simple and effective, but none the less fatiguing. When faced with a demand he did not wish to accept but was unable to refuse outright he pleaded, often justly, that it would be useless for him to agree to terms his followers would reject. If this plea failed he raised all sorts of difficulties and delays on one pretext or another, and if hard pressed, pleaded ill health, or lapsed into phlegmatic indifference. This technique of attrition—what one Italian writer called his ' *esasperante tattica temporeggiatrice* '[1]— was perhaps the best the Sayyid could have employed in the circumstances.

The discussions at al-Zuwaitina had not, however, been wasted. They had enabled Col. Talbot to know the Sayyid and, by a survey of the military situation at first hand and an initial assessment of the major problems, better to advise his Government. The discussions had made it clear that the Sayyid would agree neither to the release of the Italian prisoners nor to any further proposal unless the Allied Mission met him on the question of al-Sallum. The Sanusi received most of their supplies through this port, and if the British continued their blockade of it they would starve. Col. Talbot knew he could exact compliance in other matters in return for this concession, but he also knew that if the Sayyid did not obtain it for his people they might follow the intransigent Sayyid Ahmad, and the whole point of the negotiations was to prevent this. He felt, therefore, that he should urge the Italian delegates to meet

[1] Serra, op. cit., p. 93.

the Sayyid's wishes in this matter, both to uphold the Sayyid's prestige among his own people and to make him keep to his promises, particularly about the Allied prisoners and the Turkish officers, under threat of closing the port should he recant. There were in Cyrenaica still many Turkish officers urging the Bedouin to continue the struggle and Sayyid Idris had promised to round them up should al-Sallum be opened to trade. The question of the Turks was bound up with the al-Sallum issue because, as the Sayyid pointed out, Turkey had kept his people supplied by submarine, and while the Allies continued their blockade he could not afford to break with her.

Another problem was the immediate dispersal of the Sanusi fighting bands, or 'dors' (adwar), on which the Italian delegates insisted. It would have been foolish for the Sayyid to have disbanded his forces while discussions were proceeding, since it was their presence in the field which compelled the Allies to negotiate. He urged that it would be useless for him to agree to the dispersal of the bands, because they had no intention of dispersing and he had no means of forcing them to do so. The only result would be the loss of his prestige among his followers, who would say that he had become 'Italianized'. These bands continued to be a bone of contention between the Sanusi and the Italians for the next six years, and the issue was only settled by the military subjugation of the whole of Cyrenaica in 1932.

It was a question of importance to the Italians, because the answer to it was also the answer to what they regarded as the fundamental question of sovereignty. On this point the Sayyid was unyielding. He argued that his family, like the Arab princes of Arabia, had never accepted such demands as the Italians made, even from the Turks, fellow Muslims ruled by the Caliph of Islam; and he insisted that the British, who had everywhere shown themselves to be friends to the Arabs, should not· press those of Cyrenaica to accept Italian sovereignty, which was the issue of the war and could only be imposed on a defeated people. The British regarded the question of sovereignty as a theoretical one and could not understand why the Italians attached so much importance to it.

Col. Talbot thought they should be content with the occupation of the ports and other centres, as the British were in Egypt, without claiming sovereignty over a country their arms had failed to conquer. After they had spent, it was believed, £80 million Sterling on the war in Libya up to 1916,[1] they were still everywhere on the defensive, more or less besieged in their forts, which they could only victual and relieve by cumbrous convoys. Moreover, the Sayyid's Bedouin followers would have deserted his personal leadership had he compromised on the question of sovereignty, and there was no one else with whom the Allies could treat save Sayyid Ahmad, for only these two men could speak for the whole of Cyrenaica. If the Bedouin lost faith in Sayyid Idris, peace, the one essential for all parties, would be lost.

The British view was common sense and true to British traditions of diplomacy. It appeared to the British that the Italians, unable to conduct a colonial war successfully, wanted to gain their prize by British arms. Otherwise there was no point in pressing the Sayyid to recognize Italian sovereignty when this sovereignty had been recognized explicitly or implicitly by all the Powers of Europe. To the Italians it appeared that the British intended to secure their position in Egypt by making such terms with the Sanusi as would enable the Sanusi later to continue the struggle against Italy. There was some truth in both views. Divergence of policy arose from different aims. All the British wanted was to end the Sanusi affair quickly. They regarded it as an unfortunate incident in their war against Germany and one from which they neither expected, nor wished, profit. It was an embarrassment, freezing, at a time men and supplies were short, forces badly needed elsewhere. They demanded, therefore, besides the return of their few shipwrecked prisoners, only evacuation of the Egyptian oases, cessation of all propaganda in Egypt, and the extradition of all Turkish agents from Cyrenaica. Once the threat to their positions in Egypt and on the Canal, threatened at the same time by the Turks from Palestine, had been removed and steps had been taken to make its recurrence unlikely, the British had no further interest in Cyrenaican affairs and certainly had no intention of conquering the country for themselves or for the Italians. They considered moreover that their obligation to their Italian allies went no farther than a truce which would

[1] Colonel Talbot's Reports (unpublished).

enable the Italians to win over the Bedouin by trade, good administration, and fair dealing. Peace would doubtless break up the cohesion of the Bedouin tribes brought about by their war with Italy and wise politics could make use of the resultant cleavages. If Italy did not succeed in pacifying the country that was her affair and not England's, for she had invaded Cyrenaica on her own responsibility long before the outbreak of war in Europe. Furthermore, the British had defeated Sayyid Ahmad without receiving, or asking for, Italian support. Italian aims were more comprehensive. They not only wanted to straighten out their battered prestige but also to conquer and colonize Cyrenaica. British aims were strategic; Italian aims were political.

Thus the British were strong, but wanted no more than military security, which they could have obtained by military means, whereas the Italians were weak, but wanted complete administrative control over a country in which, after five years of military effort, they barely retained a foothold. It was clear, therefore, that the Italians would in the end have to accommodate themselves to the British view, and though the British were prepared to force Sayyid Idris to conclude an accord with the Italians, as the price of signing one themselves, they would not press him much beyond the point at which their own interests were safeguarded.

Of the two Allied partners, the British held the stronger cards and could call the play. Sayyid Idris could not hope to win the game on his hand, but he held a few good cards and might expect, if he played them well, to win some tricks. His military position was hopeless. He might have continued fighting the Italians alone, even after the Sanusi defeat in the Western Desert, but he stood no chance against the British, and he soon found that he could not separate them from their Allies. His people were weary, famished, and despondent, and wanted peace. On the other hand he was aware that the Allies were anxious to reach an agreement with him as quickly as possible. Delays which cost the Bedouin hardships to which they were accustomed cost the Allies divisions needed in their life and death struggle with the Central Powers. Also, it was as obvious to him as it was to the Allied Mission that he was the only man in Cyrenaica with whom they could treat, since the only other man who had the backing of the Bedouin, Sayyid Ahmad, despised the Italians and refused to have anything to do with them. Were Sayyid Idris to accept the full Italian demands, he would, as he said, be pulling down his position with his own hands, and he was the keystone of the whole negotiations.

The Sayyid held two other good cards at the conference table. The Bedouin of Cyrenaica did not stand entirely alone. They were still supported by the Turks, who managed to get some supplies to them by submarine in spite of the blockade, and the presence of Turkish officers in the Sanusi forces gave the struggle a wider significance than it would otherwise have had. The Arabs of Tripolitania were also, though indirectly, involved. Were negotiations to break down between Sayyid Idris and the Allies, it was probable that those Cyrenaicans who wished to continue the war would receive assistance from their western brothers, or would retire to the west to continue resistance there. If, however, the Sayyid's prestige could be enhanced among the Bedouin of Cyrenaica by an agreement which gave them supplies and left them their independence, it might be hoped that he would in his own interest oppose, and be strong enough to stop, Turkish agents and their sympathizers from involving the Arabs of Tripolitania directly in the Cyrenaican issue. England wanted to spare her troops the conquest of Cyrenaica. She wanted all the more to spare them the further conquest of Tripolitania. Sayyid Idris also held the pan-Arab card. The British had encouraged the Arabs of Arabia to revolt against Turkish rule and to gain their freedom. It seemed hardly consistent for them to bully the same Arab people in Cyrenaica into accepting Italian rule, a thing far more odious to them than Turkish rule. The successful rebellion of the Sharif of Mecca had stimulated Sayyid Idris to confirm the temporal, as well as the spiritual, power of his family in Cyrenaica and to hope for an independent Amirate, such as the Idrisis had set up in the 'Asir in 1909. It was difficult for the British to encourage Arab aspirations on one side of Egypt and to crush them on the other.

Thus Col. Talbot's diplomatic strength lay in the fact that the British could, if the Sayyid proved obdurate, starve his people by blockade and, if he proved more than obdurate, follow up their military successes in the Western Desert into

Cyrenaica itself; while if the Italians were too greedy, they could break off negotiations and limit their further participation in the Sanusi war to defensive action along the Egyptian frontier, leaving the Italians to validate their claim to sovereignty by force of arms. Italian diplomatic strength lay in the agreement by which England had bound herself that she would not conclude a separate peace with the Sanusi. They knew that the British were eager—Col. Talbot was always trying to expedite the discussions—to end their military commitments in this theatre and they were, therefore, able to bring pressure on Sayyid Idris through them. The Sayyid's strength lay in his weakness. To obtain an effective truce, the Allies would have to back him personally, and they could only do this by making concessions.

Dummy, Sayyid Idris's absent partner in this game, was his cousin Sayyid Ahmad. Till recently Sayyid Ahmad had been undisputed leader of the Sanusi, and were he to appear on the scene again, the Bedouin would probably follow him. As neither he nor the Italians were prepared to negotiate with one another, and as the British also had no wish to negotiate with him, his reappearance would mean renewal of the fighting. The only way in which it could be prevented was by making a success of the discussions with Sayyid Idris. The Allied Mission felt the presence of this uncompromising man at the conference of al-Zuwaitina, although he was far away in the oasis of al-Kharja.

II

Peace was so clearly in the interests of all that the temporary breakdown of the talks at al-Zuwaitina did not lead to further hostilities on either side, and was regarded by both as an interlude between two phases in the negotiations. The talks were resumed in the Marmarica in January 1917. The Allied Mission lived at Tubruq and the Sayyid at 'Akrama, about 40 km. distant. The Idrisis of Luxor, father and son, were again present and, as before, flitted between the two parties. The Italians were represented by Col. De Vita and Com. Pintor. Sayyid Ahmad was at Siwa.

The talks began well and by 27 March the exchange of Italian and Sanusi prisoners was at last effected. In return for the

Sayyid's goodwill in this matter the Allies conceded in principle the reopening of the markets to the famished Bedouin. The programme of al-Zuwaitina then began to repeat itself. The Italians pressed for the acceptance of terms substantially the same as those they put forward the year before and which became known as *modus vivendi* No. 1. They were unacceptable to the Sayyid, whose position had not deteriorated to any extent in the interval, and he replied with what became known as *modus vivendi* No. 2, in which he asked the Italians to make all the concessions he desired while deferring for future discussion the points in which they were chiefly interested. On the basis of the Sayyid's counter-proposals the Italians produced a *modus vivendi* No. 3 which gave the Sayyid almost all he had asked for, being in fact No. 2 with slight alterations and additions. To this the Sayyid replied with a *modus vivendi* No. 4, which altered or omitted several of the clauses in No. 3. Col. Talbot now felt that the ball had been patted backwards and forwards long enough, that the Sayyid's last effort was unnecessary, as the terms of the latest Italian proposals were practically the same as those put forward by the Sayyid himself, and that therefore No. 3 should be accepted as it stood without modifications. The Sayyid accepted it on the promise that when he did so the markets would forthwith be reopened.

At this point the Italian delegates, who were only empowered to negotiate *ad referendum*, declared, to Col. Talbot's consternation, that the Sayyid's acceptance of *modus vivendi* No. 3 was inadequate and that he must also accept No. 1 'on general lines'. It could hardly have seemed otherwise to the Sayyid than that the Italians were increasing their demands. However, he once again took Col. Talbot's advice and agreed to accept No. 1 'on general lines' on the Colonel's assurance that an acceptance of so general a nature would not fetter his future action; although the Italian interpretation of 'on general lines' was that it referred to the time and manner of implementation and not to the substance of the agreement. In the end, therefore, the Sayyid accepted No. 3 for immediate application and No. 1 on the understanding that it was to be put into force later, gradually, and subject to agreement between the parties. In reality he committed himself to very little. He had already consented to sign the terms placed before him by the British.

He signed the agreements with both Powers, with England on 14 April and with Italy on 17 April; and Col. Talbot returned to Cairo to report to Sir Reginald Wingate.

The main clauses in *modus vivendi* No. 3, for immediate application, were: hostilities were to cease at once; social intercourse and commerce were to be free between the parts of Cyrenaica occupied by Italy and those held by the Sanusiya; each party was to be responsible for security in its own territory; and neither was to create new military posts or to encroach on the territory of the other. The population was to be disarmed at a later date, it being impossible to effect this at the time; and fomentors of disorder were to be removed. Further clauses stipulated that the lodges of the Sanusiya Order occupied by the Italians were to be restored to the Order, though the Italians were to remain in those being used by them for military purposes till peace was established; that the properties of the Order were to be free from taxation as in Turkish times; that the Italians were to pay salaries to Shaikhs of the lodges, nominated by the Sayyid with Italian approval, within their zone; and that in the interior Shaikhs of lodges were to act as intermediaries should it be necessary for the Italians to have dealings with the tribes. Muslim personal law and koranic teaching were safeguarded in the courts and schools in the area under Italian control.

Modus vivendi No. 1, accepted by the parties in principle and for future application, differed from No. 3 in three particulars: the Sanusi armed camps were to be broken up and their garrisons dispersed; the tribes were to be progressively disarmed within a year; and the Italian Government was to nominate, on the Sayyid's presentation of three names, Shaikhs of lodges in their zone.

By the British-Sanusi (Talbot-Idris) agreement, to the general terms of which Sayyid Idris had assented at al-Zuwaitina, all British, Allied, and Egyptian subjects were to be handed over; all Turkish and other enemy officers and agents were to be either handed over or sent out of Africa; and no armed Sanusi were to remain in Egyptian territory, or armed gatherings to be held near the frontier. Al-Sallum was to be opened for trade, but Alexandria–al-Sallum was to be the only route by which goods, in limited quantities, might enter Cyrenaica from Egypt, and only on condition that nothing reached Turco-German hands. No Sanusiya lodges were to exist on Egyptian soil (they had already been razed to the ground in the Marmarica), though alms might be collected from Egyptian adherents to the Order. Sayyid Idris's property in Egypt was to be respected. Jaghbub oasis, though in Egypt, was to be administered by the Sayyid.

The agreement signed at 'Akrama settled affairs between the Sanusi and the British. The British got the military security

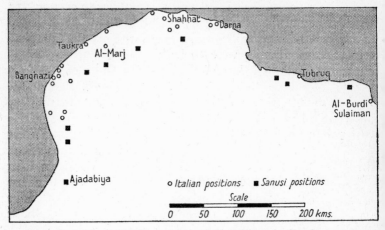

The disposition of Italian and Sanusi positions in October 1916.

they needed. The terms were very favourable to the Sanusi. The *status quo* was preserved, the Italians being left in control of those parts of Cyrenaica in which they had established themselves—the coastal towns and a few inland posts—and the Sanusiya Order retaining the rest of the country. The Sayyid had saved the organization of the Order his grandfather had founded in Cyrenaica, and though he was not formally recognized as more than the Head of a religious Order he was, in fact and of necessity, treated as though he were, as indeed he was, also the secular ruler of an independent people. The accords were signed without consultation with the Turks and without their consent, so whereas Sayyid Ahmad had fought the Italians and British as representative of the Sultan, his cousin made peace with them in his own right.

The least satisfied party were the Italians. They had embarked on a colonial war and had not been successful in waging

THE SAYYID MUHAMMAD IDRIS

it. The Sanusi attack on the British was a godsend to them, since it not only diverted Sanusi forces but brought to their side a powerful ally who, they hoped, would win their colonial war for them or, at any rate, exact from the enemy the fruits of a successful campaign. All they got from the truce was what their arms were able to maintain. Nothing in the agreements was said about their claim to sovereignty, round which there had been so much discussion during the negotiations. Some Fascist writers later blamed the Government of the day for signing 'the *modus vivendi* of Acroma', but it could not have wrung more from the Sayyid than verbal concessions, because it had not the military power to exact more. Nevertheless, the best Italian commentators have pointed out that the accord at least gave peace to Cyrenaica in the troubled years of European war and was the basis of those later accords which were to preserve it during the dangerous years of civil discord in Italy. It also gave the Italians the opportunity to spread their influence among the tribes through propaganda, subsidies, and trade. More immediate fruits were the rounding up of the Turkish and pro-Turkish elements and the widening of the breach between the Arabs of Tripolitania and those of Cyrenaica.

In the end, however, there cannot be two competing political sovereignties in the same country. The accord was a truce of convenience, on the basis, as Mondaini says,[1] of the *uti possidetis*, entered into by Italians and Sanusi because both were exhausted by the ordeal. It was 'the product of a situation particularly delicate for both',[2] and a situation which could not last.

III

The *modus vivendi* of Acroma was, as the title implies, a truce rather than a treaty. It brought military action to a close, but left political questions for future settlement. The accord embodied a fundamental ambiguity: Italy did not renounce her claim to sovereignty and the Sanusiya did not concede it to her or renounce, either explicitly or implicitly, 'the dominion which in plain fact it exercised, not only over the oases of the interior, but even over the Cyrenaican plateau

---

[1] Op. cit., p. 386. [2] Serra, op. cit., pp. 103–4.

itself, excepting the parts of it occupied by the Italians'.[1] In some respects the Sayyid found himself in much the same position *vis-à-vis* the Italian Government as previous heads of the Order had been *vis-à-vis* the Turkish Government. The authority of the Italians was limited, as that of the Turks had been, to the coastal towns and a few inland posts, and the rest of the country came under Sanusiya administration. The Order recognized their *de facto* control of the towns and they recognized the *de facto* rule of the Order in the country.

It must again be emphasized that the Sayyid signed a truce with the British and Italians without consulting the Turks and that he signed a truce with the British in his own right and not as under Italian suzerainty. Furthermore, he was defending the western frontier of Cyrenaica on behalf of the Allies, and with his own army, against possible incursions from Tripolitania. To prevent Ramadan al-Shtaiwi and his supporters making a drive into Cyrenaica, Sayyid Idris recruited a new army from the Bedouin and established a *khatt al-nar*, a line of fire, as the Arabs called it, across the Sirtica. To aid him to maintain these frontier defences the Italians had provided him with 2,000 rifles, a battery of mountain artillery, and funds. They deeply resented that later the force armed by themselves, the '*armati idrisiti*', was turned against Italy. In these circumstances it was clear that the Accord of 'Akrama would have to be supplemented by further agreements.

Domestic confusion made the task of the local Italian commanders and administrative officers very difficult. Those who had hoped that when the European war ended they would be able to give greater attention to their Libyan colonies had underestimated the moral deterioration in Italy, where disunity in the years of war was nothing to the chaos of the years which followed it. An attempt to renew the colonial war in Libya during these troubled years of 1918–22 would have created such an outcry in Italy that none of the post-war Administrations, which were always up to their ears in difficulties, could have faced the extra embarrassment. Had the Italians been able to act with promptness and decision in Libya when the war in Europe ended they would probably have met with little resistance. They had at hand men and material in plenty to

---

[1] Mondaini, op. cit., p. 388.

reconquer Tripolitania and Cyrenaica, but they lacked the will
to action. Instead, they vacillated between threats of force on
the one side and appeasements and diplomatic surrenders on
the other.

Considerable reinforcements were indeed sent to Tripolitania,
but when there were assembled there 80,000 men ready for the
reconquest of the country, the Government signed with the
Arab leaders the humiliating pourparlers of Kallet al-Zaituna
in the spring of 1919. The agreement was supplemented on
1 June 1919 by a constitution giving to the Arabs a parliament,
Italian citizenship, exemption from taxation, &c. The Arabs
were more than ever convinced of Italian impotence. In theory,
an Arab republic, the *Jumhuriya al-Trabulsiya*, founded in the
previous year under Turco-Germanic influence, now ruled the
country through its Committee of Reform at Misurata under
the leadership of Ramadan al-Shtaiwi. In fact, there was little
order of any kind. Quarrels broke out between tribes and
between tribal leaders, anyone powerful enough set himself up
as overlord of his district, the Arabs raided the Berbers, outside the narrow coastal region held by their troops Italian
officials were little more than consular agents, and when Italian
forces took part in Arab disputes they did so rather as mercenaries or allies than as rulers of a colony responsible for peace
and security in it. Meanwhile the Committee of Reform made
preparations to achieve the complete independence of Tripolitania from Italian rule by securing agreement in principle to a
Tripolitanian Amirate from an assembly of notables at Ghariyan
in November 1921. The deputation which carried this resolu-
tion to Rome, though it received no official encouragement,
found much support among Communists, Socialists, and trouble-
makers of all kinds. Its leader, Muhammad Khalid al-Qarqani,
went on to attend the Muslim Revolutionary Congress in
Moscow. Such a state of affairs could not last, and in the midst
of it Count Giuseppe Volpi was nominated Governor of Tripolitania. He was an energetic man prepared to act on his own
responsibility, and by March 1922 he had recaptured Misurata
and the whole coastal region between that town and Tunisia
and had commenced operations in the Sirtica.

During this period there was peace in Cyrenaica, the fruit of
the Accord of 'Akrama. At first the Italians did no more than

hold their posts. In 1919 they began to establish civil government in the territory under their control and to extend their
influence farther afield. On 31 October of that year Cyrenaica
was given a constitution similar to that given to Tripolitania,
and its parliament first met in April 1921 under the unlikely
presidency of Sayyid Safi al-Din, the old enemy of the Italians
in the Sirtica. The tribesmen, of course, elected their own
Shaikhs. It held altogether five sessions up to March 1923,
when it was closed down. From the Italian point of view the
best that could be said for the constitution was that it implied
a tacit acceptance of sovereignty and that a parliament brought
their officials into personal touch with tribal leaders. Writers
of the Fascist period, when the Wilsonian sentiments which
inspired the Libyan constitutions were regarded with disfavour,
strongly criticized the Government of the day for granting them.
Thus Gaibi says that they were bound to bear evil fruit and that
'the Government thought to present itself as a magnanimous
conqueror, and the Libyans thought it a beaten coward'.[1] The
Bedouin certainly distrusted and despised the Italians and cared
as little for their authority in Cyrenaica as their brothers cared
for it in Tripolitania. About 100 of their Shaikhs met at
Ajadabiya, where they issued a manifesto declaring that, constitution or no constitution, they would not tolerate the Italians
outside the coastal towns, and there only as traders. To
this insult the Government lamely responded by opening new
conversations. After long discussions between the Colonial
Governor, Giacomo de Martino, and 'Umar Pasha al-Kakhiya,
representing Sayyid Idris, and an exploratory visit by Sayyid
al-Rida to Rome, it was agreed that the *modus vivendi* of
'Akrama should be superseded by a new pact, the Accord of
al-Rajma of 25 October 1920.

By this new agreement Sayyid Idris was given the hereditary
title of 'Sanusi Amir' with the honorific address of Highness
and was created Head of the autonomous administration of the
oases of Jaghbub, Aujila, Jalu, and Kufra, with the right of
using Ajadabiya as the seat of his administration. He was
granted a personal monthly allowance of L. 63,000 (on the day
of the signing of the accord the Lira was 92 to the Pound

[1] Agostino Gaibi, *Manuale di Storia politico-militare delle Colonie Italiane*
1928, p. 531.

Sterling) and was allowed his own flag, the first place of honour after the Governor on official occasions, a salute of guns on official visits, and the use of an official steamer. Sums of money amounting to L. 93,000 were to be paid in monthly allowances to members of his family. In addition the Government undertook to pay the police and military necessary to maintain order within the area under the Amir's administrative control, and a further L. 2,600,000 to meet the Amir's general expenses, of which L. 300,000 was to be in gold, and half this sum, including the gold portion, was to be paid on the signing of the accord and the other half on the suppression of the armed Sanusi camps. The Italians also subsidized tribal Shaikhs and zawiya Shaikhs and they paid stipends to the Members of Parliament. Notables, zawiya officials, qadis, scribes, chiefs of irregular bands, political counsellors, and informers, were all on the Italian pay-roll. The Italians were, in fact, bribing the whole country to keep quiet. The Italian Government further undertook to act in agreement with the Amir in making appointments to posts within the territory entrusted to his administration; recognized his right to move about freely; permitted the oases to send representatives to the local parliament; allowed the population to keep their arms; and guaranteed exemption of the Sanusiya lands from taxation. It specifically and solemnly declared that it had no intention of expropriating Arab lands, privately or collectively owned, or endowments of the Order, in favour of colonists. On his side the Sayyid promised to aid the Government in the application of the new constitution; to suppress within eight months the camps and posts and other Sanusi organizations of a political, administrative, or military character in the territory not entrusted to his administration; to keep his army to 1,000 men, subject to increase by mutual agreement; to encourage trade and communications; and not to tax the population other than by collection of religious tithes without coercion.

It was felt by the Italian Government that though in this new pact it had to make considerable concessions it had gained in return a more definite acceptance of its claim to sovereignty over the whole of Cyrenaica, which was henceforth divided into two zones, Cyrenaica proper under direct Italian administration and the oases under Sanusiya administration. The Sanusiya, as well as Italy, had been forced to compromise. Critics of the Fascist period were later to complain that the pact was a blow to Italian prestige in that it virtually recognized 'the existence of two distinct Governments',[1] and Macaluso goes so far as to say that the making of the Sayyid into an Amir 'was the ratification of the undisputed sovereignty of the Sanusiya in Cyrenaica'.[2] Even those who defended the agreement had to admit that the Order was not being treated as a purely religious body, but as a politico-religious fraternity and that there was, therefore, doubt about what its relations with the Italian Government were supposed to be. 'Amir' to the Italians meant Honorary Prince but it had a very different sense to the Arabs. It was, moreover, uncertain whether a seat at Ajadabiya implied that the warlike Magharba tribe of the *barqa* and the Sirtica came within the Sayyid's political orbit or not. On the whole one can say that the Sayyid, or rather the Amir, as we can now call him, bargained autonomy of the oases and the hinterland for his armed camps and administrative posts on the plateau. As he did not, in fact, disband these he may be said to have had the better of the bargain. After the Accord of al-Rajma was signed the Amir visited Rome.

The accord was supplemented by a further agreement known as *Sistemazione definitiva delle zauie* of 16 August 1921 by which nomination, suspension, and transfer of Shaikhs of Sanusiya lodges were to be in the hands of the Amir, but he had to give notice of these acts to the Government, and he promised to remove Shaikhs who embittered relations between the Government and the people. The Government undertook to pay the Shaikhs of lodges (in two categories of L. 900 and L. 600 a month), to hand back to the Order all lodges in its occupation, except those being used as forts, and to pay the sum of L. 500,000 as indemnity for lodges destroyed during the war.[3]

IV

The Italians pretended afterwards that 'Umar al-Kakhiya, who closely followed political events in Italy, had in bad faith, believing that the Socialists were in the ascendant and that

---

[1] Agostino Gaibi, op. cit., p. 463.   [2] Macaluso, op. cit., p. 102.
[3] *L'Occupazione di Cufra*, 1931, pp. 62–3. On 16 August 1921 the Lira was 84 to the Pound Sterling.

Italy would therefore withdraw from her colonial adventure, advised the Amir to sign the Accord of al-Rajma in the hope that he would not have to carry out its terms. He was later to spend over 16 years in exile in Italy for his alleged duplicity. The Italians did not at this time charge the Amir with more than weakness when, after the stipulated eight months had passed, he had failed to carry out the terms of the accord, especially in the matter of the armed Sanusi camps.

These camps were supply points garrisoned by the remnants of the Sanusi army of 1917. Through them and from them the Sanusiya was exercising political control over the country and administering the tribes. The chief camps in 1917 were Ajada-biya, al-Shlaidima, Marawa, Khawalan, al-Abyar, Taknis, and 'Akrama. Each was under a *qaimaqam* and had its commandant of troops, its qadi for judicial proceedings, and its tithe collectors who collected from the Bedouin a tax on crops and flocks. With the development of the political functions of the Order alms had been transformed into taxes. Ajadabiya and al-Shlaidima had as their *nazir*, inspector, 'Ali Pasha al-'Abdiya. Al-Abyar and Taknis came under Sidi 'Umar al-Mukhtar, and Marawa, Khawalan, and 'Akrama came under Sayyid Safi al-Din.

When asked why these camps had not been broken up the Amir said that the accord had been very badly received by the Bedouin and that were it to be enforced hastily serious disturbances might ensue. He counselled caution. In addition to the continuance of the armed camps in defiance of the accord, the Italians also complained of concerted passive resistance, on the part of the Shaikhs of Sanusiya lodges and the Shaikhs of tribes, to collaboration with their officials; but either because they were not yet ready to use force or because they were convinced that the Amir was unable to dictate to his followers, and probably for both reasons, they continued to temporize.

By the further Accord of Bu Mariyam of 11 November 1921 the dissolution of the armed camps was confirmed, but it was agreed that until the Italians had strengthened their administrative control and political influence in the country the still-existing Sanusi camps should be held jointly. There were to be four so-called '*Campi Misti*', at al-Abyar, Taknis, Slanta, and 'Akrama, manned by Italian and Sanusi troops in the proportion of 5 to 4, each controlled by its own representative. To these four was later added a fifth camp, al-Makhili, so that the Italians might establish themselves at an important watering-place of the southern nomads.

The new arrangement was fantastic. Two forces, each under its own officers and flag, each opposed to the other in every particular, were jointly responsible for the security and welfare of the country. What made it even more absurd in the eyes of later Fascist critics was the fact that the Sanusi soldiers in these camps received their rations and pay from the Italian Government they did everything to flout. It was, moreover, an admission on the part of the Italians that they were unable to enforce the accords they signed with the Amir if the Bedouin did not intend to carry out their terms, and that they could not establish themselves in the country unless the Sanusiya was ready to allow them to do so. All that apologists for this new accord have been able to say in defence of it was that the Italian Government had by this time realized that nothing was in any case likely to come of all these agreements and in the end only signed it in order that, while formally respecting it, they might have time and opportunity to establish their authority among the tribes, particularly among the 'Awaqir, the western Darsa, the Bara'asa, and the 'Abaidat. The Rome Government, not wanting to increase its troubles by starting a new war in Cyrenaica, imposed a policy of appeasement on its restless Colonial Government. It was bad enough to have to face the anarchy in Tripolitania, and there was always a danger that if the situation in Cyrenaica deteriorated Sayyid Ahmad might return to raise again the standard of revolt. Sayyid Idris might be weak and at times difficult, but he was at least pacific. The harassed Governor was therefore instructed that he would have to continue the battle of words till it became feasible to open real hostilities. However, the Italian Government were mistaken in believing that the new accord would allow them to increase their influence in the country, for the Sanusiya, through its representatives in the 'Mixed Camps', came between the tribes and the Italians. It is generally admitted by Italian commentators that after Bu Mariyam the Government was only apparently in the ascendancy politically, while in fact the administration of the whole country outside the towns continued in the hands of the Order. Nevertheless, the Rome Government at the time thought, or pretended to think, that the development of events was in their favour and that their propaganda was rapidly costing the Amir and his family their popularity in the country. They constantly, as the Bedouin say when speaking of this period, pushed a stick under the pot to keep it hot till they wanted it to boil over.

The situation at this time in Cyrenaica could not, in any case, have lasted for long. It became clear to all, even before the Fascists gained control in October 1922, that hostilities would sooner or later break out again and matters were being brought to a head by the Amir's attitude on the Tripolitanian issue. The Arabs of Tripolitania, finding themselves in difficulties, sought to extend their front against the Italians by reaching an agreement with the Sanusi, with whom in the past their relations, as we have seen, had not always been cordial. Their leaders held a meeting, at which Sanusi representatives from Cyrenaica were present, at Sirt at the end of 1921 which carried the decisions of the Assembly of Ghariyan a step farther by sending a deputation to Sayyid Idris at Ajadabiya in April 1922 to offer him the Amirate of all Libya. The Sayyid refused to commit himself one way or the other, for he was aware that the Tripolitanian notables who made him the offer had for the most part little regard for his person or for his Order and were merely trying to create a diversion which might draw off some of the Italian forces operating against them. To have replied 'Yes' would have brought him into conflict with Italy. To have replied 'No' would have alienated from him those Tripolitanian Arabs who genuinely sympathized with the Sanusiya. Faced with this dilemma he pleaded ill health early in 1922 and requested the Italian Government to permit him to visit Egypt for two years for rest and treatment. He also, according to Giglio,[1] made the strange request that Sayyid Ahmad be allowed to return to Cyrenaica. Both requests were refused. So was his offer, repeatedly made, to mediate between Italy and the Arabs of Tripolitania, and he was informed, in more forcible terms than he had been accustomed to expect from the Colonial Government, that any interference on his part in the affairs of Tripolitania would be considered a breach of the

[1] Giglio, op. cit., p. 98.

Accord of al-Rajma. But the Italians were not yet ready to break with him finally, not wishing to compromise the operations they were carrying out in Tripolitania. They therefore started new discussions, conducted in person by Amendola, the Minister for the Colonies, who, on his return to Italy, expressed satisfaction with the talks and confidence in the Amir, neither of which he could have felt. In Mondaini's opinion the Government's policy of continuing to treat with the Sanusiya at so late a stage was consistent and, in the circumstances, wise, for it was believed that the greed for lucre and honours so unashamedly displayed by members of the Amir's family would bring them into disrepute among the Arabs, while the Government would be able to organize under its administration the zone of the plateau nearest its coastal bases and thus prepare for its penetration into the interior. In defence of Amendola's policy, later subjected to much criticism,[1] Mondaini further observes that the Fascist Government itself delayed action till the spring of 1923 when the Tripolitanian rebellion had been crushed.[2]

Concessions certainly did not lessen tension. The Italians felt that the Sanusiya was using the 'Mixed Camps' as a medium for anti-Italian propaganda, as indeed they were, not only through their official representatives in the camps but also through persons not officially recognized, such as the Sanusiya Shaikhs 'Umar al-Mukhtar, Salih al-'Awwami, and Khalid al-Humri; and they suspected that Shaikh 'Abd al-Aziz al-'Isawi had been sent by the Amir into the Misurata region to act as his liaison with the insurgents there. The Amir had selected for his personal advisers the most recalcitrant of the zawiya Shaikhs. They further accused the Order of responsibility for certain incidents which happened in the late summer of 1922: an attack on an Italian postal car near al-Zawiya al-Baida and the firing of some Italian property at al-Zuwaitina. Rome, said to have been misled by 'Umar Pasha al-Kakhiya, blamed the local government for these incidents and appointed a new Governor who made a further, and as it turned out final, gesture of conciliation by paying to the Amir the remainder of the money owing to him under the Accord of al-Rajma. But nothing could brake the wheels now. Already in August the Committee elected

[1] Giglio, op. cit., p. 99.   [2] Mondaini, op. cit., p. 475.

by the Assembly of Sirt had forwarded to Sayyid Idris the *madbata*, dated 28 July 1922, formally investing him with the Amirate of Tripolitania.

Sayyid Idris still hesitated. Before giving a reply he wished to consult Bedouin opinion, for it was on the Bedouin he would have to count were hostilities to break out. To this purpose he called, in October 1922, a large tribal gathering at Jardis al-'Abid. In the following month, under great pressure from his advisers, and still hesitating in his own mind, he accepted the Amirate. It must by this time have been apparent to him that the Italians intended to make war whatever course he took and that he might, in that case, just as well have the Tripolitanian Arabs as allies. In his reply to the Committee he entrusted Tripolitanian affairs to them, under their President Ahmad al-Marayid, until such time as a National Assembly could meet to draw up a constitution. Then, realizing that the fable of the wolf and the lamb was about to be enacted, he fled by caravan to Jaghbub in December 1922 and thence to Egypt, where he had long made financial preparation for this eventuality out of the Italian subsidies. He may also have felt that he had compromised himself so deeply with the Italians over a number of years that his presence in the country could only be an embarrassment to the Bedouin whose martial spirit he could understand but not emulate. He left his brother Sayyid Muhammad al-Rida and his cousin Sayyid Safi al-Din to represent him in Cyrenaica.

Sayyid Idris did not return to Cyrenaica till the third British occupation of the country during the late war (1943), though he continued in Egypt to represent the forces of resistance and, in so far as he could do so without compromising his position as a guest of a country whose Royal House was so intimately bound to the Royal House of Italy, to direct them. At the time of his flight he was 33 years of age. He gave the impression of being tall and rather portly, very unlike the slight and delicate figure he presents to-day. Nurtured, as were all the Sanusi family, in piety and learning in oasis retreats and accustomed to a refined and sedentary life, he has never been a man of action or of a hardy constitution. Though he assisted Sayyid Ahmad in organizing the Sanusi bands at Ajadabiya after the Treaty of Losanna in the first Italo-Sanusi war, he early showed that his talents lay in diplomacy rather than in the field. It is evident from the part he played in the events leading up to the truce and during the period of the truce that he is astute and a man of sound political judgement. That he is often vacillating and evasive cannot be denied, and though these characteristics may sometimes have been a wise response of the weak negotiating with the strong, and may often have served him well in the difficult circumstances in which he took over direction of the Sanusiya Order from Sayyid Ahmad, they seem to be weaknesses to which he is temperamentally prone and to have become an aversion to directness in either thought or action. Italian writers, who are, with some justification, scathing in their comments on most members of the Sanusi family, speak of Sayyid Idris with respect. They admit that he is intelligent, religious, and gifted with a profound moral sense and political intuition. He is firm in decisions once he has taken them and keeps his promises.

At the end of 1922 the Fascist revolution culminated in the march on Rome and the new Government at once made up its mind to reconquer by arms Tripolitania and Cyrenaica. It continued to temporize in Cyrenaica, partly because its position at home was not yet secure, and partly because it intended to finish operations in Tripolitania first. The Fascists felt that their prestige was at stake. The days of *socialdemocrazia* were over and military conquest, domination, and colonization were the order of the day. The ancient Roman provinces were once again to be peopled by the sons and daughters of Rome.

On 6 March 1923 the Italians, without delivering an ultimatum or declaration of war, carried out their secret and long-prepared plan to seize the 'Mixed Camps' and the Sanusi camp of Khawalan, taking about half the Sanusi soldiers prisoners. By this surprise they put out of action a considerable part of the Amir's regular forces. In a proclamation of 1 May 1923 the new Governor of the Colony, Gen. Luigi Bongiovanni—soldiers had replaced civil administrators—declared null and void all accords and conventions made between the Government and the Sanusiya. On the following day the Amir was informed of the step taken by a letter from the Italian Minister in Cairo. War had broken out again in Cyrenaica.

CHAPTER VII

THE SECOND ITALO-SANUSI WAR (1923-32)

I

THE second Italo-Sanusi war differed in some respects from the first, though the character of the fighting was alike in both. There was now, if not a new Italy, a new élite in Italy, which was eager to justify itself in the eyes of its own people and to win the respect of the Powers of Europe. Clearly, if the Fascists wanted to have the influence they thought was their due in the councils of Europe and to embark on an expansionist policy in the Mediterranean and North Africa, they would first have to show that they were capable of defeating the Bedouin of Libya. They had inherited from their predecessors in office a situation which gave them the limited choice of either full conquest at the cost of further sacrifices in life and gold or a withdrawal which might leave the half-won prize to some rival Power; for the years of compromise had shown that the Bedouin would never accept their rule, far less their colonization, until they had first been subjugated by arms. Where, in choosing the alternative of war, the Fascist Government differed from its predecessors was not in its desire to conquer and colonize Arab lands, but in its greater determination to satisfy the desire, in its vigour, and in its faith. Behind Italian arms in their second Libyan war was a will that had been lacking in the first.

The complexion of the Sanusiya had also changed. In 1911 the Order and its adherents had fought not only as allies of the Turks but also, without putting too fine a point on it, as subjects of the Ottoman Sultan. Even after Turkey had made peace with Italy Turkish officers continued to exercise command, but during the next three years the Turks slowly lost influence and the Sanusiya took over control. The resistance, with its mounting toll of Turkish casualties, became more and more a purely Arab and Bedouin struggle for freedom under the Sanusi flag. As the Sanusiya emerged as an autonomous government with direction of its own armed forces, its own finances, and its own diplomacy, the old breach between Turk and Arab gradually widened till, at the end of the war, the

Turkish Government had been eliminated militarily and politically from Cyrenaica. In its place was the Order, recognized by all as the one body which could speak for the Bedouin of the country, on whose behalf it treated with the Italian Government in the years between the two wars. Thus the first war had begun as a war against Turkey and became slowly transformed into a war against the Sanusiya. The second war was against the Sanusiya.

At first sight the Italians might seem to have been in 1923 in a more advantageous position than in 1911 to 1917, for they were united at home, at peace with the world, had established bases in Cyrenaica, and were opposed only by untrained Bedouin tribesmen instead of by Turkish soldiers who, however few and badly equipped, had nevertheless been disciplined, experienced in modern warfare, and under regular officers of distinction. But these advantages were offset by the loss of prestige the Italians had suffered in the eyes of the Bedouin since 1911. Both in Cyrenaica and in Tripolitania the Italians, if they had not been defeated, had certainly not been victorious. The Bedouin had seen them in both provinces of Libya advance in heavy columns across the country, occupy all the important centres, and then retreat in panic to the coast; and they had judged by the measure of their experience that the Italian is not a soldier. Then, in both countries, they had seen successive Italian Governors giving way to threats and trying to attain by diplomacy and bribery the ends brave men pursue by arms. Moreover, the Bedouin were far better equipped than they had been in 1911, for they had replaced their old weapons with modern rifles captured from the Italians. Col. Talbot reported in 1916 that they looked on every Italian troop movement as a gift from God. Hence energy and initiative which might have broken Bedouin morale had they been applied after the Sanusi defeat by the British in 1915–16, when expended in the opening stages of the second war did not effect the speedy crumbling of resistance hoped for. Indeed what happened in the first war was repeated in the second.

The Italians had in 1923 the same overwhelming superiority in men and equipment they enjoyed in 1911, perhaps an even greater superiority in that they could use the knowledge acquired in the European war, particularly in the use of mechanized surface vehicles and aeroplanes unknown in 1911. By the end of 1926 they had some 20,000 men in the field, mostly native troops, while after the opening round of the campaign the Sanusi probably seldom had more than 1,000 men on operational service at any one time. It was estimated that in 1923 they could put into the field 2,000 men armed with modern rifles and a few machine-guns and artillery pieces, and that in addition there were some 3,000 to 4,000 rifles among the tribes. With this superiority in mobility, fire, and numbers, the Italians were able, as in the first war, to push heavy columns in any direction they chose and to seize and fortify any point they pleased. Therefore, what is often called 'organized resistance' broke down very early in the campaign, if there can be said to have been such at any time, and gave way to guerrilla warfare in which sentries, advanced posts, supply convoys, and communications were subjected to sniping, raids, ambushes, and sabotage. Consequently the war was made up of a succession of small, and often unrelated, incidents in different parts of the country. Italian operational and intelligence reports and Bedouin stories about these hundreds of fights and skirmishes are not easily arranged into a coherent picture. The hundreds of bits and pieces are all very much alike in size and shape and colour, and the guide of any clear pattern is lacking. To attempt, therefore, to construct from them a complete mosaic of events would be a task alike arduous for the writer and confusing and unprofitable for the reader; and I shall not endeavour to do more than sketch the development of the campaign. It would, I think, be of assistance to the reader were I first to mention some very general features of the fighting, which are, indeed, features of guerrilla warfare always and everywhere.

II

The war, which was waged with increasing bitterness as the years went by, was not against all the Arabs of Cyrenaica, but only against the Bedouin, for the townsmen played no active part in the resistance, though they sympathized with it. Also, among the Bedouin, whilst there was no one who could be fairly labelled pro-Italian there were many persons, and even whole tribal sections, who remained passive, chiefly because of their vulnerability: the Baraghtha and other northern 'Awaqir sections, the 'Arafa, the Hasa, some of the Darsa, and a large part of the 'Abaidat. Most of these pacific sections, the least nomadic of the Bedouin, had a long history of intercourse with the urban population and the Turkish administration, and when Italian officials took the place of Turkish officials contact was early resumed. They tended to look northwards to the coast. The other sections, more nomadic, warlike, and powerful, and further removed from settled centres, looked southwards to the desert: the Aulad Suliman, the Magharba, the southern 'Awaqir, the Bara'asa, most of the 'Abid, the *'Ailat* Fayid, and the southern and eastern 'Abaidat. Beyond striking distance by horse patrols, these hardy wanderers of the steppe, whose history was nothing more than a long record of tribal wars, had paid scant attention to the Turks, had refused in the first Italian war to make terms, had disdainfully turned their backs on the intruder during the ensuing years of peace, and were now to offer a stubborn resistance to renewed aggression. The structural polarity exemplified in the tendency of some tribal sections to be drawn into the political orbit of the Administration while others remained politically aloof from it was earlier referred to. It corresponded to the well-known division between the *saf al-bahr*, the coastal party, and the *saf al-fauqi*, the interior party, of Tripolitania and to a political dichotomy found in some form in all countries where nomads are the social hinterland of peasants or citizens. In Cyrenaica it took the form of a pull in opposite directions by the Turkish (and afterwards Italian) Administration with its centre of attraction at Banghazi and the Sanusiya with its centre of attraction in the desert.

The more peaceful and sedentary sections early ceased to fight the Italians in the first war, and in the period between the two wars put up little outward resistance to Italian penetration. In appearance, at any rate, they had accepted Italian supervision. This was, in fact, the issue during those years: the Italians seeking to draw these sections deeper into their sphere of influence through trade and administrative liaison, and the Sanusiya seeking in its own interests to pull them back from the Government and to eliminate Italian propaganda among them. When war broke out again the Italians had the advantage, denied to them in 1911, of being in occupation of all the principal centres of the country. They believed that they had the further advantage of having, by incessant propaganda and subsidies, weakened Sanusiya influence among the Bedouin around the towns and posts. Consequently, with optimism scarcely sustained by the facts, they regarded these sections as allies against those which openly supported the Sanusiya. The coastal sections did, as the Italians expected, remain outside the war or, as the Italians called it, the rebellion, and they were, therefore, known as the *sottomessi* in contrast to the *ribelli*, the sections which resisted, and whom I shall speak of by the fitter term 'Patriots', having an objection to the language of colonial imperialism by which an honourable attempt to defend home and property against foreign aggression is labelled rebellion. They called themselves the *muhafiziya*.

It was Italian policy to deal with the collaborationist, or supposedly collaborationist, Bedouin as friends and to create between them and the Patriots a state of permanent feud. The Patriots expected the submitted sections to give them asylum when hard pressed, and to supply them with food and other requirements, and if they did not receive what they wanted, they took it by force. The Italians could not allow the Patriots to use the submitted districts as bases of operation and supply and had, therefore, for both prestige and security, either by constant patrolling to protect the submitted population from reprisals or to supply them with arms for their own protection. Both were perilous expedients. The patrols to be effective had to be highly mobile and therefore small and vulnerable to guerrilla tactics. The arms might, and did, find their way to the Patriots, the Italians becoming themselves one of the main sources of supply to their enemies. They hoped, however, that if they armed the submitted population they might, since they were Bedouin, be expected to defend their own stock against Patriot requisitioning, which the Italians called brigandage and the Patriots called payment of religious dues. It was believed that a state of civil war would necessarily result from the manifold feuds which would have to be prosecuted by bereaved families on both sides in accordance with the Bedouin law of vengeance. It was proposed to make 'furrows of blood' ('*solci di sangue*') between tribe and tribe, and between tribal section and tribal section, across which the Bedouin might exterminate each other and save the Italians much labour and danger. The policy had very limited success, for in practice the Patriots recruited from every tribe and every section. Bedouin sentiments about kinship and its obligations worked both ways. If it was a duty to avenge a slain kinsman it was no less a duty to protect and aid a living kinsman, and the sense of kin and its compelling influence in conduct, all that is meant by 'asabiya in Bedouin values, are the life and the soul of the Romany world.

It took the Italians a long time to realize that the Bedouin mind was not all of one piece but a Joseph's coat of conflicting interests. These interests excluded each other as the social situation evoked one loyalty to the detriment of another and it was, therefore, only in terms of their social structure that the apparent inconsistencies of Bedouin behaviour could be understood. Consequently the Italians were for ever suffering disappointments and accused the Bedouin, with increasing resentment and bitterness as the struggle continued, of disloyalty and treachery. Among the collaborationists, the *mtalyanin*, the Italianized, as the Patriots called them, there was every degree of participation from passivity, the refraining from taking an active part in the resistance, to full co-operation with the Italian army as spies, guides, informers, and administrative officials; but even those guilty of the worst complicity could, especially when some personal tie was involved, do the guerrillas a good turn. Many poor Bedouin near the towns joined the Italian forces as one kind or other of irregulars, police, and friendlies, and as labourers and camelmen, and it was found that these, while drawing Italian pay and rations, did not hesitate to assist the Patriots when an opportunity offered itself. Desertions to the enemy with full equipment were frequent. Italian rifles and ammunition and even pay were often handed over to the guerrillas. After an engagement the ground was left strewn with live ammunition for the guerrillas to glean. Many reported fights between the Patriots and the submitted population were undoubtedly inventions to cover gifts of ammunition, supplied by the Italians, from the Italian-sponsored irregulars to the Patriot bands. These native battalions constituted, in fact, 'a sort of supply depot of men, arms, and ammunition for the Sanusi formations'.[1] Information about Italian troop move-

[1] 'La pulizia del Gehel Cirenaico', by 'Gadria', *L'Oltremare*, Dec. 1930.

ments and plans was soon passed on to the guerrilla bands, for Sidi 'Umar al-Mukhtar had agents in every Italian post. Those *sottomessi* who were armed and paid by the Italians to protect their territories against Patriot foraging expeditions would be found among the Patriot casualties after skirmishes with Italian patrols. The submitted population, it was discovered, allowed their horses to graze far from their camps so that the Patriots could borrow them for operational purposes. The Patriots sold their animals in Italian and Egyptian markets through their submitted kinsmen, and Italian efforts to keep track of such transactions through tribal markings were, as might be supposed, unavailing. So useful, indeed, was a submitted population to the Patriots that the tribal Shaikhs sometimes arranged among themselves who among them should submit and who take the field. Even most of the Cyrenaican officials in the Italian administration did what was consistent with their safety to help their own people against their employers. Their faith unfaithful kept them falsely true. In the end the Italians came to the conclusion that they could trust no Cyrenaican, least of all a Cyrenaican Bedouin. The hearts of all were with their fighting fellow countrymen and fellow Muslims. The *sottomessi* and *ribelli* alike were all Bedouin, jealous of each other and hostile to tribes other than their own, but united by blood and a common way of life—one faith, one speech, one law. All regarded the Italians as foreigners whom one may serve but not love. 'The entire population thus took part directly or indirectly in the rebellion', wrote Graziani.[1]

The lot of the submitted sections was unenviable. They were compelled to live near Italian posts and their areas of sowing and pasturing were severely restricted. Their camps were subjected to constant inspections. Hostages were taken. Horses were confiscated. If it was discovered that they had dealings of any kind with their kinsmen in the Patriot bands they were heavily fined in animals and cereals, their camps were burnt, they were imprisoned, and sometimes shot. On the other hand, if they did not supply the Patriots with victuals or if they refused to pay taxes in support of the resistance they were subjected to punitive operations by the guerrillas. Suffering from Italian interference and Patriot levies and from punitive action

†   [1] Op. cit., p. 60.

by both sides, many came to the conclusion that they were better off fighting in the Patriot bands than living under Italian protection.

That all Cyrenaica was hard hostile rock beneath the shallowest covering of local collaboration is shown by the fact that the guerrillas kept up their numbers till the end of the war in spite of the slaughter of many times the number of men engaged at any one time in operations. Whenever a man fell there was another to take his place. Apart from the connivance of the whole Bedouin population at Patriot activities it was not easy for the Italians to tell the difference between a Bedouin who was a guerrilla and a Bedouin who belonged to one of the submitted sections. The guerrillas had no uniforms and when defeated had only to disperse and hide their rifles to become harmless shepherds. The Italians found that killed and captured guerrillas all possessed Italian identity cards issued to them when in camps in the guise of *sottomessi*. The Italians were thus victualling directly the forces opposed to them, for any holder of one of their cards could draw Italian rations. I have myself met Bedouin ex-guerrillas who, wounded in a fight, went to Italian hospitals for treatment, pretending to have been shot by the guerrillas while defending their flocks.

Italian writers who themselves experienced at first hand the sense of insecurity and the feeling, slowly mounting to a conviction, that their efforts to win over the Bedouin by bribes were as vain as their hopes of a speedy conquest, have described the situation of disillusionment in which their despondency was born. Biagio Pace writes that there did not exist, in reality, submitted and rebels, the entire population of Cyrenaica being under the control of the leaders of the rebellion, thus constituting a demographic, political, and financial whole, which maintained a force in the field. The *sottomessi* were regularly taxed to provide the guerrilla bands with food, arms, ammunition, clothes, money, and all the other requirements of war and life, and no-one escaped this levy. Pastoral nomads, urban merchants, agriculturists, even the police irregulars, made their contributions to maintain the rebellion. Even the tribal Shaikhs who received subsidies from the Government gave a tithe to 'Umar al-Mukhtar. The entire country was a capillary system of roots which fed from their hidden depths the visible foliage of resistance. It was useless to try to destroy this plant of the resistance by striking at its visible foliage, for when the fighting bands were hard pressed, they dispersed and resided among the *sottomessi* for repose, recuperation, and refitting.[1] Serra, looking back across the years of struggle, with their mixture of compromise and ruthlessness, optimism and disillusionment, tells the same sombre story. The implacable hostility of the Arabs to their Christian conquerors was as formless as it was ineradicable. Everybody and everything were against the invaders, but in a flaccid and crumbling opposition which inhibited a precise reaction. The enemy, he complains, habitually withdrew from the struggle. The environment offered nothing to the Italians and everything to the Bedouin, whose culture was unexacting and unpretentious. The Shaikhs had authority only so long as they opposed the Italians, and if they co-operated with them they lost it and could only regain it at Italian expense. The population was unstable, adventurous, and accustomed to such privations that they did not recognize the limits of resistance to the hardships of war. In one thing alone there was constancy and reality, the hatred they had for their Christian conquerors, which persisted in spite of all appearances and all protestations of friendship.[2] When Graziani took charge of the operations in 1930 he likened the Cyrenaican situation to 'a poisoned organism which sets up, on one point of the body, a purulent bube. The bube in this case was the fighting band of 'Umar al-Mukhtar, resulting from an entire infected situation.'[3]

In this semi-darkness of suspicion and uncertainty, this twilight of confidence, when every human being was a foe, the friend behind no less than the enemy in front, every thicket an ambush, and every crag and boss a sniper's nest, the campaign became distorted to unreality. It was a fantastic shadow-show in which dozens of unrelated episodes were thrown at the same time on to a gigantic screen.

---

[1] 'La pacificazione della Cirenaica', *Rivista delle Colonie Italiane*, 1932, p. 330.

[2] Op. cit., pp. 152–3. See also 'Che cosa è il Gebel Cirenaico', by the same writer, in *L'Oltremare*, May 1928.

[3] Op. cit., p. 64.

III

What gave the Bedouin the courage to endure the hardships and bereavements of the struggle? Certainly those two great sentiments, patriotism and religion. I have said that the first Italo-Sanusi war began as a war against Turkey and slowly became transformed into a war against the Sanusiya. The war against the Sanusiya also became transformed slowly into a simple struggle of the Bedouin for survival, for their lands and their freedom to live their ancient way of life; and in this struggle they felt themselves, in spite of all their cleavages and feuds, to be at one against the intruder. Beneath the surface of political expressions the issue was the same in both wars: whether the Italians could deprive the Bedouin of their lands and colonize them. Whether the Bedouin fought in the name of the Sultan or of the Sanusiya, or just fought, they always realized, from the first days of the struggle, that the issue was their right to live by their own laws in their own land. In the first war the outer bark of Turkish administration was stripped. In the second war the inner bark of Sanusiya organization was ripped off, leaving bare beneath it the hard wood of the tribal system.

The war also, as wars have a way of doing, bared the religious content in the struggle. The Caliph had declared a religious war, but when the Caliphate no longer counted in Cyrenaica, or indeed anywhere else, the war continued to be fought in the name of a religious Order. With the destruction of the Sanusiya it still went on in the name of religion. It then became simply a war of Muslims to defend their faith against a Christian Power. Deep love of home and deep love of God nourished each other. In fighting for their lands and herds the Bedouin were fortified by the knowledge that they fought also for their faith. Without due appreciation of the religious feelings involved in the resistance it would, I think, be impossible to understand how it went on for so long against such over-whelming odds or how the tribes, with a long history of feuds dividing them, co-operated as much as they did under Sanusiya guidance.

From their experiences in the first war the Italians had learned to expect that they would be more strongly resisted in Cyrenaica than in Tripolitania, and they had learned the reason for this: 'Inasmuch as in Cyrenaica the opposition to our rule was not fractionized and enfeebled by the personal ambitions and rivalries of numerous chiefs, but was retrenched and assembled around a single will, the Sanusiya, which manipulated it as it pleased.'[1] They started the war afresh in 1923 with this conclusion firmly fixed in their minds: *delenda est Sanusiya*. But they still believed, not understanding the place of the Order in tribal life, that the attachment of the Bedouin to it was superficial, that it was some kind of parasitic growth which could be cut out of the tribal system. They further believed that their incessant propaganda had already undermined the hold of the Order on the Bedouin.

The Sanusi family, as will be seen, played an inconspicuous and inglorious part in the resistance. Italian writers confess surprise that the Bedouin should have continued to show devotion to persons whose character displayed so few of those qualities Bedouin admire. The Bedouin may indeed have expected a higher standard of conduct than some members of the family lived up to, but they did not suppose that they would distinguish themselves as military leaders. They knew that the descendants of the Grand Sanusi had been brought up in the oases to a sedentary and bookish life and not in the hard way of their own children and that they were unsuited to the frugal and exhausting life of a guerrilla. Their duty, in most cases little in evidence in fulfilment, was to pursue holiness and learning that their presence among the people might bring down on them God's blessing. In the eyes of the Bedouin they lacked in full measure the manly qualities of courage and endurance that Bedouin demand in their own folk, but they were credited with the scholarship and sanctity of the religious, which Bedouin admire in their spiritual guides rather than seek to emulate in their own lives. Italian writers sometimes refer to a member of the family accompanying the guerrilla bands, as did Sayyid al-Hasan and Sayyid Saddiq, as having the role of a standard (*insegna*), a word which well describes their peculiar position in the resistance. Where in a man the qualities of *marabat*, holy man, and of *mujahid*, fighter for the faith, were combined, as in Sayyid Ahmad al-Sharif and Sidi 'Umar al-Mukhtar, the

---

[1] Agostino Gaibi, *Storia delle Colonie Italiane*, 1934, p. 344.

Bedouin followed them at great sacrifice. They were combined in many of the Sanusiya Brothers.

The Shaikhs and Brothers of the Order, with few exceptions, played a prominent part in the war, both in the field and by keeping the Bedouin, submitted and unsubmitted alike, in a ferment. The Italian soldiers and administrators constantly complained that whenever the Bedouin were tiring of the struggle the Brothers of the Order urged them to continue it. It was their example and exhortations which made it something more than the usual piecemeal resistance of a barbarous people to colonial conquest or more than a succession of raids of the kind Bedouin have enjoyed for so many centuries. Their participation made it both a national and a religious movement. It did much also to establish the Sanusiya in the hearts of the Bedouin. Some of the best-known names of the resistance, like Salih Lataiwish, 'Abd al-Hamid al-'Abbar, Saifat and Muhammad bu Farwa, Husain al-Juwaifi, Brahim al-Fallah, Fadil al-Mahashash, and Qtait bu Musa, were those of Bedouin Shaikhs, but most of the leading figures were Sanusiya *Ikhwan*, men like 'Umar al-Mukhtar, Yusif bu Rahil, Khalid al-Humri, Sharif al-Mailud, 'Abd al-Qadir Farkash, Fadil bu 'Umar, Salih al-'Awwami, and Muhammad bu Najwa al-Masmari.

The indomitable Sidi 'Umar al-Mukhtar was the soul of the resistance and the struggle is always associated with his name as similar struggles against French aggression in Algeria and Morocco are associated with the names of 'Abd al-Qadir and 'Abd al-Karim. Sidi 'Umar, 'our irreducible enemy, the faithful and able servant of Idris, the heart and soul of the Cyrenaican rebellion', as Graziani called him,[1] was that rare combination of Bedouin and Sanusiya Shaikh. He was born about 1862 of the *'Ailat* Farhan of the Braidan section of the Minifa tribe of the Marmarica and was educated first at the Sanusiya school at Janzur and afterwards at Jaghbub. He was nominated by Sayyid Ahmad al-Sharif Shaikh of al-Qasur lodge among the stubborn 'Abid tribe but only performed his duties there for two years before being summoned to Kufra to serve against the French in the Wadai. He returned to al-Qasur about 1906 and later took a prominent part in the first Italo-Sanusi war and in obstructing Italian penetration in the years of peace which

[1] Op. cit., p. 235.

SIDI ʿUMAR AL-MUKHTAR (GRAZIANI)

followed it. In 1923, when he was called to take the foremost
part in the struggle, he was already over sixty years of age.
He was a simple man, religious, courageous, contemptuous of
worldly honours and success, and with singular tenacity and
powers of physical endurance. It may well be true that, as is
reported, Sayyid al-Mahdi said 'If we had ten men like 'Umar
we would not need any more'.

IV

All the *adwar*, or guerrilla bands, on the plateau came under
Sidi 'Umar's command and he signed himself *al-Naib al-'Amm*,
the Representative-General (of the Sanusiya). Each Bedouin
tribe, as in Enver's day, maintained its own guerrilla band, some
100 to 300 men strong. Towards the end of the war the guerrillas
never numbered, all told, more than 600 to 700. Only a certain
number of men could maintain themselves on the country and
move through it with speed and secrecy. As in other guerrilla
wars, the actual fighting was done by small bands of enthusiasts,
whose success nevertheless depended on the goodwill of the
whole population. The bands suffered very heavy casualties,
but were maintained at strength by a constant stream of
adventurous spirits from submitted and unsubmitted sections
alike. Though each band was named after a tribe and its members were chiefly recruited from that tribe and fought in its
territory, they were not entirely recruited from it and they
might fight anywhere. In each tribal band there were a good
number of volunteers from other tribes and a sprinkling of
Ikhwan, Sudanese, and Tripolitanians. The 'Awaqir and Magharba had separate bands while the other tribal bands usually
fought in pairs, Hasa–'Abaidat, Bara'asa–Darsa, and 'Abid–
'Arafa. A Misuratan contingent formed a small band of its own
which greatly distinguished itself in the fighting. Each band
had a simple organization: a commander, a *qaimaqam* for civil
affairs, a qadi for religious and legal purposes, a commissariat
agent, and a number of officers, some of whom had been trained
in Turkish regular units. Sidi 'Umar maintained discipline in
the bands, and acts of pillage or personal vendetta were severely
punished. Those of the guerrillas who possessed horses rode
them. The rest went on foot. Each band had its Sanusi flag.

When things were quiet members of a band would have their
families and herds with them and live in their own tents, but
when pressed they left their women and children and beasts in
the tents of the submitted population and the only non-
combatants in their camps would then be a few female cooks.
Before the end of the war many of the Patriots, including Sidi
'Umar, had sent their families to Egypt so that they could act
more freely.

There was also a general administration for all the bands and
this came directly under Sidi 'Umar. They maintained intercommunication and worked to a common strategy. Guerrilla
headquarters had also to arrange for the collection of a tithe
from the entire population to help pay for the expenses of the
campaign. Throughout the war Sidi 'Umar's tax-collectors were
taking tithes from the submitted population, not always without trouble, and were giving written receipts for the payments.
The tithe paid by each tribe went to support its own band. Sidi
'Umar had also to arrange for caravans to bring supplies from
Egypt, and to supervise their distribution to the armed forces
and the payment of customs dues on what went to the civilian
population. Sidi 'Umar also kept up correspondence with
Sayyid Idris and Sanusi elements and sympathizers in Egypt.

The guerrilla bands were in constant contact with the enemy.
One of the most striking features of the campaign was the
frequency of the fighting. At some point or other on the plateau
a skirmish or larger engagement took place every few days for
nearly nine years during the spring and summer months. In
the account of the campaign which follows I mention but few
of these fights, those which had exceptional importance for the
campaign as a whole or as examples of the scale of the fighting.
The few mentioned are therefore no indication of the amount of
fighting. Its frequency may be judged by Gen. Graziani's statement that in the final year of the war, when resistance, compared with earlier years, was feeble and sporadic, there took
place 53 engagements (*combattimenti*) and 210 skirmishes (*con-
flitti*).[1]

This incessant fighting cannot, as I have already said, be
described in the language of text-book logistics in terms of
manœuvring, objectives, and battles. Indeed, the Italians had

[1] *Rivista delle Colonie Italiane*, vol. vi (I), 1932, pp. 52–3.

to adapt themselves to the kind of fighting which seldom fails to upset the orthodox military mind. Text-book strategy does not apply to an enemy who wanders at will over a country with which he is familiar from birth, among a friendly people ready to provide him with exact intelligence, and in small mobile bands; and whose strategy is little more than the guerrilla imperatives—strike suddenly, strike incessantly, strike hard, get out quick. An army can only be manœuvred to inflict defeats on the enemy and to destroy his armed forces when he has an opposing army which can be brought to decisive engagements. The Italians were fighting a people, not an army, and a people can only be defeated by total imprisonment or extermination.

If the Bedouin had had anything which could clearly have been isolated as 'armed forces', these could easily have been destroyed by Italian superiority in men and machines. But they had nothing which could, properly speaking, be called an army, and they had no lines which could be pierced or turned and no strongholds which could be taken or in which troops could be contained. Against Bedouin it was of little profit to occupy towns and villages, for they retired to less accessible regions or circulated gaily between the Italian garrisons. Control of the roads and ports was also of little benefit. Roads were meaningless to the Bedouin and they were independent of overseas trade since they could live on the country for immediate necessities and obtain from Egypt what few additional supplies they required to carry on the war. To ease the supply problem, as well as to be of maximum nuisance to the Italian garrisons and convoys, the guerrilla bands were kept as small and mobile as possible. Their smallness and mobility confused the slow and unwieldy Italian columns. If the columns split up they were liable to be surrounded by concerted action of the bands and annihilated, whereas if they kept together, the cost of formation was the loss of speed and surprise. There seemed to be no enemy forces to fight, yet attack was incessant. There were no fixed points of opposition. It was indefinite and disseminated.

Even when contact could be established with the guerrilla bands and they could be defeated, as they often were, their defeat could not be turned into more than a temporary rout, for there was no highly organized tactical system to be upset, no large-scale operational plan to be thrown out of gear. The defeated band just dispersed and faded into the background of the *sottomessi* where their Bedouin garb was an effective camouflage. Italian bewilderment was further increased by the fact we have already noted, that when they claimed to have pacified a district and to have received the submission of its tribal Shaikhs it often meant no more than that the Bedouin of the district had made formal submission while their sons and food continued to go to the support of the guerrillas, thus confusing the issue and making even the field of operations wholly theoretical, besides adding heavy police duties to the already crushing burden of the campaign. The blows the Italians struck at Sidi 'Umar's bands were like the batterings Brer Rabbit gave the Tar Baby: they sank into a solid sticky mass of formless opposition.

The patternless pattern of the war is well summed up by Teruzzi, one of the Governors of Cyrenaica during the campaign, in a passage in which, scarcely attempting to conceal his irritation at the parsimony of the home government, he concludes his apology for his stewardship. He says that Italian superiority in men and arms was a vain illusion, because the struggle was not against an organized enemy who resisted, but against an enemy who had no consistency of form. It was equally an illusion that it was possible to maintain, in the struggle against the rebellion, the initiative of action. For the most part the Italians had to remain on the defensive. The rebellion was like a fire creeping deceitfully over the whole of the vast territory of the Colony. One might have wished to make it blaze into a single point to limit and subdue it, but this could not always be done. 'Thus, against 200, 500, 1,000, 2,000 rebels, dressed in picturesque rags and badly armed, often 5,000 or 10,000 of our soldiers are not sufficient, because the rebels are not tied down to anything, are not bound to any impediment, have nothing to defend or to protect, and can show themselves to-day in one place, tomorrow 50 km. away, and the following day 100 km. away, to reappear a week later, to vanish for a month, to disperse to fire from afar on an unarmed shepherd, on a patrol of inspection, or on a column which files along the edge of a wood, or at the foot of a hill.' An overwhelming superiority in numbers was required to act on the offensive against so fractionized and elusive an enemy.[1] Corrado Zoli (later Governor of Eritrea) tells the same story, how after 1923 began a long cycle of exhausting '*campagne di grande polizia*', repeated every year, and frequently two or three times in the same year, against an elusive enemy who kept the Italian forces in constant movement and alarms by endless surprises, incursions, raids, and ambushes; making use of his great mobility, powers of dispersal, tactical independence, and perfect knowledge of the insidious terrain, to avoid decisive encounters.[2] And in *Cirenaica Pacificata* Graziani tells us how the Arabs spoke during the long campaign, right up to its conclusion, of the two Governments of Cyrenaica, Italian and Sanusi, as 'the Government of the Day and the Government of the Night'.

V

In January 1923 the position was as follows: Italian posts to the south of Banghazi were up to some 50 km. from the Capital on the line Qaminis–al-Tailimun–Suluq; in the region between Banghazi and Talmaitha on the line al-Rajma–al-Marj–Qasr Libiya, running to a mean distance of 25 km. from the coast; and in the Shahhat area on the line al-Fayidiya–al-Qubba up to some 40 km. from the coast. In the region of Darna and between Tubruq and the Egyptian frontier the country was tranquil and was, in appearance at any rate, controlled by the Italian civil and military authorities as far as the southernmost encampments of the 'Abaidat. The Italians considered that the northern 'Awaqir, the 'Arafa, the Darsa, the Hasa, the northern Bara'asa, and the 'Abaidat were organized on the basis of the constitution of 1919.[3] In fact, however, their authority was negligible beyond the immediate vicinity of the towns and military posts. To the south of the Italian posts were the 'Mixed Camps' of al-Abyar, Taknis, Slanta, al-Makhili, and al-'Akrama, in each of which there were between about 100 and 300 Sanusi troops and rather more Italian troops, though the Italian garrisons were at the mercy of the Sanusi, since they were isolated in unfriendly country. The Sanusi had also estab-

---

[1] Attilio Teruzzi, *Cirenaica Verde*, 1931, pp. 338–9.
[2] 'La completa Conquista e l'Occupazione definitiva della Libia', *Rivista delle Colonie Italiane*, 1932, p. 169.
[3] Mondaini, op. cit., pp. 480–1.

lished on their own account, and the Italians considered
illegally, a camp at Khawalan of about 100 men and a number
of small posts, shown on the map, with about 15 to 30 men in
each. Their headquarters force was at Ajadabiya.

As stated at the end of the last chapter, Gen. Bongiovanni
seized the 'Mixed Camps' on 6 March 1923. Though this day
may be regarded as the date of the recommencement of hostilities

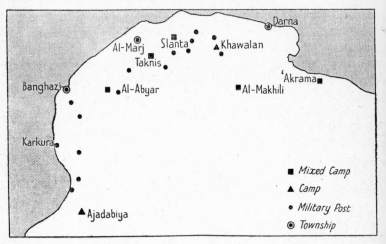

Distribution of Sanusi forces in March 1923.

in Cyrenaica, the first operational phase proper was a drive to
the south of Banghazi. The country there offered fewer difficulties to mechanized movement in the grand style than the
plateau country, and it was near the main Italian base. The
objective was the little village of Ajadabiya, the Sanusi seat of
government and military headquarters, called grandiloquently
by Bongiovanni after its capture the '*Roccaforte della Senussia*'.[1]
The Italians seem to have believed that they had only to take
it for resistance to collapse everywhere, much as it had collapsed
in Old Tripolitania after the chief centres had been occupied.
The Sanusi forces, under their Commander, Qajja bin 'Abdalla,
a Qur'ani of Tibesti, were unable to defend the village against
so large and well-equipped a column, and after they had been
worsted in several fights they retired, leaving the jubilant

---

[1] *Proclama alle popolazioni*, 1923, p. 5.

Italians to occupy it on 21 April, the Birthday of Rome. This proved to be less favourable an augury than was hoped, for early in June two of their columns advancing from Ajadabiya on Marsa al-Braiqa were almost annihilated by Magharba tribesmen.

Their experience in the *barqa* taught the Italians afresh the lesson of 1911 to 1915, that against Bedouin unwieldy columns advancing without concealment in a direct line on definite and fixed objectives could lead to little more than skirmishes, for the enemy was too wise to become involved in decisive action and mobile enough to avoid it; so they adopted the new tactics of making surprise raids by mechanized units on the Bedouin encampments, slaughtering man and beast indiscriminately, and destroying the grain stores. In these raids, on what in a non-colonial war would be regarded as the civilian population, the purpose was to kill as many of the Bedouin as possible, striking terror into the hearts of the shepherd folk of Cyrenaica. When the rains came and mechanized transport could no longer be used, the camps were bombed and machine-gunned from the air. The Bedouin suffered greatly from this persistent strafing, the Italian estimate of their losses—I must repeat that Italian figures are highly suspect—from 6 March to 3 September 1923 being 800 killed, 230 captured, and 1,000 wounded, besides about 700 camels and 22,000 sheep killed or confiscated. These losses were incurred only in the western part of Cyrenaica, for during the opening phase the rest of the country was quiet, except for minor skirmishes between Sidi 'Umar and the Italians in the Marmarica. At the end of the year the Sanusi forces had retired to country where they were less vulnerable, roughly to south and east of the line al-Braiqa–al-Qatafiya–Msus, with infiltrations everywhere along it towards the Italian posts.

The ease with which they had entered Ajadabiya and had raided and overcome resistance in the *barqa* generally had misled the Italians into believing that they would encounter little resistance elsewhere. They were further misled by the number of submissions they received at the commencement of the campaign: by the end of May 1923, 10,380 in the Ajadabiya zone, 3,417 in the Banghazi zone, and 7,000 in the zone of al-Marj; a total of 20,797 with 6,028 tents and more than 10,000 head of livestock, on which fines were levied for having taken part in the resistance. These submissions were from the less warlike Bedouin, those within easy reach of administrative centres, who had been taken by surprise and overwhelmed by the size of the Italian forces and their mechanized equipment, especially their planes, against the indiscriminate bombing and machine-gunning of which they had neither protection nor reply. They lacked the forest covering of the plateau tribes and the desert wastes into which the tribes of the Sirtica could retire. Moreover, the Italians had not yet realized that submission to protect families and herds did not exclude help in men, supplies, and intelligence to the fighting bands which continued resistance in country better suited to guerrilla warfare. The quietness of the plateau also deceived them. The Bedouin, unlike themselves, did not have an army ready to hand which could be sent into action at a moment's notice. It took the plateau tribes time to grasp what was happening and to form guerrilla groups. It also took the leaders of the Bedouin, both tribal Shaikhs and zawiya Shaikhs, time to accommodate themselves to Sayyid Idris's defection and vacillation, which seriously affected morale in Cyrenaica and Tripolitania and caused much coming and going between Cairo and the battlefields.

As the war entered its second phase in 1924–5 it soon became evident that neither the ponderous spectacular movements nor the mechanized raids on the camps which had been used in the flat *barqa* country were suited to the rugged and wooded plateau. The campaign rapidly assumed the character of guerrilla warfare, some of the features of which I have already outlined, with its tedious record of countless skirmishes and surprises. When the operational season opened in March 1924 the advanced Italian dispositions were on the west–east line al-Shlaidima–al-Abyar–Sidi Salim–Taknis–Marawa–Slanta–al-Fayidiya–Khawalan–al-Makhili. The Sanusi 'regular army', mixed with tribal volunteers from the Magharba and southern 'Awaqir, was still unbeaten under al-Qazza in the eastern Sirtica between Ajadabiya and the Wadi al-Farigh. The tribal guerrilla bands under Sidi 'Umar were mostly on the southern slopes of the central plateau. They were chiefly recruited from the Bara'asa, 'Abid, and 'Awaqir tribes which had from the earliest days of the Italian occupation of Cyrenaica shown themselves most hostile to penetration, though they were assisted by contingents from the Darsa, Hasa, and 'Abaidat.

In the fighting between March and June of 1924 the Italians reckoned that about 600 men of the 'Abid, Bara'asa, and northern 'Awaqir had been killed and 25,000 head of their livestock had been captured. In the summer and autumn at least another 250 were killed and about 1,500 camels and 17,000 sheep and goats captured. In spite of these, what were to them very heavy, casualties, the Bedouin continued to harass Italian posts and communications. Salih Lataiwish with his Magharba tribesmen menaced Ajadabiya; Abu al-Qasim al-Zintani with an 'Awaqir band threatened the advanced Italian bases at al-Abyar, al-Rajma, and Banina; Sidi 'Umar with the 'Abid tribal band contained the posts in the al-Marj sector, and detachments under his lieutenant 'Ali bu Rahayyim operated against communications between al-Marj and Talmaitha; Husain Juwaifi's Bara'asa band worried the garrisons at al-Zawiya al-Baida, al-Fayidiya, and Slanta; and Qtait bu Musa with his Hasa and 'Abaidat volunteers was camped opposite Khawalan. Behind these detachments were the camps of the Bedouin who had not submitted, even in appearance, in the *sirwal*, the *barqa al-baida*, and along the southern slopes of the plateau everywhere. The Italians found it necessary to pause to consolidate gains of territory and to carry out a reorganization of their operational units.

Sidi 'Umar's strategy at the time, both as Commander of the 'Abid band and as Commander-in-Chief of all the guerrilla forces on the plateau, was to hold its southern slopes. Their rugged desolation prevented the use of mechanized forces against him and gave him tactical superiority over foot and horse patrols. From the slopes he was able both to menace the Italian posts and communications on the plateau and to cover the families of his fighting men in their camps to the south of it. The Italian answer to these tactics was obvious. They could not prevent guerrilla bands from circulating on the plateau in the cover of forest and deep ravines, but they had by this time established themselves in sufficient strength on the margin of the plateau, and had gained sufficient experience in the handling of mechanized patrols to attack the camps of non-combatants in the flat steppe country to the south. These camps were easily

4936
N

spotted by planes and either bombed or machine-gunned from the air or destroyed by armoured cars.

As a result of the operations in 1924 and the spring of 1925 the Bedouin bands were pressed eastwards away from the main Italian bases at Banghazi and al-Marj. However, Italian control of much of the country from which they claimed to have driven the Patriots was less secure than the disposition of their advance posts suggests, for the guerrilla bands continued to operate in it. Nevertheless they were now able to mass men in these posts in such numbers, and to equip and supply them so well, that a Patriot attack on them had small chance of success. Sidi 'Umar had therefore to fall back on such operations as could be conducted by his small guerrilla bands, now deprived of any secure bases, mostly in and from the thick forest country to the south of the watershed between Marawa and al-Qaiqab and in the broken country of the Wadi al-Kuf area, where they had protection from air-reconnaissance and mechanized patrols and the advantage of superior intelligence and knowledge of the terrain.

The Italians had to adapt their tactics anew to the kind of warfare most favourable to the enemy. Gen. Mombelli's new operational plan was to establish a line of forts to act as *perni di manovra* from which the whole country could be ceaselessly patrolled to prevent the Patriot bands from massing against any point, to destroy their herds and crops, and to keep them constantly on the run. The main concentrations for these operations were al-Abyar, al-Marj, and Shahhat. The plan at first appeared to give the desired results but as time went on it gave less satisfaction. It was found that while it allowed the troops greater freedom of movement it was they, and not the Patriots, whose strength was worn out and finally exhausted. The Bedouin countered the new measures by attacking the smaller Italian patrols and dispersing before the larger. They solved the supply problem by living on the country, exacting food from the submitted sections, in whose country they also quartered their families, sowed their crops, and pastured their herds, so that the Italian patrols did not know what belonged to the *sottomessi* and what to the *ribelli* and they could only destroy the crops and beasts of the Patriots if they destroyed at the same time the crops and beasts of the quiescent part of the population, thereby irritating them into renewed rebellion. The net result was that while the Italians could prevent the Bedouin bands from massing, the Bedouin could make them pay too high a price for dispersing, and without dispersing they could not ensure mobility. Mombelli's plan was found to be too costly and fatiguing for the rather meagre results obtained.

Early in 1926 occurred a spectacular interlude which focused attention away from the plateau. The Italians sent an imposing column to take the little oasis of Jaghbub, the historic seat of the Sanusiya Order and the burial-place of its founder. The column met with no opposition and the oasis was surrendered by the Shaikh of the zawiya there, Husain al-Susi, on 7 February. Once again the Italians were jubilant and hoped that their troubles had ended, believing that the capture of the sacred city of the Sanusiya would so adversely affect Sidi 'Umar's prestige that his followers would forthwith desert him. These hopes showed great lack of understanding of the Bedouin mind. In fact, the expedition to Jaghbub, though it showed technical ability, had no strategic significance and was politically a disappointment.

So convinced had the Italians been that Sidi 'Umar would attempt to save Jaghbub that they conducted at the same time a vigorous offensive on the plateau intended as a diversion to prevent him using part of his meagre forces for the purpose. The beasts and crops of the Patriots were systematically destroyed where they were found in the area of guerrilla operations. Italian figures for Patriot losses in the ensuing engagements were 303 killed and 100 horses, 2,300 camels, and more than 30,000 sheep and goats either killed or captured. Their own losses were 3 officers, 25 Italian O.R.s and 24 native troops. In spite of Patriot losses, doubtless magnified by those who reported them, Rome was not satisfied with the achievements of the Military Governor Mombelli and he was replaced at the end of 1926 by Gen. Teruzzi, a good Fascist who had earlier seen service in Tripolitania. Indeed, some indication of the dissatisfaction felt by the Fascist hierarchy at the inability of their Governors to break the resistance of a few Bedouin may be judged by the fact that there was a succession of no less than five of these between 1923 and 1933: Bongiovanni, Mombelli, Teruzzi, Siciliani, and Graziani.

Teruzzi soon discovered that matters appeared in a different light to those in charge of the operations in Cyrenaica from that in which they appeared to those sitting on committees at Rome. In spite of all their successes, their occupation of the main strongholds of the country, and the submission of the greater number of the tribal sections, the Italians of all ranks were far from happy. The enemy was still protean and ubiquitous. It was like fighting mosquitoes. They have to be killed one by one and there are always a few left. Next sunset they are back again in the same numbers as before. Italian difficulties were increased by the absence of any single policy towards the tribal sections taking no open part in the struggle. Teruzzi found in the five Commissariats five different formulas of political action.[1] In the Banghazi district the submitted Bedouin were placed under strict surveillance, being organized into armed groups to defend their property against guerrilla raids. This separated them from the Patriots but meant entrusting to the Bedouin a function rightly belonging to the Government. In the Barce (al-Marj) district, on the other hand, relations between the submitted and the guerrillas were tolerated. This enabled the Italians to make propaganda in the Patriot camps, but it still more effectively allowed the Patriots to incite the submitted to further resistance or to exact from them tribute as the price of tranquillity. In the Cirene (Shahhat) district the Hasa tribe had submitted and was concentrated in the cages (*reticolati*) of Marsa Susa and Shahhat. In the Darna and Marmarica districts the 'Abaidat tribesmen, who had submitted as early as 1915–16 and had remained peaceful since the renewal of hostilities in 1923, thereby relieving the Italians of the necessity of sending a large body of troops to eastern Cyrenaica, were becoming restless and were purchasing quiet by payment of tribute in money, provisions, and volunteers to Sidi 'Umar. Taking all in all, there was lacking in the submitted districts good administration, effective propaganda, and adequate force to back decisions.

Teruzzi also found that, although almost unbroken success had been reported month by month in every part of the country ever since the war began, even as late as the middle of 1927 the Italians had little real control beyond the immediate vicinity

[1] Op. cit., p. 37.

of their forts. In the bend of the Sirtica they occupied only Ajadabiya, joined by a corridor to the little port of al-Zuwaitina. Farther to the north they held a territory running from the coast to the line Qaminis–Suluq–al-Shlaidima–al-Rajma–al-Abyar–Jardis al-'Abid–Taknis–al-Gharib–Talmaitha. There was a gap between this territory and the tract of country held farther to the east, running from the coast at Marsa Susa to the line al-Zawiya al-Baida–Slanta–Jardis al-Jarrari–al-Fayidiya–Bilqis–Khawalan–al-Qaiqab. This gap, the Wadi al-Kuf area, was entirely in guerrilla hands and necessitated communication by sea between Banghazi and Darna. In the Darna and Tubruq districts Italian control was uncertain, and political rather than military.[1] The people there were quiet only because the Italians left them alone. Moreover, in the spring of 1927, when Teruzzi's first campaigning season began, the Patriots still had, according to Italian records, some 1,000 men in the eastern Sirtica, some 1,600, about a quarter of whom were horsed, on the plateau, and about 100 in the Marmarica. However, these estimates were almost certainly magnified to excuse failure, and although the war dragged on for many more months the issue, if ever in doubt, was decided during Teruzzi's term of office in 1927 and 1928. His plan to hasten the end of the war was twofold: to clear the Wadi al-Kuf area of guerrillas and to clean up the Sirtica.

Local actions began their usual seasonal run in the spring of 1927 and included one of the rare Italian defeats in a hard fight at al-Rahaiba, to the south of al-Marj, on 28 March, in which they lost 6 officers and 306 native troops. Otherwise Sidi 'Umar's men suffered heavily, especially in two encounters with the Italian forces in the middle of July, and their consequent dispersal enabled Teruzzi to carry out his plan of combing the Wadi al-Kuf area, where deep ravines and dense undergrowth had always given the guerrillas a refuge when hard pressed, and by so doing to link up the western (Banghazi and al-Marj) and eastern (Shahhat and Darna) sectors. This was accomplished during the summer and considerably eased Italian communications. During an 80 days' campaign the Patriots lost, according to Teruzzi, 1,296 dead, 2,844 camels and 5,000 sheep slaughtered, and 842 camels, 18,000 sheep, 172 head of cattle, and 26 horses

[1] Op. cit., pp. 43 seq.

captured, against 2 Italian officers, 5 airmen, and 61 native troops dead. The 'Abid and Bara'asa, the two tribes which from the beginning were the most tenacious supporters of Sidi 'Umar, were the most severely hit. The 1927 summer campaign left the Patriots dispersed and they had now clearly lost the initiative in the more open country. They still held out, however, in the more broken and wooded area of the *jashsha* in the neighbourhood of Bir Qandula, Shnaishan, and the Wadi Mahajja, and to the south of Jardis al-'Abid, where they could more easily escape detection from the air and disperse before superior forces. Here Sidi 'Umar reorganized his guerrilla bands. His difficulties and casualties were becoming formidable. Indeed, in the summer of 1928 Teruzzi could speak with some justice of the war on the plateau as large-scale police action. In evidence of his success in the work of pacification he cites that between May 1927 and February 1929 he recovered 3,755 rifles from the Bedouin. Fighting still went on, it is true, and raids against the submitted sections, particularly against the Hasa tribe, even became fiercer, but the area of guerrilla activities was more restricted. On the last day of March 1928 the Patriots suffered an unusually severe defeat in the southern steppe country, in which they lost 200 dead, 70 prisoners, and 1,500 camels and 20 horses killed. Sidi 'Umar was forced, for the first time, to make contact with the Italians and treat with them for a truce.

The development of operations in Tripolitania had pointed to greater co-ordination between the forces attempting to crush Arab resistance in that country and those attempting the same in Cyrenaica, so at the end of 1928 the two colonies were placed under the single direction of Badoglio, and early in 1929 Teruzzi was replaced in Cyrenaica by Siciliani with the rank of Vice-Governor. Badoglio marked his appointment with a flamboyant proclamation offering the Arabs the choice between unconditional surrender and extermination. Its tone defeated its end, if peace was its end, though Italian writers assume that it influenced Sidi 'Umar in making his approach to the Italians in June 1929, together with the noted guerrilla leader Sidi Fadil bu 'Umar and Sayyid al-Hasan al-Rida, a boy of the Sanusi family who accompanied the guerrilla forces on the plateau. A truce was agreed to by both sides and continued for five months while negotiations for peace dragged on. The Arab and Italian accounts of these negotiations are very different and in many particulars contradictory. Graziani's account is certainly tendentious and I see no reason to doubt the Arab statements that Sidi 'Umar would not sign terms unless they were witnessed by observers from Egypt and Tunisia and agreed to by Sayyid Idris. As he was thus claiming to be the representative of the Head of a sovereign State the Italians would not agree to these conditions and discussions broke down. The Italians, however, prevailed on the boy al-Hasan to sign an agreement in their favour, and greatly to his own personal advantage, at Banghazi. This agreement was at once repudiated by Sidi 'Umar, and Sayyid al-Hasan deserted him, followed by most of the Bara'asa-Darsa band, which Sidi 'Umar's followers nicknamed 'The Army of Flour', chiding them for selling themselves for rations. Fighting broke out again in November and on 8 January 1930 Sayyid al-Hasan's followers, who had been kept under supervision, resisted the Italian attempt to disarm them and 80 of them were killed while another 100, including the Sayyid, surrendered. Ten days later Sidi 'Umar's own force was beaten on the Wadi Mahajja, he himself being wounded and barely escaping with his life. From February 1929 the Patriots had lost another 800 men killed, 2,000 camels, and a vast number of sheep and goats. About 2,000 Bedouin had fled with their animals and goods into Egypt. Against these losses the Italians had lost only 6 officers, 6 other nationals, and 102 native troops.

VI

It is here necessary to leave Sidi 'Umar fighting his desperate guerrilla fight on the plateau to note developments in the Sirtica, which Teruzzi had decided to clean up in 1927. After their drive on Ajadabiya at the commencement of hostilities in 1923 the Italians had been content to sit in the village, leaving the Bedouin in control of the country around it. But operations in Tripolitania had drawn Italian forces slowly farther away from their coastal bases towards the south and east and were now being held up because the Tripolitanian elements which still resisted were able to retire into the Sirtica and its hinterland, where they were difficult to contact and could rely on recruits and supplies from their Cyrenaican kinsmen. The situation which had developed there in 1915 seemed likely to develop again. Concerted operations from Cyrenaica and Tripolitania were, therefore, planned. To facilitate them from the Cyrenaican side the Italian line was advanced in March 1927 from Qaminis–Tailimun–Suluq–al-Shlaidima to Ajadabiya–Sawunnu–Msus; and Teruzzi, always an advocate of combining political with military action, decided to try what

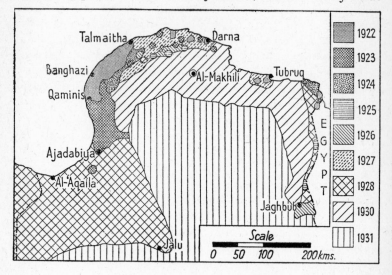

The Italian conquest of Cyrenaica.

diplomacy could do to ease the task of the soldiers. He had some success, with the aid of the treacherous Sanusiya Shaikh Sharif al-Ghariyani, in that he was able to arrange a meeting in June in the *barqa al-baida* with a number of tribal Shaikhs and to persuade 13 of those belonging to the Magharba Shammakh to make submission. This pacification of the Magharba near Ajadabiya, indispensable to operations in the Sirtica, had an immediate result in the uncontested occupation of al-Qatafiya towards the end of September and of al-'Aqaila a few days later. Sayyid Saddiq al-Rida collected a small force to the south of the Wadi al-Farigh to prevent a further advance but neither he nor his father, a man lacking both vigour and spirit, had the character of the Bedouin and both were wavering. The son entered into correspondence with the Italians and the father left his camp near Jalu oasis and surrendered himself to them at Ajadabiya at the beginning of 1928 when he knew that they intended to strike southwards. He was sent to Sicily. Had the Italians kept their word and allowed him to reside at Banghazi his sons al-Saddiq and al-Hasan would probably have surrendered also.

The long-planned operation followed. In February and March 1928 the oases of the 29th Parallel, the Saukna group, Zalla, Marada, and the Jalu group, along which is an important caravan route to Egypt, were occupied by either the Tripolitanian or the Cyrenaican army; the powerful Sirtican tribe of the Aulad Suliman was heavily defeated; and the greater part of the Magharba tribe was disarmed. However, small Bedouin bands still remained at large and from time to time raided towards the coast from the interior. The most active of these were under Salim bu Krayyim of the Zuwaya tribe, a man of over eighty years of age, and Salih Lataiwish, the leader of the Magharba tribe. The Italians were able to bring overwhelming force against these small bands. In the open country in which they had to operate they were easily located by planes and run to earth by armoured cars and troop-carrying vehicles. Their bases, the oases of Tazirabu and Kufra, were defenceless against the bombs rained on them.

The combined operational programme for 1929 was to disarm the tribes of southern Tripolitania, to reoccupy Fazzan, and to capture the distant oasis of Kufra. It has not been thought necessary to describe the development of the war in Tripolitania which pursued its course parallel to, but for the most part independently of, the war in Cyrenaica. Accompanying sketch-maps show the advance year by year in the two countries. The Cyrenaican part of the 1929 programme, the occupation of Kufra, began, as described, by driving the Sanusi bands from the hinterland of the *barqa al-baida* and the Sirtica, and while this was happening the whole of Fazzan was conquered. It remained only to undertake the arduous journey across a vast expanse of desert to Kufra and to destroy the last Bedouin bands from the *barqa* and the Sirtica which still offered in the oasis archipelago a stubborn and forlorn resistance under Salih Lataiwish, ‘Abd al-Salam al-Kizzih, ‘Abd al-Jalil Saif al-Nasir, and ‘Abd al-Hamid bu Matari. There was no more strategic

advantage to be gained by the capture of Kufra than there had
been by the capture of Jaghbub, but the magnitude of the undertaking, in both preparation and execution, and the opportunity
it gave to inflict a last humiliation on the Sanusi family by
planting the Italian flag in '*la Mecca della Senussia*', as Graziani

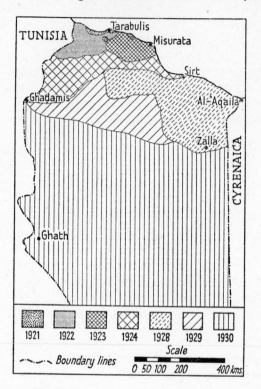

The Italian conquest of Tripolitania.

in a characteristic phrase calls the oasis, made an irresistible
appeal to the Fascist politicians and generals. The operation
again showed Italian skill in large-scale technical undertakings
in which fighting is not required. Serious opposition could not
have been expected, for there were at most only 600 armed men
to defend the archipelago against over 1,000 native troops led
by 100 Italian officers and N.C.O.s. The Italian force advanced
in three columns, largely mechanized: the main column from
Jalu and the subsidiary columns from Zalla and Wau al-Kabir.

On 19 January 1931 the combined columns defeated the Sanusi garrison at the oasis of al-Hawari and on the following day the Italian flag flew over al-Taj, the shrine of Sayyid al-Mahdi al-Sanusi. There was no alternative to flight for the remaining heroes of the *barqa* and the Sirtica. Four possible routes of escape were open to these Bedouin and the civil population of Kufra, all hazardous enough in time of peace: straight across the desert to the Egyptian oases, to the oasis of Siwa, to al-'Awainat and the Anglo-Egyptian Sudan, and to Tibesti. With sickening cruelty Badoglio ordered Graziani, who had replaced Siciliani as Vice-Governor of Cyrenaica from 13 March 1930, to follow the caravans without quarter, and they were systematically bombed and machine-gunned to make them abandon food and water.

The Sanusi family had, as usual, deserted their comrades and followers. The sensual Sayyid Muhammad 'Abid had represented Sanusi interests in Kufra since 1917, when he was driven from Fazzan by a group of pro-Turkish adventurers. From Kufra he had from time to time made advances to the Italians, but his emissaries had either been captured by Patriot forces or, having reached Banghazi, received little encouragement from the Italians. The Zuwaya of the oasis finally tired of his treachery and compelled him to flee to the Borku in January 1929. His place at Kufra was taken by Sayyid Shams al-Din bin Sayyid 'Ali al-Khattab, who, after a vain effort to negotiate with the Italians in October 1929, fled to Egypt, leaving his younger brother Hasan the sole representative of the Sanusi family in the seat of the Order. Sayyid Saddiq al-Rida had already, early in 1929, given up resistance and fled to Egypt.

VII

We can now return to the plateau where Sidi 'Umar and his gallant men faced inevitable defeat and almost certain death. By 1930 all their bases had gone and they lived like hunted beasts in the juniper forest between the Italian posts of Jardis Jarrari, Slanta, al-Fayidiya, and Khawalan. Sidi 'Umar's losses had been, for so small a population, enormous, and the destruction of the livestock on which his men relied for sustenance had been staggering. Nevertheless, till Graziani arrived in Cyrenaica to take over the command, Sidi 'Umar had, in spite of almost invariable defeats, kept the initiative. Mobility, knowledge of the country, and daring still enabled his men, worn out though they were by long years of hardship and hunger, to strike where they would, keeping Italian posts, patrols, and convoys always on the alert. Graziani now closed on them from both the plateau and the steppe country to the south. All the earths were stopped. The view-halloo was given wherever they broke. Flight to Egypt alone could save them, and this they would not take.

Graziani was determined to wrest the initiative from the guerrillas. He reorganized his forces for the last round in the '*guerra senza quartiere*' into small mobile patrols to keep the whole of the forest country under surveillance and to attack the enemy wherever they met him, giving him no rest. To prevent the guerrillas from obtaining supplies and reinforcements from the civilian population he disarmed the tribesmen, confiscating from them thousands of rifles and millions of rounds of ammunition, and made possession of arms a capital offence. He instituted the '*tribunale volante*', a military court flown from point to point to try, and execute, all who had dealings of any kind with the guerrillas. He reduced the Libyan units by more than two-thirds, with the intention of disbanding them altogether later. In the meanwhile he distributed among the 750 Libyans retained in service rifles of a different calibre from rifles in Patriot hands to prevent leakage of ammunition. At the same time he closed the Sanusiya lodges, confiscated their estates, and exiled their Shaikhs to the Island of Ustica. He also much improved the communications of the colony, thereby easing his supply problem and economizing man-power.

It may be doubted whether all these measures would have been effective if he had not also started his immense concentration camps for the entire tribal population of Cyrenaica, about whose feelings the General had no illusions. In taking this step the Italians were doing no more than others had done before them and have done after them, for an army fighting guerrillas is fighting an entire population. The first concentrations of January 1930 were found to be too near the area of military operations, for the prisoners, in spite of close surveillance, still managed to supply the guerrillas with some of their requirements ;

so most of the Bedouin were removed to the *barqa al-baida* and the Sirtica. In this bleak country were herded in the smallest camps possible 80,000 men, women, and children, and 600,000 beasts, in the summer of 1930. Hunger, disease, and broken hearts took a heavy toll of the imprisoned population. Bedouin die in a cage. Loss of livestock was also great, for the beasts had insufficient grazing near the camps on which to support life, and the herds, already decimated in the fighting, were almost wiped out by the camps.

The guerrillas thus found themselves cut off from local sources of supply and forced more and more to rely on Egypt for the bare necessities of life and of war. For years a considerable part of their supplies had come from there, paid for by Bedouin produce, money raised by customs charges, and funds collected throughout the Arab and Muslim world. Supplies came through the port of al-Sallum, and the Egyptian Frontiers Administration must have closed its eyes to supplies going into Cyrenaica as tightly as to refugees going out of it. The Marmarica had been declared by the Italians a military zone, its people being removed to concentration camps, and the closed frontier was patrolled by armoured cars and planes with instructions to destroy any caravans they spotted, but, in spite of these precautions, supplies continued to reach the Patriots. Graziani therefore decided to run a line of barbed-wire entanglement from the sea to Jaghbub and into the dunes to the south of it, a distance of over 300 km. The work was completed early in September 1931 and control along the wire was operated through fortified posts, a telephone system, and aviation camps. Perhaps nothing shows more clearly the slow imprisonment of the people of Cyrenaica than the use of barbed wire on an ever-increasing scale to imprison them in concentration camps within their country and to shut them off from the outside world: in 1922–3 the Italians spent only 27,000 Lire on barbed wire in Cyrenaica but by 1930–1 they could boast of spending 14,111,000 Lire.[1]

In spite of all Graziani's energy and threats Sidi 'Umar and his men would neither surrender nor flee the country. In 1930 the bands of the Bara'asa, 'Abid, and Hasa-'Abaidat were still harassing Italian detachments and raiding the herds of those who had submitted. Nevertheless, Italian activities had now

---

[1] *La Nuova Italia d'Oltremare*, 1933–4, vol. i, p. 239.

the character of mopping-up operations and there is little to record beyond a succession of isolated skirmishes in which the guerrillas lost several of their most experienced leaders. In mid-September 1930 Fadil bu 'Umar had been killed in one such encounter and on 11 September 1931 Sidi 'Umar himself was wounded near the tomb of Sidi Rafa', pinned down by his horse, and captured. He was taken to Suluq where on 16 September, still suffering from his wound, he was hanged before 20,000 Bedouin and the urban notables of Cyrenaica, brought there from confinement to witness his end. The Italians were exultant. They believed, this time rightly, that the rebellion had been stamped out.

The resistance died with Sidi 'Umar al-Mukhtar. The remaining fights were twitches of an already lifeless body. There were still about 700 guerrillas on the plateau but there was no one of Sidi 'Umar's prestige to lead them. Three of his faithful lieutenants tried with about 100 of their men to break through Graziani's wire into Egypt. Of the three only 'Abd al-Hamid al-'Abbar succeeded. 'Uthman Shami then surrendered himself and on 19 December 1931 Yusif bu Rahil was killed, fighting with great gallantry, in an engagement in the Marmarica. This seems to have been the last fight of the war, which Badoglio declared in an Order of the Day to have been brought to a successful conclusion on 24 January 1932. Except for the five months' truce in 1929 there had been just under nine years of constant fighting. In those nine years 'Cirenaica verde di piante' had, as Mussolini wrote, become 'rossa di sangue'.[1]

[1] Introduction to Cirenaica Verde, p. 11.

CHAPTER VIII

ITALIAN RULE AND COLONIZATION (1932–42)

I

THE two Italo-Sanusi wars had broken the Bedouin and desolated their country. It is not easy to estimate from Italian figures Sanusi casualties, nor to assess their reliability. The Bedouin population was probably reduced by half to two-thirds by death and emigration between 1911 and 1932. Losses of livestock are even more difficult to estimate but they were certainly enormous. The herds seem to have been slaughtered indiscriminately by the Italians.

The Italians had suffered too. It is true their casualties were not nearly as high as those suffered by the Bedouin and were mostly among their native troops, but the cost of the war imposed a grave burden on the Italian people. Loss of prestige in the eyes of the world for failure to break the resistance of a few Bedouin within weeks and for their cruel conduct of the war must also be taken into account if we are to appreciate fully the determination of the Italian leaders that there should be no third Italo-Sanusi war. To ensure that the dying embers of resistance should not again be fanned into flame it seemed necessary as the most immediate measure to prevent the Sanusiya Order reconstituting itself. The Order appeared to be destroyed but the Italians were never quite certain what was happening under the surface and watched ceaselessly for any sign of its rehabilitation.

By the end of the second Italo-Sanusi war the Sanusi family were, with the exception of those few members who had fallen into Italian hands and were considered by their captors too lacking in character to be a danger, scattered in exile. Nevertheless the Italians never felt entirely secure while Sayyid Muhammad Idris was in Egypt. It is true that he had promised the Egyptian Government not to engage in politics and was closely watched by the Italian Embassy, but while he was alive and free the Sanusiya Order might be said still to exist in his person. He and his cousin Sayyid Safi al-Din were potential trouble-makers who would certainly try to stir up a rebellion in Cyrenaica should the Italians find themselves at war with a European power. Efforts to obtain the extradition of the Sanusi leaders in Egypt were unsuccessful.[1]

The organization of the Order within Cyrenaica had been entirely disrupted during the years of war. The zawiyas had been destroyed by gun-fire, had fallen into ruin through neglect, or were being used as military posts by the Italians. Their Shaikhs had been scattered by the years of war and in 1930 had been rounded up and exiled at the same time as the properties of the Order had been confiscated on the grounds that while the Sanusiya existed as a corporation it would continue from its lodges to spread disaffection. The confiscation of the estates of the Order was viewed as the final act in its extirpation.[2]

When the Italians invaded Cyrenaica in 1911 they hoped that the Bedouin might remain neutral. They therefore declared repeatedly during the early stages of the war that the privileges of the Order and the customs of the people would be respected.[3] It can hardly be doubted that they did so in bad faith, for Giolitti had won support for the war among the peasants of southern Italy by promising them the exploitation of an Eldorado in Libya. Certainly, as the Italians themselves had to confess, they were not believed.[4] In retaliation for the support the Order gave the Turkish cause the Italians began to sequestrate its estates in those parts of the country where they had obtained a footing. At the end of 1913, Gen. Ottavio Briccola, the first Governor of Cyrenaica, ordered sequestration of its lodges and in the following year further instructions provided for seizure of the properties of the twelve lodges at that time in Italian hands. It is doubtful, however, whether these measures were intended to constitute complete and final confiscation. It is more likely that, as the Italians themselves say, they were temporary war measures to prevent the resources of the Order being used to support Sanusi forces operating all over the country against them, as a retaliation, and to provide a pawn with which to bargain when the Sanusiya decided to come to terms.

---

[1] Giglio, op. cit., p. 110.
[2] 'Italia e Senussia', *L'Oltremare*, Aug. 1930.
[3] Bourbon del Monte Santa Maria, *L'Islamismo e la Confraternità dei Senussi*, 1912, p. 240.
[4] *Norme Sommaire* for Political Officials, Aug. 1912, pp. 5–6.

The *modus vivendi* of 'Akrama of 1917 declared that the Sanusiya lodges occupied by the Italians were to be restored to the Order, together with their properties, which would be exempt from taxation. The Italians were also to pay salaries to the Shaikhs of the lodges. On 29 July 1919 the Governor of Cyrenaica, Giacomo De Martino, issued a proclamation in which he spoke of the *'Venerabile Confraternità dei Senussi'* from which the Government sought co-operation for the moral and economic advancement of the country and for the maintenance of security, and of the *'Venerabili Zauie e i loro Capi'* to whom were confirmed their traditional privileges and full freedom to exercise their beneficial functions.[1] The Accord of al-Rajma, which replaced the truce of 'Akrama in 1920, re-affirmed the right of the Order to its endowments. On 16 August 1921 a further agreement, the *Sistemazione definitiva delle zauie*, again reaffirmed it, and the Italians promised to pay an indemnity for lodges destroyed by their action during the war and again undertook to pay the salaries of the Shaikhs of the lodges.

In 1919 the Government of Cyrenaica, in order to put into execution Article 5 of the *modus vivendi* of 'Akrama, had nominated a Mixed Commission presided over by the Head of the Land Registry at Banghazi, Judge Colucci. Sayyid Idris appointed a representative on this Commission, and the Shaikhs of the lodges were co-opted when the lands of their lodges were being registered. The terms of reference limited the duties of this Commission to registration of lands indicated by the Shaikhs as belonging to their lodges, examination of documents relating to these properties, and interrogation of tribal Shaikhs representing those sections which had made the endowments. Moreover, the Commission was to register the immobile properties of only fourteen of the Sanusiya lodges, those which the *modus vivendi* recognized as being in the Italian area of occupation.

In 1922 the new Fascist Government at Rome decided to crush the Sanusiya Order once and for all and to seize its lands and colonize them with its own nationals. Gen. Bongiovanni's declaration of 1 May 1933, rendering invalid all accords and conventions entered into with the Sanusiya, revoked by implication the guarantees of inviolability of the estates of the Order. Even

---

[1] *Bolletino Ufficiale*, Bengasi, Jan.–Feb. 1919.

so, to avoid offence to Muslim opinion outside the Order, he was careful to announce in the same proclamation that the Sanusiya Order would be free to function as an Islamic fraternity.[1]

When Bedouin resistance had been overcome, except for its final guerrilla spasms in the more inaccessible parts of the plateau, the Italians no longer hesitated to grasp the prize they had aimed at for so long. By the Royal Decree of 22 December 1930 the articles of the various pacts between the Italians and the Sanusi which recognized the property rights of the Order were formally revoked and the closure of its lodges and sequestration of their goods were ordered. The Head of the Cyrenaican Land Registry was instructed to register without delay the properties of the Order in the name of the Colony. This Royal Decree set out to destroy the economic foundations of the Order as completely as military operations had destroyed its political foundations.

In execution of the decree Judge Valenzi was instructed in 1931 to complete the registration of as many of the Sanusiya lodges as political circumstances permitted and to inscribe their properties as patrimony of the colony. A technical survey and, therefore, final registration, were completed for only eighteen of the lodges. The disturbed state of the country, in which guerrilla bands were still operating, forced the Government to be content with compiling inventories of the properties of the remaining lodges from depositions made by tribal Shaikhs in concentration camps. It was intended to make a technical survey of these when circumstances allowed, but the work does not seem to have been done. During Italo Balbo's Governorship of Libya, from 1 January 1934, the Italians took what they wanted of the Sanusiya estates for their colonists and for other purposes, and the Shaikhs of the lodges on their return from captivity, or anyone else who wished to do so, cultivated on what was not immediately required by the State, though all the land belonged to the Colony and would eventually have been taken over by the Government without compensation whenever it suited its purpose.

The confiscated lands of the Order were given, when suitably placed, to Italian colonists under the *Ente* scheme of demo-

---

[1] Op. cit., pp. 7–8; also the Governor's speech on 6 Mar. 1923 at the opening of the spring session of the Cyrenaican Parliament.

graphic settlement. Some of the richest arable lands in Cyrenaica,
forming part of the endowments of the plateau lodges, were used
for this purpose, and the lands of a number of other lodges came
within the area marked out for future metropolitan colonization. The lands of yet other lodges lying outside this area were
earmarked for Arab agricultural settlement schemes. The only
Sanusiya lands which were not to be colonized were those in the
less-favoured parts of the country. The date-palms and gardens
of the Order in the oases were also confiscated.

As soon as the Italians had been powerful enough to seize
the endowments of the Order they had seized them. Their action
can only be called theft. It was a violation of the Shari'a law,
repeatedly proclaimed inviolable by the Italians, and of the
constitution they drew up for Cyrenaica in 1919. Their plea
that the Order had opposed them in both political and military
fields and had fomented rebellion in the Colony would have
carried more weight if they had not seized the lands for their
own nationals, for they could quite as effectively have broken
the Order by using its revenues for general religious and
charitable purposes. Some Italians were, indeed, troubled about
such barefaced robbery, but their lawyers were able to fall back
on the specious argument, so often used before to excuse similar
expropriations, that the State has unlimited powers and must
use them for its own safety and the welfare of the community
regardless of the traditional rights of individuals and associations, and of God.

II

The elimination of the Sanusiya deprived the Bedouin of the
leaders they had learned to follow but it did not make them any
more favourably disposed towards the Italians. The efforts of
the Administration to overcome this dull hostile turning away
from their conquerors, to their acceptance of them only in
resignation to the will of God, had only from 1932 to 1940 to
become effective, and it was so little successful that I do not
consider a detailed account of Italian native policy and measures
to be required. I shall endeavour nevertheless to indicate
briefly in the present section the general lines of their policy
from 1911 to the entry of Italy into the last war and to illustrate
its development by describing briefly in the following sections

the changes in the legal status of the Arabs of Cyrenaica during those years and how the lands of the Bedouin were confiscated to provide farms for Italian colonists. In the final section of the book I give a résumé of events leading up to what is, I hope, the threshold of Cyrenaican independence.

The Italians detested the Bedouin. Long years of campaigning against guerrilla bands had irritated them more than governments are usually irritated by Bedouin and made them increasingly flamboyant and brutal. In the whole Italian literature on Cyrenaica I have not read a sentence of understanding of Romany values. Because they lived in tents without most of the goods the peasant, and even more the townsman, regard as signs of civilization the Italians spoke of them as barbarians, little better than beasts, and treated them accordingly. The arguments they used to justify their treatment of them have a familiar ring.

Graziani has described the Bedouin in his usual uncompromising language and his opinions were doubtless shared by most army officers and government officials:

> 'Anarchist, lover of the most complete liberty and independence, intolerant of any restraint, headstrong, ignorant, unconquerable and boastful (*bluffista*) hero, it is sufficient that he possesses a rifle and a horse; he often masks, under the pretence of the necessity of moving his tent, the desire of gaining the end of withdrawing himself from every governmental contact and control.'

And again:

> 'Rebellious against every tie of discipline, used to wandering in territories often immense and solitary, bold in mobility and ease of movement, bemused by the fascination of independence, always ready for war and raiding, the nomads have always resisted every governmental restraint.'[1]

Graziani was a plain-spoken soldier. When the conquest phase of colonization had passed and it was no longer fashionable to believe in naked *refoulement*, administrators found it expedient to express themselves more temperately. The soldier-politician Badoglio, in his directive to subordinates in Libya for the year 1933, forbade further talk of '*ribelli*'. The war, the rebellion as it had been called, was over and the past must be forgotten in a

---

[1] Op. cit., pp. 119–20.

common effort to reconstruct the life of the country. The first object of the Government was now to increase the Bedouin population, not to destroy it, for the country could never be prosperous in its present depopulated state. At least 20,000 refugees had taken refuge during the war in Egypt and elsewhere and they could not be expected to return unless a more conciliatory policy were pursued.

Selected Arab officials were attached to the Italian Consulates in Egypt to do propaganda among the refugees, and those who returned were given food, clothing, and beasts. This policy met with some success. In Egypt, where most of the refugees lived, the Bedouin were faced with the choice between becoming wage-earners or leading a gipsy life on the edge of the cultivations. The temptation to return to their country, where they were used to a life of freedom and plenty, was too great for many of them, in spite of Italian occupation. It was, as they say, *yakhtar akhaf al-dararain*, the choice of the lighter of two evils. Between 5,000 and 10,000 must have returned by the middle of 1940. Besides a general amnesty to induce the refugees to return, pardon was granted to almost all political prisoners, and by 1939 only a very few remained in jail or enforced exile. Instructions were given for this fact to be made widely known to neutralize anti-Italian propaganda in Arab countries.

It was possible to adopt a milder policy because the Bedouin had been disarmed and were unable to cause further trouble. It had long been recognized that while they possessed arms they would use them against the Italians if given an opportunity. As early as August 1912, in the very premature *Norme Sommarie* for Political Officers, it was stressed that the Bedouin regard rifles as essential as horses and that no amount of persuasion would make them part with either, especially as 'there is not an Arab in the country who, in asking himself why we have come, does not reply to himself and to others, "To take our lands, our beasts, our women" '. Because of the strong feelings of the Bedouin on an issue which touched their manhood no very determined attempt was made to disarm those tribal sections which submitted to the Italians till the second Italo-Sanusi war was well advanced, and it was not till Graziani was made Vice-Governor in March 1930 that total disarmament of the civilian population was aimed at.

In 1932 the Bedouin were released from the concentration camps into which they had been herded in 1930 and were allowed to return to their tribal territories. In spite of their losses in manpower, stock, and arms, it was felt that the closest watch must still be kept on them. Local officials were, therefore, instructed to keep detailed lists of distribution of tents, and soldiers were posted to picket the camps and prevent any movement without a permit from an Italian official. Any breach of the regulation, which was in force till 1938, was punished with imprisonment. This supervision by what amounted to a strict pass system was finally given up by Balbo, as it was found that it irritated the Bedouin without serving any useful purpose.

Like other governments that have had dealings with nomads, the Italian bureaucrats in charge of the administration could not abide that they should live free from their interference. It was held that it was wicked to be a nomad and that it was the duty of an administration to compel them to settle. Graziani declared that the nomads are 'enemies, and destroyers, of agriculture. Everywhere, in fact, the nomad has passed he has destroyed woods, trees and fields.' Therefore, 'the nomads have no justification and no right to claim to stay in areas of assured development, such as those of the Cyrenaican plateau, rich in promise of tree and cereal culture, but ought to be excluded from it for ever, leaving room for thousands and thousands of Italian arms which are stretched out there, anxious to begin again to till and make fruitful this ancient Roman earth'. Graziani held, furthermore, that not only must the Bedouin be kept off the fertile plateau, but must be stabilized in the country on the edge of the steppe where, in his opinion, they had sufficient and suitable land for pasturing and sowing. They would there find themselves in an environment perfectly responding '*alla loro natura di rapsodi del deserto*'. Here their every move, every halt, every camp ought to be under rigid supervision by government officials. Braida adds that by 1935 Graziani's plan had been put into operation in its main proposals.[1] The plateau was reserved for metropolitan colonization and the steppe for the Bedouin, who were subject to such rigorous control that it might be regarded as a prelude to

[1] Graziani, op. cit., p. 123; Vittorino Braida, *Memoria per l'Ufficiale dei Reparti indigeni della Cirenaica*, 1935, pp. 61–3.

stabilization in native reserves. Zones of pasturing were fixed, it was forbidden to camp in places other than those laid down by the political authority and, as mentioned above, no move might be made without written authorization. The Italian aim was in the end to abolish the traditional Bedouin way of life altogether and to make them peasant-tenants of the State and wage-labourers. 'It is necessary', said Graziani in his address to the Fascist Institute of Culture at Banghazi on 23 November 1931, 'to compel them to build houses, abandoning the tents.' Balbo later held the same view and it was shared by some writers of the liberal period.

In any case, the Italians intended to take the best arable of the country for themselves and I describe later in this chapter how they planted by mass emigration colonies of metropolitans on extensive stretches of the best tribal lands, excluding the Bedouin from the whole tableland, both for pasturing and for sowing, section by section as it was taken over for exploitation. The inevitable prosecutions for trespass of stock on the expropriated lands followed. Since it was recognized that the Bedouin must move north–south to pasture their flocks and sow, passages for transport of stock across the reserved area were marked out, as shown in the map on p. 224, and the staging points fixed. All that was left to them in northern Cyrenaica were the narrow coastal belt, the more rugged parts of the first terrace which would not yield to Italian methods of cultivation, and the bleak southern slopes of the plateau. Under Balbo's scheme of development, which aimed at destroying the Bedouin way of life, they were to be settled as far as possible in village communities in these areas, where they would live and cultivate under the same rigid State control to which the Italian nationals were subjected. The whole of northern Cyrenaica was thus expropriated for State purposes, the more fertile areas for metropolitan colonists, and the less fertile for urbanized and semi-urbanized Arabs or such Bedouin as could be induced to submit to State direction and forsake their traditions. It was originally intended to establish sheep farms in those parts of the country more suitable for pastoral than agricultural exploitation, but experience showed that the Italian settlers did not make successful shepherds and, in any case, the development in this direction was in opposition to a colonization of people rather than of capital. For these and for political reasons the plan was abandoned and Balbo decreed in 1939 that only the Bedouin might own herds for nomadic pastoralism. This excluded both Italian colonists and urban merchants and left most of the southern slopes of the plateau, the steppe at their termination and on the *barqa*, and Cyrenaica's two arid wings, the Marmarica and the Sirtica, to those Bedouin who preferred to continue their ancient shepherds' way of life.

The loss of their best land could not by itself disrupt the social life of the Bedouin. It was necessary at the same time to destroy their social organization. As a first step in this direction an attempt was made to undermine the influence of the tribal Shaikhs. In the early days of their partial occupation of Cyrenaica the Italians continued, because they had no choice, the Turkish administrative divisions and their policy of consultation with the Shaikhs, confining the duties of Italian officials to inspection and advice, though native participation was illusory.[1] This policy was carried to excess in the Basic Law of 1919 which gave extensive powers to a local Parliament of representatives elected from the tribes and urban centres with ex-officio and nominated members who were not to exceed in number a sixth of the elected members. For administrative purposes the Shaikhs of each sub-tribe and the Shaikh al-Mashayakh of each tribe were recognized as such by decree. By official recognition as tribal Shaikhs of large numbers of men of no great importance in tribal life the status of Shaikh was lowered in the eyes of the Bedouin, and official subsidies to these Shaikhs occasioned much rancour between individuals and sections.

The Fascists revoked the Law of 1919 and reversed the tribal policy of the liberal period. Administration was in future to be as direct as could be—straightforward military rule of a beaten people without use of intermediaries and without tribal co-operation through their leaders. Graziani told his audience at the Fascist Institute of Culture: 'Direct rule will not be an empty phrase, because chiefs and sub-chiefs are going to be abolished; I have withdrawn them from circulation.' He went on to say: 'They will be replaced by old battalion N.C.O.s (*graduati*) made worthy of such employment by services

[1] Mondaini, op. cit., p. 327.

rendered in fighting faithfully for Italy.' On this point Balbo, who replaced Graziani, was equally emphatic: 'Chiefs do not exist any more—there are only citizens with equality of duties and rights.'[1] Tribal Shaikhs, therefore, were not asked to advise the Government or to co-operate with it in any official capacity and the subsidies they had received in the pre-Fascist and early Fascist periods were withdrawn. Cyrenaica under the Fascists was administered by decrees issued by a Governor directly responsible to the Minister for the Colonies at Rome. Under the Organic Law of 1927 a General Council with very limited advisory functions was allowed for, and Arabs chosen from the notables of the sedentary population and Shaikhs of the Bedouin tribes could be nominated to sit on it by the Minister for the Colonies on the recommendation of the Governor. Its constitutional importance was nil, because it never came into operation. It was replaced by the Law-Decree of 1934, by which Tripolitania and Cyrenaica became a single colony with the seat of its administration at Tripoli. The new colony was divided into four commissariats (Tripoli, Misurata, Bengasi, and Derna) and a military territory of the Sahara. Each commissariat came under a Prefect and was divided into administrative sections: departments, residencies, and districts, all under Italian officials. It was recognized that the Bedouin were divided into tribes and sub-tribes. At the head of each was a Shaikh chosen in accordance with tribal custom and nominated by the Head of a commissariat. The Shaikh of a tribe was personally responsible to the competent Italian authority for order and security within the tribal territory. His functions and powers were those accorded him by tribal custom. The Shaikhs of the sub-tribes came under his control and had within their sub-tribal areas functions analogous to his. All that this meant was that certain tribal Shaikhs were recognized as such in so far as they were held responsible for any shortcomings of the Bedouin, but were accorded no privileges and had no representation. Consultative councils, where allowed for, were composed of administrative officials. So long as the Bedouin obeyed the Government and submitted to whatever curtailments of their freedom and rights it chose to enact, they could stew in their own juice until the

[1] Italo Balbo, *La Politica Sociale Fascista verso gli Arabi della Libia*, 1938.

Italians had more leisure to devote to breaking up tribal life altogether.

The final decree of the Fascists affecting Arab status was issued in 1939. It incorporated Tripolitania and Cyrenaica within the Kingdom of Italy, and to quiet any dismay this might cause among the Effendiya of the towns it offered them certain privileges, mostly nominal. The decree in no way affected the Bedouin. Indeed very little of the unceasing flow of legislation which poured from the Italian bureaucrats and lawyers in the form of Laws, Royal-Decrees, Royal-Law-Decrees, Ministerial Decrees, and Governatorial Decrees affected the Bedouin. The vast majority of these rules and regulations in no way touched their lives and they remained in blissful ignorance of their content. They had little or no money, they settled their own cases with the aid of their Shaikhs and religious teachers, they made their own trading arrangements, they provided their own labour, and so on. Where a law affected them it could often be eluded or circumvented. As the Bedouin themselves say, '*Sama' min gher ta'a*', 'To hear without obeying', is one of their chief characteristics. The Italians in any case, sitting comfortably in their offices and entirely out of touch with the people, relied on their Cyrenaican police and minor officials to report breaches of regulations, and if they did not choose to do so, the law became a dead letter. Also it cannot be assumed that because there were regulations great efforts were always made to enforce them. 'The gap between the letter of the law and daily practice, wide in all countries, becomes an abyss in Italy.'[1]

With all their regulations and petty interference the Italians were most careful not to offend Arab opinion in religious matters. From the moment of their invasion of Libya they vociferated their respect for Arab custom, culture, and religion. Thus the Minister Bertolini said to the Arabs in a discourse at Tripoli in 1914: 'We will respect your religion and your customs; we know the splendour with which your civilization has already illumined the world and we do not intend in any way to threaten it. . . .'[2] The Italians prided themselves on their Islamic policy and claimed that as a result of it and of their justice and of their

---

[1] James Meenan, *The Italian Corporative System*, 1944, p. 340.
[2] Mondaini, op. cit., pp. 327–8.

care for the material welfare of their Muslim subjects their colonies were the only ones in which the Muslim subjects of European powers were not in a state of suppressed revolt.[1] Balbo said:

'The Government has never favoured in Libya any form of religious proselytism directed to the conversion of Muslims to another faith. On the contrary it has shown its interest in favour of Islamic cult by making important donations for the restoration of old mosques and for the construction of new ones, even in the desert territories where the nomads have never till now been able to kneel to the Almighty in sacred precincts.'[2]

They built mosques, restored the tombs of well-known saints, including that of the most famous of Cyrenaican saints, Sidi Rafa', which their troops had destroyed in the fighting, and celebrated zawiyas (other than those of the Sanusiya Order). They respected Islamic law and custom. While the civil, commercial, and penal codes and their rules of procedure were as in Italy, the personal status and law of inheritance of Muslims were guaranteed in all laws and decrees from the beginning of their occupation, and nothing might be taught in the schools contrary to Islamic principles. They issued ordinances defining the status and duties of the mufti and of qadis and to ensure the proper functioning of the Shari'a Courts and the *auqaf* (religious endowments) administration. They founded a religious training college at Tripoli to serve the two Libyan countries and make it unnecessary for students to go to al-Azhar in Egypt or al-Zaituna in Tunisia for koranic instruction, for in those places they were subject to anti-Italian propaganda. Their prefects attended Islamic ceremonies on important feast-days, especially on the Birthday of the Prophet, and distributed alms on these occasions. The Prefect of Darna even re-established the *zarda*, a festal excursion at the beginning of spring, for the students of the town, though this was hardly an Islamic function. They went further. They built mosques in their concentration camps. They permitted the kuttabs (local koranic schools) to remain open although they disapproved of them. They gave special facilities for the pilgrimage to Mecca and established an Italo-

---

[1] R. d. C., 'L'Italia per i suoi sudditi musulmani', *Riv. delle Col. It.*, 1938, pp. 1177–91.
[2] Op. cit., p. 9.

Muslim hospice at al-Madina for the pilgrims. They ensured that the meat of their Muslim troops was prepared in the pre-scribed manner. In 1937 Balbo, at the request of some of the Muslim notables, forbade the sale of alcoholic drinks in the month of Ramadan. Exhibitions of fakirism by the ecstatic religious Orders were prohibited in 1935 to please the *'Ulama* who regarded them as an undesirable innovation. Mussolini thought, like Napoleon, that it was good policy to build up for himself a reputation of being the defender of Islam. The supreme moment of this burlesque was when the notables of Tripoli presented him on his visit to Libya with 'The Sword of Islam', an event commemorated by a huge equestrian statue in the middle of the town.

The Bedouin was not impressed with this Islamic propaganda, which even the more impressionable townsman thought highly ridiculous, especially the building of mosques by Christians. Those the Italians built outside the towns were neglected, for the Bedouin preferred to use his own prayer-places or the mosques of the Sanusiya lodges, where these had not been destroyed, when he felt the need to pray at all. Government qadis were of little interest to him, for in law and custom he followed tribal tradition, and such priestly services as he required were performed by his faqihs and zawiya Shaikhs. If the Italians liked to restore the tombs of his saints he was un-concerned. If they liked to encourage the pilgrimage, so much the better for those who felt the need, unfelt by himself, to make it. The Bedouin was a Sanusi and the Italians had driven the revered Heads of his Order into exile and had plundered and abolished the Order itself. He could hardly be expected to feel, and certainly did not feel, that the Italians were sincere in their professed respect for Islam.

The Italians based their claim to Arab regard on two con-siderations, their respect for Islam and their social services. I shall not describe in detail Italian measures designed to raise the standard of culture and living among the Bedouin, for their efforts in this direction were little advanced by 1940, but it is necessary to refer briefly to their educational policy. The Turks had provided instruction only in the towns, only during the last years of their rule, and only on a very modest scale. The only schools in the Bedouin districts were those of the Sanusiya lodges. The Italians, who had some small schools in Libya even before 1911, gave considerable attention to educational matters from the earliest days of their occupation. The first educational programme for Libya, drawn up by the Arabist C. A. Nallino, was not accepted by the Central Government because it was felt that the proposals did not give the Administration effective control over the schools and that consequently education could not be sufficiently directed to political ends. Military conquest must be consolidated by moral conquest. This feeling hardened under the Fascists into an educational policy designed to meet the new programme of colonization. Mixed schools and classes were abolished in favour of schools for Italian boys and schools for Arab boys or, where they had to be taught in the same building, separate classes for each. Teaching, except of the Koran to the most junior pupils, was entirely in the hands of Italians. In the curriculum Italian took precedence over Arabic and it was intended that it should become eventually the sole medium of instruction. Arab boys learnt under the system to write Italian with greater facility than their own language. The aims of this education were to satisfy the cultural ambitions of the Arabs, while keeping them under control and preventing them from reaching a level of cultural equality with the Italians, and to provide minor government officials and a means of intercommunication by which the Arabs could more easily be employed in menial work.[1] It seems that by 1940 there were twenty-three schools for Arabs in Cyrenaica. Some of these were in centres within reach of Bedouin and a number of medical clinics were also opened in Bedouin areas. Less use was made of the schools than of the clinics.

Thus in every department of public life power and authority were retained by the Italians in their own hands and the people of the country had no representation in the Government and were not consulted about plans for their future. It was, however, necessary for the Italians to employ a number of Arabs in minor administrative posts, because they could not themselves make contact with the people, and in the Islamic courts, where they could not themselves function. After 1935, when Italy

---

[1] Dr. R. Micacchi, 'L'Instruction publique en Libye de 1912 à 1924', *Institut Colonial International*, 1926, and 'L'Enseignement aux indigènes dans les colonies italiennes dépendant directement de la Couronne', ibid. 1931.

found herself in none too friendly a world with the added cares of an imperial power, efforts were made to identify more closely with Italian interests those of the better-educated section of the Arab population through this bureaucratic *élite*. If it was to be an asset in the future it would have to be given a larger stake in the administration of the country. Balbo emphasized this requirement in his plan of development. He said in 1938 that he wished to raise the cultural and social level of the Arabs by allowing them to collaborate in greater numbers and more positively in public offices and duties. If such collaboration was still limited and the participation of Arabs in posts of responsibility was still rare it was due 'to the poverty of capable and reliable elements, and certainly not to an obstinate prejudice on the part of the Government'.[1]

This *élite* had to be very small to begin with, for suitable material was, as Balbo wrote in the passage quoted above, hard to find in Cyrenaica. Excluding persons employed in such menial offices as sweepers, door-keepers, and office messengers, and the large numbers of Cyrenaicans in the army and police under Italian officers and N.C.O.s, there were in 1940 only about 150 Arabs employed in the Civil Service. About 100 of these were administrative officials, advisers, mudirs, and sub-mudirs, and the rest were religious functionaries, qadis and officials of the religious courts. The administrative officials had no real authority, their duties being limited to collecting information about the Arab population and circulating among it the instructions of the Government. They were treated as servants in the domestic rather than in the public sense and they were ill-paid. Nevertheless, through their many social contacts with their fellow countrymen they exercised more influence than the Italians would have wished, and the Italians were, owing to their ignorance of Arabic and of Arab ways of life and thought, very largely in their hands. They undoubtedly deceived their masters to their own advantage and in the interests of their fellow countrymen. These Arab bureaucrats were townsmen, mostly from Banghazi and Darna. Some were members of respectable urban families of Turkish days, such as the Banghazi families of Bin 'Amir, Bsaikri, Biju, and 'Anaisi, and the Darna families of Bannani, Darbi, Dillal, and

[1] Italo Balbo, op. cit., p. 15.

Jarbi, and had been educated in Turco-Arab schools in the country, and a few at Istanbul. Most, however, were less reputable and had a record of close and active collaboration with the Italians as informers, spies, guides, interpreters, leaders of 'friendlies', and overseers in concentration camps. When the fighting was over the Italians felt under an obligation to these men, their only friends in the country, and rewarded them with administrative posts for which they had few qualifications. It is not surprising that later they often found them an embarrassment and had to admit that the Bedouin for preference avoided their company. Before the last European war they were being slowly replaced by a new class of officials brought up in the towns under Italian rule and educated in Italo-Arab schools. These *évolués* showed a marked preoccupation with their own affairs and little inclination to use their superior education for the benefit of their own people in the towns, while their repugnance to the Bedouin made them regard a posting to one of the country districts as a punishment. But if they had no strong sense of loyalty to their own people they likewise had none to their masters. They might join Fascist clubs and syndics and apply for special Italian citizenship but they did so passively, without conviction that these things would mean more to them than payment of subscriptions. They knew moreover that the swarms of Italian immigrants settling like locusts on Cyrenaica would spell disaster to them no less than to the rest of the Arab population. It is not surprising, therefore, to find that during the late war the Italians watched them closely for *disfattismo politico*, and not without cause, for they showed themselves very ready to co-operate with the British during their first two occupations of Cyrenaica, and some, including ten senior officials, showed themselves so openly anti-Italian during these periods that they thought it wise to retire with the British forces in their second retreat to Egypt.

The Bedouin accepted all these Italian measures, good and bad, with resignation and indifference. They were powerless to oppose them, but as far as possible they ignored them. Plagued with concentration camps, loss of stock, confiscation of arms, rape of sowing and pasture grounds, the pass system, corrupt officials, and neglect of their Shaikhs, they found the odd mosque, school, and clinic poor consolation and retired

into the strongholds of their tribal and kinship systems. Two
exclusive societies, the colonial and bureaucratic Italian community and the Bedouin tribal community, lived side by side
with the most slight and occasional contact between them.
For the most part Italian and Bedouin lived as though the
other did not exist. Brought up against a tribal solidarity which
excluded them and ignored them, the Italians began to realize
that they would not make any impression on the Bedouin
without totally destroying their tribal and kinship institutions.
This Balbo set about doing. 'Patriarchal agriculture' was to
be broken down and replaced by individual ownership within
Fascist corporations. Tribal and lineage ownership of wells was
abolished. 'The epoch of the clan is about to pass for ever in
these provinces.' A new type of Italo-Libyan citizen was to be
created who would fit into the structure of the corporate Fascist
state.

> 'The participation of the Libyan Arab in our social life begins
> at the tenderest age, whether in the company of scholars at our
> schools established at every centre or with the enrolment of the
> boys in the formations of the G.A.L.;[1] becomes perfected by mili-
> tary service; will continue afterwards, whatever may be the
> occupation of the individual in the following years, assiduous and
> uninterrupted, so that the personality of each emerges from the
> traditional and primitive ethnic group to integrate itself within
> the ambit of the Municipalities, of the Residencies, of the Depart-
> ments, of the Prefectures, and of the Colony.'[2]

The stress placed on the building up of an Arab personality
based on participation in various State organizations in place
of the traditional Bedouin personality moulded in tribal and
kinship groups was, of course, particularly Fascist. 'Therefore,
for the Fascist', wrote Mussolini in the *Enciclopedia Italiana*,
'everything is in the State, and nothing human or spiritual
exists, much less has value, outside the State.'[3] In the midst of
their conceit and ignorance the Fascists had at least this grain
of virtue: they said that they were trying to do what they were
trying to do. Aiming in their native policy at a combination of
political domination with social justice, they repudiated what
they regarded as the British system of a small ruling class of

---

[1] The Arab Fascist Youth organization.   [2] Ibid., pp. 21–2.
[3] 'The Doctrine of Fascism', 1932.

Weisse Götter, who avoided all contact with the natives that was not unavoidable, and they rejected also the French policy of cultural assimilation and social and political equality with the *évolués*.[1] In 1938 the Under-Secretary for Italian Africa, Teruzzi, the ex-Governor of Cyrenaica, described the fundamental principle of Fascist native policy as a steering between the Anglo-Saxon colour bar and the French policy of assimilation which was not merely a middle course but an entirely new direction. At the same time he rejected the concept of indirect rule 'which leaves to the native chiefs very wide autonomy, not only administrative but also political, and which leads therefore inevitably to a slow detachment of the colony from the mother country'. The Italian policy was to regard their colonies as extensions of Italy beyond the seas.[2]

Had the Italians been content, as in the first years of their occupation, to restrict their immigration to the towns, where there was scope for a new element as traders, artisans, officials, and professional men, a symbiosis might have developed, for the Arabs were at that time incapable of these functions on an adequate scale, and the problem of adjustment might never have become acute; but when they began to organize mass colonization of the country-side, questions of status and racial interrelations appeared to present no other solution than that proposed. Even had racial miscegenation not been prohibited it could hardly have taken place between Catholic Italians and Muslim Arabs. Cultural assimilation was also unlikely because both Italians and Arabs were civilized peoples with a long cultural history behind them and it was most improbable that the Arabs would give up their religion, law, and language. No other solution seemed feasible, therefore, than that advocated by Balbo, the policy of parallel development in cultural matters and structural co-ordination within the framework of the Fascist State. The Arabs were to remain Arabs in speech, religion, personal law, customs, and manners, but their tribal structure was to disappear and its place was to be taken by political and economic institutions similar to those of their Italian fellow Libyans. 'We shall have in Libya not rulers and ruled, but

[1] Oskar Schmieder and Herbert Wilhelmy, *Die faschistische Kolonisation in Nordafrika*, 1939, pp. 79–80.
[2] Italo Neri, 'Politica Indigena', *Riv. delle Col. It.*, 1938, pp. 1391–2.

Catholic Italians and Muslim Italians, the one and the other united in the enviable fortune of being the constructive elements in a great and mighty organism, the Fascist Empire. Rome will thus show herself to be once again and always the grand and fruitful Mother of peoples.'[1] Arabs and Italians would share like institutions in the same corporate State, though remaining culturally and racially distinct, it being understood, however, that the institutions would be like, not common, and that the Italian colonists and officials would always occupy a superior position politically and economically.

It was hoped that when the Bedouin tribal and kinship structure had been broken down and their social life had been remodelled on Fascist corporative lines, both Arabs and colonists would accept a situation they could not alter and tolerate each other in the realization that, though their immediate interests might sometimes clash, co-operation was to the final advantage of both. It was believed also that any jealousy the Arabs might feel about the disparity between the political status and economic privileges of the two peoples would be overcome by the natural aptitude of all Italians for meeting other peoples as social equals. In the end the two races would feel themselves bound together by a community of economic interests in loyalty to a common *Patria* and a common *Duce*. Clearly such rugged individualists as the Bedouin were did not fit into this picture. The Bedouin would, therefore, have to go.

In pursuance of this policy of parallel development the Italians under Balbo's direction made serious efforts to improve the material condition of the Arabs. New wells were dug, stock was improved, zootechnical stations were started, and educational and medical services were expanded. An effort was made to persuade the Arabs that they would receive consideration commensurate with that accorded by a paternal administration to its own nationals. Arab agricultural villages were built as well as metropolitan agricultural villages, metropolitan schools were balanced by Arab schools, the hospitals had Arab wards as well as Italian wards, there were Colonial battalions and Libyan battalions, there were Colonial Fascist organizations and Arab Fascist organizations, and the Government built mosques as well as churches. It may be doubted whether these

[1] Op. cit., p. 22.

measures would have convinced the Bedouin that they were compensated for the loss of their kinsmen, their lands, and their independence. In the event they were inadequate and they came too late.

Italian policy in Cyrenaica, like the colonial policies of other European powers, was full of contradictions. It is not within the scope of this book to discuss them, but I would draw the reader's attention to the changes this policy underwent during the thirty years between their occupation of the country and their embroilment in the late war. They were tactical changes demanded by the development of local, domestic, and international situations. There was no fundamental difference between the aims of the Fascist Government and the aims of pre-Fascist Governments. All intended to wrest Cyrenaica from its inhabitants by force of arms and by peopling it with Italians to exploit it for Italian economic, political, and above all strategic, purposes. They were attempting no more than other Colonial Powers had done before them, but they had waited too long, till the tide of colonial expansion was turning and the right of Europeans to rob native peoples of their lands was beginning to be challenged. Even so, it was not of their choosing or out of deference to humane considerations, but on account of military weakness and incompetence, that they made a truce with the Sanusi in 1917, and on account of domestic difficulties that they prolonged this truce to 1923. As soon as Mussolini had restored order in Italy he resumed the war Giolitti had begun, although he had been one of the most hostile critics of it at the time. When Graziani had crushed resistance the original plan of colonization was acted on. The migratory swarms from Italy of peasants, officials, traders, and hangers-on of all kinds, threatened the very existence of the Bedouin, who saw themselves being forced either to eke out their lives in the desert as a scarcely tolerated class of shepherds or to sink to the level of landless wage-earners in the country districts and of unskilled labourers in the towns. The Italians intended this to be their fate,[1] and it might well have been if events in Europe had not

---

[1] Giuseppe Daodiace, 'Latinità e colonizzazione nell' Africa del nord', *Riv. delle Col. e d'Oriente*, Feb. 1927, pp. 13–14; Filippo Lo Bello, *Rivista Coloniale*, 1925, p. 38; and Paolo D'Agostini Orsini di Camerota, *L'Italia nella politica africana*, 1926, p. 132.

first caused misgivings in Rome and afterwards led to the destruction of the Italian armies in North Africa and their ejection from the continent. A sullen Arab population in Cyrenaica and Tripolitania and a hostile Arab and Muslim world were, in view of the coming storm, so clearly contrary to Italian interests that a more conciliatory policy, at any rate in words, was adopted and Balbo was entrusted with the difficult task of putting it in effect against a background of slaughter and repression. Once again the Italians had waited too long.

III

The ups and downs of Italian fortunes in Cyrenaica and in the world are reflected in the various decrees which defined the juridical status of the Arabs. In giving a brief account of these decrees it must be kept in mind that whilst they referred to the whole Arab population they really affected only the Arabs of the towns, and even in the towns only those few persons, mostly officials, who actively collaborated with the Italians; and that till 1932 the Italians had no certain or complete control outside the towns.

At the beginning of the first Italo-Sanusi war the Arabs were in law Turkish subjects. By a Royal Decree of 5 November 1911, Tripolitania and Cyrenaica were declared to be under the full sovereignty of the Kingdom of Italy. The status of the Cyrenaican Arabs was fixed by the Royal Decree of 6 April 1913, which declared all born in the country, wherever resident, to be *sudditi italiani*, provided they were not Italian citizens or foreign citizens or subjects. They retained their Muslim personal law, but were subject in other respects to whatever regulations the Italians saw fit to impose on them. They were permitted to hold posts in the armed forces and administration of the colony, and persons desirous of acquiring Italian citizenship might apply for it if they possessed residential qualifications, though by taking it they became subject to Italian personal law. These early decrees were more in the nature of administrative than constitutional law. A constitution, in the continental sense, was promulgated in 1919 after the Italians had signed a truce with the Sanusi.

The agreements entered into with the Sanusi between 1917

and 1922 and the efforts made by the Italians during those years to build up a democratic system of government in Cyrenaica were, as we have seen, largely due to defeatism and political unrest at home, but they sprang also from a genuine belief in peace and Wilsonian principles among the men at that time in power in Italy. It is possible that the local Governor, Giacomo de Martino, also believed in them. Early in his term of office the Royal Decree of 31 October 1919, called the *Legge Fondamentale per la Cirenaica*, was promulgated. The natives of the country who were not *cittadini italiani metropolitani* were defined as *cittadini italiani* and thus received status equal to that of Italians, but not identical with it, because the Arabs kept their Muslim personal law. They also enjoyed guarantees of personal liberty, inviolability of domicile and property, the right to compete in military and civil careers and professions, even in the Kingdom of Italy, electoral rights (a local Parliament was set up at Banghazi), the right of petition to the National Parliament, and rights of sojourn and emigration. Respect of religion and local custom was guaranteed, liberty of the press and right of meeting were recognized, citizens could not be conscripted for military service, no fiscal tribute could be imposed which was not the same for all or without consent of the local Parliament, revenue from taxes was to be used for Cyrenaican purposes exclusively, the Arabic language was compulsory in the teaching of certain subjects in the schools and in certain official publications, and no precepts contrary to Islam were to be taught. In general, all the inhabitants of Cyrenaica, whether Arab or Italian, were equal before the law. An adult Arab could acquire metropolitan citizenship if he fulfilled certain conditions. The decree revoked the earlier one of 6 April 1913 relating to Italian subjects, and other decrees and laws, though not formally abrogated, seem to have lapsed by substitution save in so far as some of the administrative machinery created by them remained of necessity in operation.

This basic law of 1919 was as unwise as it was generous. The Bedouin may have enjoyed the elections, but to have formally handed over the country to the Arabs was detrimental to Italian prestige, for it was a confession that the Italians were unable to control it themselves. Moreover, the Chamber of Deputies, which was to the Bedouin a glorified *mi'ad*, or Shaikhs' gathering, was expected to run the country with machinery with which they were totally unacquainted. Arabs being what they are, and circumstances being what they were in 1919, the constitution could hardly have been other than a failure. Indeed it is not surprising that Fascist writers later poured scorn on these well-meant efforts of pluto-democracy.[1] They were particularly shocked by the grant of Italian citizenship to the Arabs, especially as these same Arabs were exempted from compulsory military service. Under Federzoni, the first Fascist Minister for the Colonies, policy was in this matter, as in others, completely reversed. All agreements with the Sanusi were, as has been noted, torn up, and into the waste-paper basket with them went the local Parliament and the constitution of 1919. In its place was issued by the Royal Decree of 26 June 1927 the *Legge Organica per l'Amministrazione della Tripolitania e della Cirenaica*. In a sense this was a new, and Fascist, constitution though its constitutional content was subordinated to its administrative and judicial content. By it the Arabs ceased to be *cittadini italiani* and became *cittadini italiani libici*, they lost the right to free exercise of military and civil careers outside the colonies, electoral rights (parliament had in any case been abolished), the right to petition to the National Parliament, &c., and there was no mention of the liberty of the press, of the right of meeting, of freedom from military conscription, and of the protection of the Arabic language in public instruction. In general, the Arabs were no longer equal with the Italians before the law. Metropolitan citizenship might still be asked for under certain conditions. Application of this decree was several times postponed and it appears never to have come into operation.

Bedouin resistance in both Tripolitania and Cyrenaica still caused the Italians much trouble even as late as 1929 and on both military and political grounds it was deemed advisable to place the two countries under single direction. This was done by the Royal Decree of 24 January 1929 which placed the two colonies under Pietro Badoglio and by the Royal Decree of 3 December 1934, *Ordinamento Organico per l'Amministrazione della Libia*, which, as described in the last section, divided the single colony into four provincial commissariats and a mili-

---

[1] Alberto Stern, 'Il nuovo Ordinamento Fondamentale della Tripolitania e della Cirenaica', *Rivista delle Colonie Italiane*, 1934, p. 1027.

tary command of the Sahara. The other Articles of the 1934 decree were designed chiefly to meet the new conditions arising, or likely to arise, from colonization by nationals. In no important respect did it alter the status of the Arab population or what rights it still possessed. In the first enthusiasm of turning Libya into a metropolitan colony the Arabs were of secondary interest to those who made the laws.

In view of the coming struggle between the powers of Europe, already seen by Mussolini to be inevitable, the Italian Government considered it advisable to pay more attention to the feelings of its colonists and native peoples. To encourage the colonists already in the country and those about to join them from Italy a Royal Decree was promulgated on 9 January 1939 declaring Libya to be an integral part of the Kingdom of Italy, its four provinces becoming the ninety-seventh, ninety-eighth, ninety-ninth, and hundredth provinces of the Kingdom. The military status of the Libyan Sahara remained unchanged. The colonists no longer had to feel that they had left their fatherland for inhospitable shores. The *Colonia* had become *Terra Italiana*. The *Quarta Sponda*, Italy's Fourth Shore, had become a political fact. At the same time, to quiet any uneasiness which the incorporation of their country in the Kingdom of Italy might create among those educated Arabs whose services the Italians needed, and to implement the promise Mussolini had made during his tour of Libya in 1937 that he would remember the part played by Libyan volunteers in the Ethiopian campaign, the Decree offered the Arabs a new special citizenship which took the place of the right of acquiring metropolitan citizenship allowed in the earlier decrees and now abrogated. That the Italians had attached importance to the partial assimilation of a small *élite* of natives is shown by the retention of the right of acquiring metropolitan citizenship through all the decrees and laws, from the invasion of Libya in 1911 till the present decree, in both pre-Fascist and Fascist times. It had been found, however, that the Arabs had not availed themselves of the privilege. Employees of the administration could not feel that any advantages they might derive from it could compensate them for loss of status before the religious courts in matters of personal law, a loss considered shameful even by whole-hearted collaborators. Also, the new special citizenship, *cittadinanza italiana speciale*, was more in accordance with Balbo's policy of parallel development than acquisition of metropolitan citizenship.

The new special citizenship could be acquired, without prejudice to Muslim personal law, by persons who had reached the age of eighteen, provided they had a good record and had in some way or other served the State or could read and write Italian. The status carried with it certain privileges: the right to bear arms, the right to be inscribed in the Arab Blackshirt Organization, the right to a military career in Libyan units (now withdrawn from other Libyans), the right to become mayor in Arab communities and adviser in mixed Italo-Arab communities, and the right to come under the *Ordinamento sindacale-corporativo*, an ordinance by which the Fascist guild system had been adapted to suit colonial conditions, and to take some part in the activities of these guilds. These rights could be exercised only in Italian African territories and no Arab could, in any case, occupy posts or practise professions which would necessitate Italians serving under him.

The reception of the new decree by the colonists and by Arab employees of the Administration was enthusiastic. It may be doubted, however, whether the sentiments expressed by the mudirs, the qadis, and some of the richer merchants, in the telegrams of thanks they sent to Mussolini and Balbo were felt. It was tacitly assumed to be a condition of continued employment that special citizenship should be applied for. The first batch of diplomas included ninety Cyrenaican names, almost all of native officials and government pensioners of the urban centres: the decree could not have been of the slightest interest to the Bedouin. Conscription for military service followed shortly afterwards. Of their bounty the Italians had given to the Arabs of Cyrenaica a *Patria*, *l'Italia Fascista*, and they were expected to show their gratitude by fighting for it. On 10 June 1940 Italy entered the war on the side of Germany.

Thus in 1911 the Arabs of Cyrenaica became enemy subjects and were afterwards declared to be Italian subjects. In 1919 they became Italian citizens. When the Italians renewed operations against them in 1923 those who resisted were declared to be *ribelli*. Under the Fascists they lost the Italian citizenship they had been granted under the democratic régime of 1919 and became instead Italian-Libyan citizens. In 1939 they were granted the privilege of applying, if they had the necessary qualifications, for a special Italian citizenship, a status half-way between that of the ordinary Arab of the country and that of the Italian colonists. There were, therefore, in Cyrenaica in 1940 three categories of citizenship, that of the *cittadini metropolitani*, Italian settlers and officials, that of the *cittadini italiani speciali*, a small intermediate urban class of educated Arab officials, and that of the *cittadini italiani libici* (*musulmani*), which comprised almost the entire native population of the country. These changes in the civil status of the Arabs were to a considerable extent a response to the development of the political situation in Cyrenaica itself. The Royal Decree of 1913 was an optimistic anticipation of easy victory; the Royal Decree of 1919 was an acknowledgement of political and military failure; the Royal Decree of 1927 was a sign that apathy and compromise had given way to determination to fight the Bedouin if necessary, and even by preference, to the point of extermination; the Royal Decree of 1934 marked the end of all resistance and envisaged the settlement of Italian colonists on the best lands of the country; and the Royal Decree of 1939 signalled the realization of this programme and at the same time made a bid for co-operation of the Arab intelligentsia. But to an equal extent the changes in civil status were determined by political events in Italy and in Europe. The Royal Decree of 1913 was a plain colonial declaration such as any European Power would have made in similar circumstances. In 1919 Italian politics were defeatist, demagogic, socialist, and internationalist, and the Royal Decree of that year was a stew of these ingredients. The Royal Decrees of 1927 and 1934 were typical Fascist pieces of legislation with emphasis on State requirements rather than on citizenship and the rights of the individual, and showed a strong bias towards bureaucratic centralization and hypertrophy. The Royal Decree of 1939 bore the stamp of empire.

IV

The Bedouin were altogether unimpressed either by Italian propaganda or by their social services, and they did not believe in their promises of future benefits. *'Bukra al-'id'*, 'The feast day is always just ahead', as they say. Nothing could compensate them for the loss of their lands taken from them to make farms for Italian immigrants.

When the Italians invaded Libya in 1911 they did so not only to keep other European powers out of it but also to provide an outlet for their surplus population.[1] Sentiment also played a great part in their plans, especially under the Fascists. In classical times and for over a thousand years Europeans had flourished in Cyrenaica, and the country had once been part of the Roman Empire. To sentiment were added plausible arguments of an economic kind. Italy imported some of her elementary requirements, such as grain and oil, from countries controlled by other European powers and it was hoped that her Libyan colonies might supply part of these and so, through colonization, make a contribution to the autarchy its rulers aimed at. But sentiment and demographic and economic aims weighed less in the calculations of Italy's leaders than the political and strategic advantages likely to accrue from the adventure, both of which would be served by colonization.

It was, of course, well known to the Italians that only a small portion of Cyrenaica, part of the plateau, was suitable for European colonization. The findings of the Anglo-Jewish commission of 1908 had been far from encouraging, for they expressed the opinion that Cyrenaica could not take more than about three hundred thousand colonists in addition to the existing population, even when the maximum point of exploitation had been reached.[2] Many Italians also were sceptical about the advantages of the country for colonial settlement, but most took the more optimistic view and believed, or affected to believe, that an America lay opposite their shores. Indeed, as Despois observes, many Italian books and articles on colonization of Libya 'lack the most elementary competence or the least critical sense.'[3] But though there was much disagreement about the saturation point most Italian writers accepted that political control and colonization must go hand in hand.

In the first years of Italian occupation political conditions did not permit colonization on any scale. It was restricted to cereal culture in comparatively safe areas near Banghazi and

---

[1] Mondaini, op. cit., p. 257, seq.
[2] Gregory, op. cit., pp. 12–14.   [3] Op. cit., p. 137.

behind barbed wire in the vicinity of al-Marj and al-Abyar, and up to the end of 1926 there were only 13 colonists, possessing 630 hectares. Even by the end of 1932, in spite of Teruzzi's fervent efforts and the personal interest of Mussolini, there were still only about 90 Italian farms in the whole country and the farming, mostly by concessions and private company settling, was often uneconomic and incompetent. Exploitation of this kind clearly did nothing to relieve over-population in Italy and was certainly not at all what had been advertised as '*coloniz-zazione di popolamento*', so in 1932 there was formed by the State, and coming as time went on more and more under State control and supported by public funds, a parastatal corporation called the *Ente per la colonizzazione della Cirenaica* and, after its extension to operate also in Tripolitania, the *Ente per la coloniz-zazione della Libia*. The *Ente* began in a small way in Cyrenaica in 1933. The lands immediately allotted to it were 30,000 hectares in the black soil country of Shahhat-Safsaf, 4,000 hectares near al-Zawiya al-Baida, and 5,500 hectares in the neighbourhood of al-Marj. The first experimental operations were begun in the Shahhat and al-Zawiya al-Baida areas, a fertile region with a climate like that with which the colonists were familiar in their homeland. In this smiling country of the juniper, the lentisk, and the cypress began to spring up the little white Italian farms: in 1933 at Beda Littoria and Luigi di Savoia, in 1934 at Luigi Razza and Giovanni Berta, and in 1936 at Maddalena. But the progress of colonization was not quick enough for the Fascist junta—only some 300 families had been settled—and it was decided to quicken the pace, especially in view of the rapidly deteriorating situation in Europe. By the spring of 1937 there were over 700 colonist families in Cyrenaica. The pace was forced in 1938 by State-directed im-migration in mass. The unit of this demographic immigration was the family, so that each farm would be a self-contained economic unit run on its own labour. The farms had been pre-pared and the houses built in advance and furnished down to the last pot and pan. Each farm was part of a village and attached to a centre comprising all that a paternal State con-sidered necessary for the bodies, minds, and souls of its citizens: a clinic, a granary, a school, a Fascist club, administrative offices, and a church and priest's house.

The first 20,000 new colonists for Libya were given a tre-
mendous send-off in March 1938 and their settlement was
completed during the following eight months. Those who came
to Cyrenaica, probably more than half of the 20,000, partly went
to complete the villages already in existence and partly to
occupy the new holdings prepared for them at Baracca, Oberdan,
D'Annunzio, and Battisti. The Cyrenaican quota of another
20,000 immigrants, the second wave of demographic colonization, was supposed to have followed in October 1939 to constitute the population of the newly constructed villages of Mameli,
Sauro, and Filzi, but not all of them appear to have arrived.
These two waves of mass immigration brought the number of
farms to over 2,000 and the number of agricultural colonists to
over 15,000 persons, making round about 50,000 Italian colonists
of all kinds. Northern Cyrenaica had become in population and
in appearance, as well as in law, part of Italy. Banghazi and
Darna had become modern Italian towns which might well have
been on the shores of Sicily or southern Italy. Modern roads
cut through the plateau and for mile after mile were lined with
Italian farmhouses and every few miles bisected Italian village
centres. A railway ran from Banghazi to Suluq and from
Banghazi to al-Marj and was in process of extension to Darna.
An aqueduct was being built to carry water from Mara, near
Darna, to the colonial villages as far to the west as those on the
farther edge of the plain of al-Marj. Banghazi had been made
into a modern port. Airlines to Banghazi ran from Rome,
Tripoli, and Tubruq.

I have given a short sketch of Italian colonization of Cyrenaica
only in order that the effect it had on the Bedouin may be better
understood, for what concerns us is the fate of Muhammad,
Mehemmed, Ahmad, and Abu Bakr, who with their flocks and
herds were driven from the more fertile parts of the plateau to
make way for Michele, Antonio, Italo, and Cesare. For over
twenty years the Italians had been unable to colonize Cyrenaica
for, as Graziani bluntly observed, 'It is plain that when one is
making war one cannot plant trees, neither can one sow corn.'[1]
Once resistance had been overcome it was merely a question of
finding a legal formula for depriving the owners of the land of

---

[1] 'Panorama economico della Cirenaica', *Rivista delle Colonie Italiane*,
1933, p. 295.

their rights in it, and this presented no more difficulty to the lawyers than the discovery of a formula to cover confiscation of the Sanusiya properties had done.

Ancient rights in the lands of Cyrenaica rested with the *Sa'adi* tribes and whatever tribal fragments they permitted to reside there by grace. Disputes about ownership had been settled either by war or through discussion between the groups concerned in them, sometimes with the aid of Turkish officials or Marabouts, particularly of the Shaikhs of Sanusiya lodges after the Order had become established in the country. In 1858 the Ottoman Government, under pressure of Western ideas, promulgated a land code in all parts of the empire, and to put it into effect in Cyrenaica the Governor, Khalil Sami Pasha (1863–8), appointed a committee which declared the lands round Banghazi and Darna to be for the use of these towns and the rest of the country for the use of the tribes in occupation of it, except for barren hills and deserts which, like woods and roads, were regarded as the natural demesne of the State. The tribal boundaries of to-day were finally fixed by this committee, though the fixing of them was less an adjudication than a recording of existing conditions.

The new Turkish land code operated in the towns and just outside them and was not applied to tribal lands and grazing grounds, and the tribes were not asked to acquire a title to their lands by registration of them. This would have been an impossible task, and the Turks were in any case too wise to meddle with Bedouin lands, knowing that the Bedouin would not have consented to change or interference of any kind. Nevertheless the State claimed all tribal lands not bearing buildings or plantations as *miri*, public demesne, and from a legal point of view it was in virtue of this absolute and residuary ownership that it taxed the tribal occupiers and users of the land. This was a legal formalism which made no difference to anyone since the Government had neither the wish nor the power to exploit the lands and accepted that the tribes had rights of use, the *tassaruf*, in them in perpetuity. The Italian Land Registry, created in 1913 on the basis of the Turkish registers, followed Turkish practice in this matter, classing tribal lands as State demesne in which the occupiers had rights of use, and also in allowing tribal disputes to be settled by tribal custom, which the Italians called *Sa'adi* law. In 1923 the Land Registry, which had hitherto restricted its attention to urban properties, took the first steps towards an assessment of tribal lands and by the end of 1932 had registered in the name of the Colony 120,790 hectares, a large part of which was already marked for colonial settlement. The lands were acquired by 'natural right' (9,124 Ha.), by purchase, expropriation, and renunciation (43,441 Ha.), and by confiscation of Sanusiya estates (62,225 Ha.) and of properties of persons fighting in patriot bands and classed as rebels against the State (6,000 Ha.). However, expropriation for purposes of public utility and purchase were found to be slow, expensive, inadequate, and, in the political circumstances, inopportune methods of acquiring land for colonial settlement. Both also led to most complicated disputes about the distribution of the compensation in a country where every member of a tribe had preemptive rights of some degree in all its lands. In 1928 a new system was therefore adopted. The State in virtue of its supreme authority asked the owners of the lands considered useful to the State to renounce their rights in them. Compensation was to be divided equally among the various participants in the *tassaruf*.

No action of the kind allowed for in the new decrees was, or could be, taken till the Bedouin had been subdued. It would have been useless to attempt to register the lands of the Bedouin in the name of the State on those parts of the plateau in which the guerrillas still operated freely, and to have attempted to register them in the submitted areas would merely have driven the population to renewed revolt. Action does not seem to have been taken till 1935–6 and it was then taken in a form which is said to have disgusted even some of the lawyers. Proclamations covering the lands required for colonial settlement were drawn up and it was stated in them that the particular lands to which each referred were State property and that if no objection were raised by a certain date they would be registered in the name of the State. The proclamations were published by being fixed to official notice-boards in the Land Department and municipalities, but they were not published on the lands concerned, or anywhere near them, so that the Bedouin, even had they any idea of what the procedure was, and even could they have read the proclamations, did not in

any case see them. Consequently no objections were raised—
had they been raised no attention would have been paid to
them—and there was legal presumption of State ownership in
the fullest sense. The judges, therefore, ordered registration of
the new lands in the name of the Colony. They comprised
about 450,000 hectares, about a quarter of which were immediately allotted to the *Ente* for colonization. It will be noted
that the State had already, before this action was taken, been
bare owner of the lands as heir to the Turkish *miri* property.
What it now gained in addition was, in the opinion of its lawyers,
the *possesso utile*. They held further that compensation of those
deprived of the use of the lands, while perhaps unnecessary,
added to the juridical rigour of the proceeding. In other words,
in order to make it look a little less like common robbery it was
decided to make a parade of indemnification. The areas to be
taken over were estimated in a non-technical way by a surveyor
and a clerk of the Land Registry, and the supposed owners were
summoned, told that their lands were worth so much, and that
this sum would be handed over to them by the Government.
Tables of succession showing the share in the land of the various
members of the local group who owned it had already been
prepared, and if the representatives of this tribal section agreed
to the proposal the money could then be paid over on demand.

Whether the Bedouin took the money offered in compensation
or not they still lost their lands. For this reason most of them
took it. Though compensation was in this way offered, the
document to which the recipients of it had to affix their seals
or thumb-prints was not a contractual agreement for sale and
purchase nor an edict of expropriation for public utility purposes, but it was a simple declaration by the owner that he
renounced all his rights in the land and transferred them to the
State. The Italians had now got all the lands in Cyrenaica
which were of any immediate use to them. They had only to
allot them to colonists and register them technically as they
were required for settlement. The target figure for the zone of
colonization was 900,000 hectares.[1]

There remained the question of the Bedouin who had been
driven off the lands of their fathers. Clearly they could not be
allowed to lead their nomadic life amid the Italian cultiva-

---

[1] *La Nuova Italia d'Oltremare*, vol. i, p. 552.

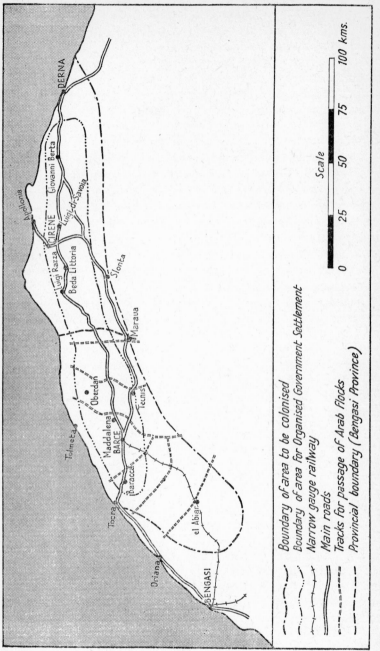

The Italian plan for the colonization of northern Cyrenaica.

Boundary of area to be colonised
Boundary of area for Organised Government Settlement
Narrow gauge railway
Main roads
Tracks for passage of Arab flocks
Provincial boundary (Bengasi Province)

Scale

0   25   50   75   100 kms.

DERNA
Apollonia
Giovanni Berta
CIRENE
Luigi di-Savoia
Luigi Razza
Beda Littoria
Slonta
Maraua
Oberdan
Tecnis
Tolmeta
Maddalena
BARCE
Baracca
Tocra
el Abiar
Driana
BENGASI

tions and gardens. On the other hand, it was recognized that if they were to be able to lead a nomadic life at all, and they had to do so if they were to rear their animals, they must have access to water-supplies and grazing-grounds, and that this would sometimes mean their crossing the plateau through the area of Italian colonization. To solve this problem corridors running north and south across the plateau were, as explained in an earlier section, marked out for the transit of Bedouin flocks and herds.

It was envisaged that the Bedouin would continue to lead a predominantly pastoral life on the more rugged parts of the first terrace of the plateau, on its southern slopes, and in the steppe country of the *sirwal*, the *barqa*, the Marmarica, and the Sirtica. It was thought that they had in these areas all the land they needed for grazing and catch-crop cultivation, though it was evident that in years of drought they could not have managed to survive without summer grazing on the plateau. Nevertheless, efforts were made to raise the economic level of the Bedouin by improving their methods of cultivation and stock-raising so that, as both producers and labourers, they might be more valuable an adjunct to Italian husbandry, and might become more dependent on the State and more closely linked with metropolitan activities. It was intended that they should constitute a cheap reserve of labour for general unskilled work and for seasonal labour on the farms of the colonists. By using them in this way it was hoped that it would be possible to avoid the growth of a metropolitan proletariat.[1] These efforts included, largely for political reasons, the creation of Arab colonization centres. Agricultural villages and farms were to be built by the *Ente* similar to, but smaller than, those built for the Italian immigrants. The first two such villages, Fiorita and Alba, were built in 1939. Each Arab farming family was provided with a house, a well, a camel, a cow, and farm implements. Like the Italian, the Arab colonist was to be first salaried labourer, then partner with the State, then mortgagor, and finally owner. As only thirty-two holdings were prepared at Fiorita and Alba the contribution to native agriculture cannot be regarded as more than a token one. Moreover, the Italians experienced difficulty in finding Arab colonists for even these

[1] Ibid., p. 622.

thirty-two holdings, for the Bedouin showed no inclination to work as serfs the lands they had worked as freemen: 'In their daily attitude coldness and scepticism were apparent so that the part they took in collaborating was purely formal.'[1] A pastoral village, furnished with veterinary and stud services and offices for the collection, classification, and weighing of wool, was built at Nahiba (Jardis al-'Abid) and another was planned to be built at Verde (Jardis al-Jarrari). Some may consider that these measures are evidence of Balbo's sincerity. The Bedouin believed that he intended to destroy them by guile as surely as Graziani had destroyed them with machine-gun and bomb.

V

When Giolitti landed troops in Cyrenaica and Tripolitania in 1911 he started his country on the road to ruin. The first Libyan war was from 1911 to 1917. In the midst of it Italy was involved, from 1915 to 1918, in the first Great War. From 1921 to 1932 she was again engaged in prosecuting her colonial war in Libya, first in Tripolitania, then in Cyrenaica also. From 1934 to 1936 she participated in the Spanish civil war. In 1935 and 1936 she conquered Ethiopia. In 1939 she seized Albania. From 1940 to 1944 she was engaged in the second Great War. It was appropriate that disaster should overcome the Italians in Cyrenaica, that the Bedouin of that country who had suffered so much at their hands should witness their humiliation, and that it should fall on the head of Graziani, who became Governor of Libya when Balbo was killed at Tubruq on 28 June 1940.

As the day of retribution drew near the Italians showed some uneasiness about the situation in Cyrenaica and, as I have recorded, they made belated attempts to conciliate the Arabs. Their uneasiness was partly due to the presence of the Sanusi leader Sayyid Idris and of a number of notable Cyrenaican and Tripolitanian Shaikhs in exile in Egypt. It could hardly be doubted that they would approach the British with offers of assistance should Italy enter the war on the side of Germany. This is what happened. In October 1939, when Italy's participation seemed imminent, the Cyrenaican and Tripolitanian

[1] Giuseppe Palloni, *The Action of the Italian Government in Favour of the Lybian Agriculture*, 1945, p. 31.

Shaikhs met at Alexandria and informed the British Ambassador in Cairo that they recognized Sayyid Idris as their Amir and that he could speak on their behalf. At a second meeting of these Shaikhs in Cairo on 9 August 1940, after Italy had declared war, it was decided to form a Libyan force to co-operate with the British army in the Western Desert. Though some of the Tripolitanian notables refused to associate themselves with this offer, wishing to make a separate offer on their own account, it was gladly accepted by the British authorities, and the British-Arab Force, later known as the Libyan Arab Force, was recruited from among the Sanusi exiles in Egypt and later also from Sanusi prisoners of war, who had taken the first opportunity of surrendering to the British. It was officered by British and Arabs, including some of the veterans of the Italo-Sanusi wars, and at its maximum strength consisted of five battalions and a depot. The force was not trained and equipped for the kind of fighting which took place in the Western Desert, but it performed useful ancillary duties to which Mr. Eden paid a tribute in the House of Commons on 8 January 1942, when he declared that His Majesty's Government was determined that the Sanusi should not come again under Italian domination. It took part in the first and subsequent occupations of Cyrenaica by British troops, and two battalions served in the defence of Tubruq in 1941. The little Sanusi army fought under its own flag and Arab commissions in it were in the name of the Amir. The Bedouin of Cyrenaica also rendered services to the British army as guides and agents and in assisting escaped prisoners of war and men detached from their units during our two withdrawals to Egypt. They gave further assistance by their eager co-operation with the three British Military Administrations of their country, although those who were known to have rendered the British special assistance were shot by the Italians on our withdrawals.

When in 1943 Sayyid Idris visited Cyrenaica for the first time since his hurried departure from it in 1922 and was received with wild enthusiasm by the whole country, it was just a century after his grandfather had founded his first zawiya in it. During that century the Sanusiya Order had seen many changes and had itself changed. Even in the Grand Sanusi's time it had some political functions. The best Italian historian of the Order, Carlo Giglio, could write that at the death of its founder the

Order was 'not a true and proper State but something very similar'.[1] We have seen how these political functions were further developed under the rule of Sayyid al-Mahdi and how under the rule of Sayyid Ahmad al-Sharif what may justly be called an embryonic State came into being. The Head of the Order was by this time less the religious Head of an Islamic fraternity than the leading representative of a nascent nationalism which became increasingly conscious of itself in the long struggle against the Italians under Sanusiya leadership. In this struggle the Order became more and more a political organization which directed, administratively, economically, and militarily, the entire Bedouin population, and morally the entire population of Cyrenaica, Bedouin and townsmen alike, against the common enemy. When truce was made in 1917, whatever the Italians and British may have asserted to the contrary, they had, in fact, to treat with Sayyid Idris not only as the Head of a religious Order, but also as the Head of a political organization which represented, and alone represented, the political aspirations of a people. As events turned out, the Italians, by destroying the Sanusiya organization, cut out the intervening structure of lodges and Shaikhs and made more evident the political status of the Head of the Order.

What has happened during the century which has passed since the first Brothers of the Order began to build the lodge and till the soil at what is now al-Zawiya al-Baida must be viewed in relation to Bedouin tribal structure. A man coming from outside and with religious authority established himself as Head of the acephalous Bedouin society of Cyrenaica, and circumstances in which that whole society was forced to act for a long period of time against external enemies transformed his religious fraternity into a political organization. The Sanusiya Order from the first identified itself with the Bedouin and laboured to bring about tribal unity under its aegis. Under Turkish rule nationalist tendencies, as distinct from, and overriding, tribal loyalties, were latent, and the role of the Sanusiya within the frame of the Ottoman Empire was still predominantly religious rather than political; but when the Italians sought to subjugate the Bedouin their resistance, in the very clear moral issue presented to them, manifested itself

[1] Op. cit., p. 11.

as a nationalist movement, with a corresponding effect on the character of the Sanusiya Order and on the status of its Head. The final stage in the transformation of a religious revival into a political movement was brought about by the clash of European arms. Amid the roar of planes and guns the Bedouin learnt to see themselves more clearly as a single people, the Sanusi of Cyrenaica, in a wider world, and came to be regarded as such by those engaged in the struggle.

CYRENAICAN PLACE-NAMES FREQUENTLY MENTIONED IN THE TEXT

Spelling in the text	*Italian spelling*
al-Abyar	el-Abiar
Ajadabiya	Agedabia
'Akrama	Acroma
al-'Aqaila	el-Agheila
al-'Arqub	el-Argub
Aujila	Augila
al-'Azziyyat	el-Ezzeiat
(al-Zawiya) al-Baida	Zauia el-Beda (Beda Littoria)
al-Banba	Bomba
Banghazi	Bengasi
Banina	Benina
al-Burdi Sulaiman	Bardia
Dariyana	Driana
Darna	Derna
al-Fayidiya	el-Faidia (De Martino)
(Bir) Hakaim	(Bir) Hacheim
al-Haniya	el-Hania
Jaghbub	Giarabub
Jalu	Gialo
Janzur	Gianzur
Jardis al-'Abid	Gerdes el-Abid
al-Jikharra	Gicherra
Khawalan	Chaulan
al-Makhili	el-Mechili
Marawa	Maraua
al-Marj	el-Merg (Barce)
Massa	Messa (Luigi Razza)
Msus	Msus
al-Naufiliya	en-Nofilia
al-Qaiqab	el-Ghegab
al-Qasur	el-Gsur
al-Qatafiya	el-Gtafia
al-Qubba	el-Gubba (Giovanni Berta)
al-Sallum	es-Sollum
Shahhat	Sciahhat (Cirene)

Spelling in the text	*Italian spelling*
al-Shlaidima	esc-Sceleidima
Slanta	Slonta
Suluq	Soluch
Susa (Marsa)	Susa (Marsa) (Apollonia)
al-Tailimun	Tilimun
Taknis	Tecnis
Talmaitha	Tolmeta
Tart	Tert
Taukra	Tocra
Tubruq	Tobruch
al-Zuwaitina	ez-Zuetina

A SELECT BIBLIOGRAPHY

ONLY the most important authorities, and those I have made most use of, are cited. There is a very considerable literature on Cyrenaica, mostly in Italian and of very uneven quality. I have published part of a more comprehensive bibliography elsewhere.[1]

AGOSTINI, ENRICO DE, *Le Popolazioni della Tripolitania*, Tripoli, 1917.

—— *Le Popolazioni della Cirenaica*, Bengasi, 1922–3.

BELARDINELLI, ARSENIO, *La Ghibla*, Tripoli, 1935.

CANEVARI, EMILIO, *Zauie ed Ichuan Senussiti della Tripolitania*, Tripoli, 1917.

COLUCCI, MASSIMO, *Il Regime della Proprietà Fondiaria nell' Africa Italiana*, vol. i, *Libia*, Bologna, 1942.

DELLA CELLA, PAOLO, *Narrative of an Expedition from Tripoli in Barbary to the Western Frontier of Egypt in 1817*, translated (from the first Italian edition of 1819) by Anthony Aufrere, London, 1822.

DEPOIS, JEAN, *La Colonisation Italienne en Libye: Problèmes et Méthodes*, Paris, 1935.

DEPONT, OCTAVE, and COPPOLANI, XAVIER, *Les Confréries Religieuses Musulmanes*, Alger, 1897.

DUVEYRIER, H., *La Confrérie Musulmane de Sidi Mohammed ben 'Alî es Senoûsî et son Domaine géographique en l'Année 1300 de l'Hégire = 1883 de notre ère*, Paris, 1884.

GAIBI, AGOSTINO, *Storia delle Colonie Italiane*, Torino, 1934.

GIGLIO, CARLO, *La Confraternità Senussita dalle sue Origini ad Oggi*, Padova, 1932.

GRAZIANI, RODOLFO, *Cirenaica Pacificata*, Milano, 1932.

Handbook on Cyrenaica (by several authors), Cairo, 1944–7.

HASSANEIN, A. M., BEY, *The Lost Oases*, London, 1925.

LAMMENS, —., *L'Islam*, Beyrouth, 2nd ed., 1941.

La Nuova Italia d'Oltremare (edited by Angelo Piccioli), Roma-Milano, 1933–4 (2 vols.).

LE CHATELIER, A., *Les Confréries Musulmanes du Hedjaz*, Paris, 1887.

MACALUSO, GIUSEPPE, *Turchi, Senussi e Italiani in Libia*, Bengasi, 1930.

---

[1] *African Studies*, 1945 and 1946.

MONDAINI, G., *Manuale di Storia e Legislazione Coloniale del Regno d'Italia*, Roma, 1927 (2 vols.).

MUHAMMAD AL-AKHDAR AL-'ISAWI, *Raf' al-Sitar 'amma ja'a fi Kitab 'Umar al-Mukhtar*, Cairo, 1936.

MUHAMMAD IBN 'UTHMAN AL-HASHAISHI (Mohammed ben Otsmane el-Hachaichi), *Voyage au Pays des Senoussia à travers la Tripolitaine et les Pays Touareg*, translated by Serres and Lasram, Paris, 1912 (first edition, 1903).

MURRAY, G. W., *Sons of Ishmael*, London, 1935.

PACHO, JEAN RAIMOND, *Relation d'un Voyage dans la Marmarique, la Cyrénaïque et les Oasis d'Audjelah et de Maradèh*, Paris, 1827.

RENZI, EDMONDO DE, *Nozioni sull' Islam con speciale riguardo alla Tripolitania*, Tripoli, 1918.

RINN, LOUIS, *Marabouts et Khouan*, Alger, 1884.

SALIM BIN 'AMIR, A series of articles on the Grand Sanusi in Cyrenaica in *Majallat 'Umar al-Mukhtar*, Banghazi, 1943–4.

SAVARESE, ENZO, *Le Terre della Cirenaica*, Bengasi, 1926–8.

SERRA, FABRIZIO, *Italia e Senussia*, Milano–Roma, 1933.

TERUZZI, ATTILIO, *Cirenaica Verde*, Milano, 1931.

INDEX

PRINTED IN GREAT BRITAIN
AT THE UNIVERSITY PRESS, OXFORD
BY CHARLES BATEY, PRINTER TO THE UNIVERSITY